First published in the UK in March 2021 by
Journey Books, an imprint of Bradt Travel Guides Ltd
31a High Street, Chesham, Buckinghamshire, HP5 1BW, England
www.bradtguides.com

Text copyright © 2021 Michael Lynch
Edited by Samantha Cook
Cover illustration by Neil Gower
Layout and typesetting by Ian Spick
Map by David McCutcheon FBCart.S
Production managed by Sue Cooper, Bradt & Zenith Media

ISBN: 978 1 78477 833 0

British Library Cataloguing in Publication Data
A catalogue record for this book is available from the British Library
Digital conversion by www.dataworks.co.in
Printed in the UK by Zenith Media

To find out more about our Journey Books imprint, visit www.bradtguides.com/
journeybooks.

About the author

Michael Lynch was born and raised in County Tipperary, Ireland. There, he developed an interest in Irish history, and played a lot of football. At an early age, he took a break from a 'proper' job and left to travel around Australia. On the way, he stopped off in London, and never made it any further.

At a later age, on a break from another 'proper' job, he travelled around South America. It was here that he was able to indulge his interest in Irish history and in football. The result is this book.

Now back in London, he is currently planning his next escape.

Author's note

This text was written in 2011–2012 and some details – although accurate at that time – are no longer applicable at the date of publishing (eg: Ñuble, noted as a province in *Chapter 8*, was designated a region in 2018 and, in *Chapter 14* Everton's win/loss record reflects their position in 2011). I thought it best to leave such details as they were at the time they were written.

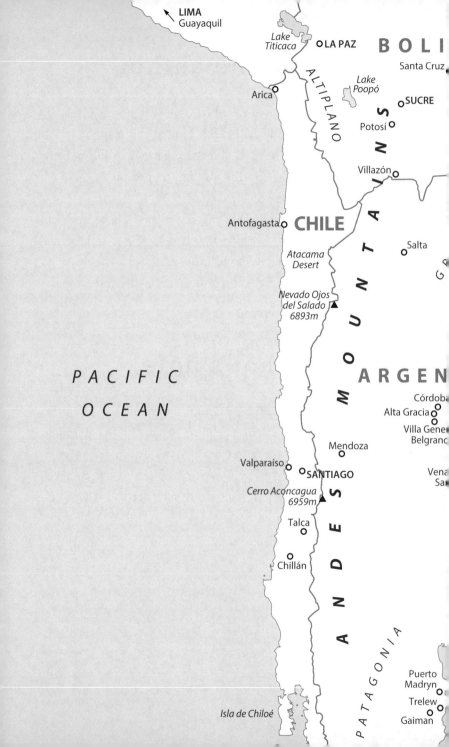

1

I last stayed in a hostel two months ago, in Puerto López, Ecuador. The room there was hot and clammy, the loo had no toilet paper and the taps had no water. The bulb in the bedroom barely emitted light, but this was probably a good thing, as it meant I didn't get a close look at the buzzing and crawling things that were keeping me company. I swore off hostels that night. Now, after weeks of hotels, travel and tours, a creaking bank balance means that I must think again about cheaper accommodation. Last night, just arrived in Chile, I took a single room in a hostel in the centre of the country's capital, Santiago. It was, at least, bug-free. But I'm not won over. This morning, I'm switching back to a hotel.

My guidebook leads me to Hotel Paris, on Calle Paris (Paris Street), parallel to the city's main thoroughfare, Avenida Libertador Bernardo O'Higgins (Avenue of the Liberator). It is a great location, a small neighbourhood tucked away in the heart of the city, its narrow streets paved with flat, slate-black cobbles. My modest, first-floor room faces on to Calle Paris and although cat-swinging is off the agenda, it is comfortable. The smell of disinfectant from the bathroom is quite strong. It makes me wonder how bad the original smell was that the disinfectant now masks. I drop my bags, flop on to the bed and flick through cable TV channels. 'Los Momentos de Freak del Casting de Factor X' has a giggle at Chilean X-Factor no-hopers.

It is mid-morning and it is cold and cloudy. From the hotel entrance, a short distance to the right, Calle Londres cuts through Calle Paris and leads to Avenida Libertador Bernardo O'Higgins (thankfully, this mouthful is more commonly known as the Alameda). Several blocks west, an enormous flagpole sits in the centre concourse of this very broad avenue. Its giant Chilean flag barely stirs in the slight breeze.

Close by, parallel to the Alameda, Calle Moneda leads back east. This is the Financial District and I stop for coffee here, at Café Bombay. The café is packed. Clearly, it is very popular. It soon becomes clear that its popularity may not be due entirely to the quality of its coffee. In South American cafés, waitress service is the norm, and Café Bombay employs quite a few. What is unusual about the waitresses in Café Bombay is that they don't wear very much clothing. Each girl has on a 'uniform', an extremely short, skin-tight, flower-patterned dress. The dress is held together by a zip that runs up the front, from bottom to top, leaving very little to the imagination. Sheer tights and gaudy, silver stilettos complete these almost-ensembles. The girls wear heavy make-up and are very pretty. It is perhaps no surprise then that Café Bombay's clientele is 99% male. Nearly all of them are businessmen, and regulars are greeted and sent on their way with hugs and regulation South American kisses on the cheek.

I finish my coffee and consider extending my stay in Bombay over another cup. Instead, I tear myself away and continue strolling east on Calle Moneda. Soon I'm wandering through a grid of pedestrianised avenues and cross-streets lined with shops and restaurants and office buildings. I pass Café Caribe, a close relation of Café Bombay. Inside, three beautiful, bored waitresses in matching, minuscule dresses lean against the counter. Business is slow in Caribe. Perhaps customers have moved on, to a nearby shopping mall, where Café Jany has blacked-out windows and doors. There may be more than coffee on offer here. Later, my guidebook informs me that this Santiago coffee-shop phenomenon is '*café con piernas*', coffee with legs.

That evening in my hotel room, recovering from the trip to Bombay, I hear the faint sound of chanting from the street. I expect it must be *los estudiantes radicales* (radical students). Earlier, their homemade banner was hanging from a building at the corner of Paris and Londres.

I quiz the lady at reception about where to go for a beer and she points me to a bar opposite the hotel entrance. But I'm keen to see more of the city, and decide to ramble further. I veer left out of the hotel and on to Calle San Francisco, which runs through Paris on the way to the Alameda.

I hear the wail of the sirens first. Moments later, a small convoy of armoured people-carriers zooms past. Military personnel hang from the sides of a jeep that brings up the rear. People walking in my direction cover their faces with scarves and raised sweaters. There's a sour tang in the air, my throat is irritated and my eyes sting. On the Alameda, litter bins are smouldering; one or two are in flames. The tear gas is stronger here and I pull the collar of my fleece over my mouth and nose. More sirens screech and army vehicles speed by. A crowd is dispersing; whatever had been going on is finished now.

I can't find anywhere for a beer on the Alameda and return to Calle Paris. The bar opposite the hotel is quite busy, with youngsters mostly (*estudiantes radicales,* at a guess) and there's a lively atmosphere. TV screens in the top corners of the room blast out Latin music videos. They're popular favourites, judging by the cheers that greet them, and the communal singing that follows. More youngsters arrive, to great shouts and occasional chants.

I pluck up my Spanish-language courage and ask the barman about the shenanigans on the Alameda. Something goes awry between the forming of the Spanish words in my brain and their tumbling out of my mouth (this is not unusual), and the barman answers by telling me the name of my beer! My mouth is half-open to ask the question again. But I figure that, with my rubbish Spanish, and the loud music (but mostly my rubbish Spanish), this has the makings of a drawn-out struggle of a conversation. I shuffle back to my table. Three small bottles later, I leave the *estudiantes* to their videos and return to the hotel.

It's been an interesting first full day in Chile: coffee at an intriguing establishment (if Carlsberg made coffee shops, they probably wouldn't be the best in the world, because they're already here, in Santiago), followed by what seems to have been the aftermath of a riot! As introductions to a country go, I figure this might be difficult to beat.

2

I have been in South America for three months now. In London, at the end of a long-term IT contract, I was worn out and in need of a break. I considered retreating to my home place in Ireland. Instead, I rented out my flat and booked a two-month holiday in Ecuador: four weeks of Spanish classes in Quito, followed by a month exploring the country. After that, I wasn't sure. But with my flat rented out, I figured that if I liked the place, I might stay for a bit.

After Quito, I crossed to Ecuador's beautiful coastline, and stuttered south. Four weeks later, my departure date almost due, I had no intention of returning home. I delayed my flight by three months (later, I would postpone it by a further two) and kept on moving. Four weeks after that, I am in Santiago.

Clearly, since Ecuador, the nature of my stay in South America has changed. It is no longer a fixed-length holiday; it is open-ended, extended travel. I move from place to place as I please. If a location is pleasant, or if the company is good, I stay for as long as I wish. I am enjoying myself. Previously undiagnosed, pent-up London-ness is draining from me. I am a very content, accidental traveller.

En route to Chile, I stopped off in Peru. Here I received conclusive proof that my four weeks of Spanish lessons in Quito had not equipped me as I had hoped they might. Until then, I had persuaded myself that my Spanish was adequate. Mainly, I did this by not actually speaking the language; I resorted instead to using standalone words, and pointing. In Lima, the final nail in the coffin of any linguistic aspirations I might have had was delivered by a passer-by who I had stopped to ask, in Spanish, for directions to an internet café. He asked me to repeat my question, this time '*en español, por favor*'. My Spanish would not improve. I resorted again to using standalone words, and became an expert pointer.

In the absence of Spanish-language skills to help me pass time with locals, I bought a small laptop, a notebook, for company. And in the course of mindless browsing, I discovered irlandeses.org, the hugely informative website of SILAS (the Society for Irish Latin American Studies), its pages full of Irish links to the continent, almost all unknown to me. Soon I decided to assign a vague purpose to my vague ramblings. Where I could, I would visit places with an Irish connection.

There are vast distances to cover in South America and bus travel is the norm (train services do exist, but mostly only within urban areas). The quality of bus services can vary enormously. Top-of-the-range companies operate *cama* (sleeper) and *semi-cama* buses (the latter have almost fully reclinable seats, blankets, hostesses, meals, air conditioning and rolling movies). Many companies offer a perfectly decent, standard service. And others don't quite reach that mark. Guidebooks warn of unsafe travel, and in some countries, stories of horrific bus crashes are not rare. In Ecuador, on long-distance journeys, I would always choose a seat towards the middle or rear of a bus. Only in hindsight does it seem odd that my choice of seat was determined not by availability or comfort, but by the marginally increased chances of avoiding death in the case of a head-on collision.

Bus services, it seems, are provided by private companies. At their most basic, these consist of a two-man operation, a single bus operated by a driver and a sidekick. The sidekick collects fares and advertises the service. This usually involves standing around at a bus station, shouting his destination at passers-by while pointing at his bus. This can make bus stations very noisy places.

Mate (pronounced *mah*-tay) is popular here. *Mate* is a drink made by steeping the dried leaves of the yerba mate plant in hot water (yerba mate is a species of the holly family; its evergreen leaves contain caffeine). It is drunk from a calabash gourd through a metal straw, a *bombilla*. With a filter at one end, the *bombilla* acts as both a straw and a strainer. The gourd is three-quarters filled with dried leaves (a much greater volume of leaves than, say, in tea), and then filled with water, hot, but not boiling. Drinkers carry a *termo*, a thermal vacuum flask, for hot water top-ups. Drinking *mate* can be a communal experience, and sharing is common. In Bolivia, I accepted a sip from an Argentinian couple; the *mate* dissolved the gum I had tucked away in a corner of my mouth.

3

Next morning, in Santiago, TV stations report that, on the Alameda last night, 30,000 people demonstrated against government plans to build a hydro-electricity plant in an area of pristine wilderness in Patagonia (most of Chile's rivers rush westwards from the heights of the Andes to the Pacific; many are ideal for generating hydro-electricity). The number of protesters took police by surprise. And the organisers too, it seems. The march had been due to start at 7pm, but was delayed as crowds continued to gather. It also extended beyond the expected 9pm finish time, at which point it turned nasty. Sixty-seven people were arrested and seven injured. The use of *gas lacrimógenas* (tear gas) would make headlines on TV and in newspapers for much of the week.

I ramble out into the chilly morning and retrace my steps of yesterday, west along the Alameda. Opposite the giant Chilean flag, on the other side of the road, is La Moneda Palace, the official seat of the president of Chile. Originally the Royal Mint (*la moneda* – coin, currency), it took on its current role in the mid-1800s. The building has been centre-stage in Chilean life ever since, not least on September 11, 1973, when a military coup, organised by General Augusto Pinochet, overthrew the government of Salvador Allende.

In 1970, Salvador Allende became the world's first democratically elected Marxist head of state. In Chile, a shift to the left had been ongoing for decades. Allende himself had contested three previous presidential elections. In 1964, he had received 39% of the vote and lost out only because the right, sensing their own electoral demolition, did not put forward a candidate.

The new president's aim was to create a socialist state by constitutional means. He wanted to break the power of the oligarchs, those great landholders and capitalists who had wielded power in the country for centuries. He planned to nationalise mining, industry and banking, and in this way, place the levers of power in the hands of the state.

During Allende's first twelve months in office, Chile enjoyed a boom. After this, the economy went into free-fall. Soon, inflation was pushing 180%. Industrial production fell. For the year 1973, agricultural output was down by almost one-sixth. Industries were nationalised, including the subsidiaries of multi-nationals, like Ford. Great landholdings were broken up, but only a small number of the rural poor benefited. Land reform upset all parties involved: those whose lands were expropriated, and the peasants, who were unhappy that it wasn't happening quickly enough.

As the economic crisis deepened, the hard-left advocated the immediate, armed overthrow of the capitalist state. Allende remained insistent on a constitutional route to socialism. The moderate-left favoured this approach, as a means of keeping the middle classes on board. But support from this quarter was draining away. White-collar workers went on strike. In Santiago, in the 'March of the Empty Pots', 5,000 middle-class women took to the streets, banging saucepans to complain about food shortages. An eleven-month truckers' strike disrupted the whole country. In an attempt to ward off any possible attempted coup d'état, Allende brought three military commanders into his cabinet.

Congressional elections in March 1973 were inconclusive. No single party achieved an overall majority – all were left frustrated. Inflation was now running at an annual rate of 600%. The hard-left had begun to arm themselves. The right wanted the military to intervene, but Allende retained the support of the head of the army, General Carlos Prats. After more strikes and disturbances, however, his fellow officers forced Prats to resign. On August 23, 1973, he was replaced by General Augusto Pinochet. The general informed Allende that he was 'ready to lay down (his) life in defence of the constitutional government (that the president represented)'. Over two weeks later, Pinochet organised a coup d'état, to begin at 6am on September 11, 1973.

On the morning of the 11th, in La Moneda, the president refused all calls to stand down. Before the final ultimatum expired at 11am, government snipers had taken to the surrounding rooftops. By noon, there were tanks on the streets. As Hawker Hunter jets slammed the palace with rockets, Allende moved deeper into the building. He had with him a Kalashnikov rifle, given to him by Fidel Castro. He set the rifle to automatic, placed it between his legs and aimed it at his chin. Two shots ripped off the top of his head.

This morning at La Moneda, military activity is of a less unpleasant variety. In a yard behind the palace, the Changing of the Guard is coming to a close. Departing soldiers in white jackets follow a military band around the far side of the building and down a side street. Others, in brown jackets and now on duty, march through the palace gates. A small crowd watches from a raised pathway at the edge of the yard. Two cavalrymen linger for tourist photographs.

Nearby, on Calle Moneda, the working week is done and the Financial District is quiet. Café Bombay is closed. The waitresses have packed away their things (this can't have delayed them too long) and departed for the weekend.

Off Calle Moneda, the pedestrianised streets of the city centre are busy with Saturday morning shoppers. Coffee comes from a 'conventional' café on Paseo Ahumada (perpendicular to the Alameda, this street has the most expensive retail space in South America). The cappuccino, in a stemmed glass with a metal handle, is topped with a dollop of cream tapered like a 99 ice-cream cone. The cream melts slowly and seeps into the coffee, sweetening and cooling at each sip.

*

Having brushed up against riot police last night, I'm expecting a less eventful search for a beer this evening. From the Universidad de Chile Metro station on the Alameda, an underground train travels directly to Baquedano, the stop for Bellavista, the city's main nightlife area. It's a standard fare, 560 pesos (c. 75p), for all single journeys.

A short walk from the Metro at Baquedano, a bridge leads over the Mapocho river. At the moment, the river is a trickle. In its concreted bed, a low wall runs down one side, close to the bank. What water there is seems to have been diverted down this channel. Across the bridge is Pío Nono, Bellavista's main thoroughfare. Part-way down Pío Nono, off the road, patioBellavista is a development of upmarket bars, restaurants and sellers of tasteful tat. The sign at the entrance has had a designer makeover – the letters of patioBellavista are purple except for the 'e', which is orange and back-to-front. The area is well laid-out. A raised wooden walkway links its various parts; people pose for photographs beside sculptures in a small courtyard. There are some tourists about, but mostly it's Chileans who are enjoying the nice ambience, the fading light and the high prices.

Back on Pío Nono, customers sit at tables outside bars and restaurants. The drink of choice is a shared, screw-top, litre bottle of Escudo, the local brew. Escudo also comes in larger volumes. On some tables, a clear tube, about half a metre high and the breadth of a pint glass, is filled with beer. Glasses are topped up via a tap in the contraption's fat base.

Bellavista is quiet tonight and as I stroll along Pío Nono my urge for a beer subsides. Soon, I'm back on the Metro, bound for Paris.

4

No 'central agency' planned the Spanish conquest of South America, according to Edwin Williamson in *The Penguin History of Latin America* (the Spanish ventured south from Central America in the 1520s). It was improvised and driven by the desire of *conquistadores* for precious metals, and their subsequent need for a labour supply (ie: the indigenous peoples). Their main ambition was to acquire the wealth required 'to achieve noble status' and their lordship over others. To achieve what Williamson calls this 'seigneurial way of life', the Spanish went to those parts of the continent that already had metals and labour, broadly those areas previously conquered by the Incas (and, further north, by the Aztecs).

To manage their vast colonies, the Spanish set up a viceregal system. All 'power and authority issued from the person of the monarch…through his viceroys and the royal bureaucracy'. Initially, there were two viceroyalties. New Spain, with its capital at Mexico City, stretched from Panama northwards (it also included part of modern-day Venezuela). The Viceroyalty of Peru had its capital at Lima, and covered most of Spanish South America. These enormous territories were subdivided further into provinces (ruled by a governor), which, in turn, were made up of *corregimientos* (administrative units); in a *corregimiento*, each town had a *cabildo* (municipal council). Other, separate administrations, captaincies general (Chile was a captaincy general), were technically under the realm of the viceroy, but actually conducted business directly with Madrid.

Spain alone was permitted to trade with its colonies, and it enforced this monopoly by ensuring that all commerce across the Atlantic was channelled through a restricted number of ports. On the peninsula, Seville was the main entry/exit point. At first, in the Americas, only three ports served the empire's vast territories. Goods to and from Mexico and Central America passed through Veracruz. Nombre de Dios and later Portobelo, both in Panama, serviced Peru and Chile, while Cartagena de Indias dealt with imports to, and exports from, New Granada (present-day Colombia).

Guilds of merchants on either side of the Atlantic were granted exclusive rights to trade, and these monopolists kept prices high to ensure large profits. With the discovery of silver in South America, and the booming towns that resulted, Spain was no longer able to furnish the New World with all the goods it required. Other European merchants supplied the deficit, either legally through Seville merchant houses, or illegally through smuggling.

Official sailings to and from the colonies were known as the *carrera de Indias* (the Indies run). In the latter half of the sixteenth century, when the export of silver increased, the vessels that brought home the booty were protected by galleons (the *galeones* fleets). These treasure ships attracted the attention of Spain's foes. Silver was 'the fuel that drove the Spanish war machine', and her enemies tried to cut off its supply.

The *galeones* fleets also drew interest from mainly French, English and Dutch pirates (these were the days of the pirates of the Spanish Main). Chief among them was Sir Francis Drake. *El Draque* operated in the Caribbean in the early 1570s, before turning his attention to the Pacific coast of South America later in the decade. His activities were not confined to American shores during this time. In Ireland, from

1571 to 1575, the Enterprise of Ulster was an attempt to colonise that province's eastern counties, a task devolved to individual entrepreneurs. Walter Devereux, 1st Earl of Essex, mortgaged his estates in England to finance an expedition to colonise Antrim. He ended up in a war with Sorley Boy MacDonnell (Somhairle Buidhe, Sorley of the Yellow Hair). In 1575, on the earl's orders, Francis Drake and John Norreys (a prominent Elizabethan soldier) landed on Rathlin Island, off the Antrim coast. The MacDonnells occupied a castle there. The castle's 200 defenders surrendered, but were put to death. A further 400 women and children of the Clan MacDonnell, hidden in caves on the island, were slaughtered. Ultimately, the Enterprise of Ulster ended in failure. For his losses, Queen Elizabeth I compensated Devereux by making him Earl Marshal of Ireland. Her Majesty seems to have neglected to offer compensation to the MacDonnells.

El Draque had started as he meant to go on. Some years later, on the west coast of South America, his activities were infamous. Sara Wheeler, writing in *Travels in a Thin Country*, says that 'his conduct up and down the Chilean and Peruvian coasts was so barbarous that his name entered the language as a synonym for terror and destruction'.

5

It is freezing in Santiago. It is May, we're in the South American winter, but my room at Hotel Paris has no heating, and the head of my bed is underneath an old, metal-framed window that has no insulation. A thin curtain does little to keep out the cold draught. Next morning, I wake to a sore throat, a blocked nose and a cramped stomach. The hotel's name, I think, conjures up an image of grandeur, one entirely at odds with the level of comfort it actually provides. I've re-christened it Hotel Siberia.

Today, I plan to visit Cerro Santa Lucía, a small hill in the centre of Santiago, where the city was founded. In colonial times, once a band of conquistadors had conquered and settled an area, the *adelantado* (chief conquistador) was obliged by the Crown to establish a town. At the centre of each town was a plaza, around which was built the Cabildo (town hall), church and main residences. Parallel and perpendicular streets then divided the surrounding area into blocks (*cuadras*). Cerro Santa Lucía is a short walk from the capital's central square, La Plaza de Armas (*la arma* – weapon, arm). The main square of many South American towns and cities has this name, a reminder of a past when these central locations provided a mustering point to which settlers retreated when attacked by indigenous peoples.

Santiago's Plaza de Armas is at the end of Paseo Ahumada. The sizeable space is mostly paved, with a central fountain and tall pine trees that sprout from small, well-tended splotches of greenery. On this cold and bright Sunday morning, a military brass band in sand-coloured uniforms plays on the plaza's covered bandstand. At a nearby junction, two samba dancers wear outrageous head plumes and little else. The girls dance and shake to a persistent drum beat. The drummers wear *Keiko Presidente* T-shirts (Keiko is a candidate in the upcoming Peruvian presidential election). It is unclear what the girls are doing here, so far from home, but they're proving very popular. Men gather round, craning their necks to ogle the dancers' minimally covered, juddering body parts. Wearing so little, the girls should consider a job in a Santiago coffee shop.

A series of terraces at different levels on Cerro Santa Lucía are natural resting points on the climb to the hill's summit. One, Terraza Neptuno, offers a good view of the city from behind a disturbingly low railing. Or it would be a good view, if it wasn't for the perma-smog. A soupy cloud of it lies low in the mid-distance. From Neptuno, sets of steep steps zigzag up the slope; at every turn, teenagers canoodle on benches. At the top, a short climb leads to a small turret. Here, a low railing around the crenellated edge offers minimal protection from a sharp drop over the side.

In 1535, the conquistador Diego de Almagro left Peru to explore what is modern-day Chile. Almagro found none of the precious metals he was looking for, and two years later he returned north. The Spanish showed no further interest in the country until the arrival, in 1540, of Pedro de Valdivia. And it was here, on Cerro Santa Lucía, in February of the following year, that Valdivia founded Santiago de Nueva Extremadura – Santo Iago is St James, Extremadura was Valdivia's birthplace in Spain, and Nueva Extremadura was the name originally given to Chile.

The absence of any mineral wealth meant that conquistadors were not particularly attracted to Chile. By the end of the sixteenth century, only 5,000 or so Spaniards had migrated here. It was in this early colonial period that vast tracts of land were distributed among the conquerers. And for centuries, a small elite was to control most of the country's wealth and political power.

Towards the end of the colonial period, the population of Chile was approximately 500,000. This number did not include those aboriginal peoples yet to be subdued, most of whom lived south of the Bío-Bío river. In south-central Chile, the Bío-Bío formed *la frontera*, the frontier between Spanish-ruled Chile and Araucanía, home of the Mapuche (La Frontera can also refer to the territory of Araucanía, as opposed to the border itself). Five hundred kilometres south of Santiago, the city of Concepción lies near the mouth of the Bío-Bío and, in the 1780s, it was governed by an Irishman, Ambrose O'Higgins.

Ambrose O'Higgins was born c.1721, at Ballynary, County Sligo (the family later moved to Summerhill in County Meath). As a young man, he moved to Cádiz, Spain, where he worked for an Irish merchant house. From there, he travelled to South America. Unsuccessful business ventures meant that by 1761 O'Higgins was back on the peninsula, looking for more steady employment. He joined the army as a lieutenant *ingeniero delineador* (engineer draughtsman) and three years later returned to South America as an assistant to an engineer, Irishman John Garland, formerly a cadet with the Hibernia Regiment in Spain.

Garland was appointed military governor of Valdivia. In northern Patagonia, 1,000 kilometres south of Santiago, Valdivia was deep in Mapuche territory, and at that time, not much more than a walled military camp in the midst of hostile neighbours. There, O'Higgins was successful in wars against the native population. By 1780, he was commandant general of the army, and in 1787 he was appointed captain general of Chile, the highest post in the country's administration.

South again from Valdivia, the town of Osorno was even further into indigenous lands. Founded in 1558, it was destroyed by the Mapuche early in the following century. O'Higgins wanted the town rebuilt, and he gave the task to John Mackenna (in Chile, the name is recorded using a lower-case 'k'). Mackenna was born in 1771 at Clogher, County Tyrone (some sources give his birthplace as Monaghan). His uncle was Alexander O'Reilly, named Condé de O'Reilly (Count Alexander O'Reilly) and Visconde de Cavan by Charles III of Spain (at the time, O'Reilly was the leading infantry commander in the Spanish military). After three years at the Royal Academy of Mathematics in Barcelona, Mackenna joined the army as a cadet. He fought in a number of European campaigns, was made captain in 1795, and left for America the following year. Appointed governor of Osorno by O'Higgins, Mackenna made a success of rebuilding the town.

A small chapel, Ermita Mackenna, sits at the edge of a terrace on the climb to the summit of Cerro Santa Lucía. Today, the ground around it is unsafe, and access to the building is restricted by tape across the path leading to its entrance. The *ermita* holds the remains of Benjamín Vicuña Mackenna, grandson of John. Vicuña Mackenna was a prodigious journalist, author and historian, a senator and, in 1875, an unsuccessful presidential candidate. In 1851, he had taken part in a revolution to overthrow the government and was jailed, only to escape dressed as a woman. He lived in exile in North America for a time, studied in England and visited Ireland, before eventually returning to Chile.

Ambrose O'Higgins was a success as captain general of Chile and in 1795 he was appointed viceroy of Peru, the most prominent position in Spanish South America. Along the way, he also acquired the titles Marquess of Osorno and Baron of Ballenar. While crossing the Andes from Argentina to Chile, O'Higgins came up with the idea of constructing a chain of *cobertizos* (shelters) along the route. This enabled the establishment of a postal system between the countries and allowed for the year-round transportation of goods. He fortified Valparaíso, Concepción and Valdivia and built the roads from Santiago to Valparaíso, and from Concepción south to Chiloé. In moves which did not endear him to local elites, he advocated reforms in the Catholic Church to benefit the poor. O'Higgins also finally abolished *encomienda*, a system whereby Spaniards received labour from the aboriginal population in return for protection, wages and religious instruction (in practice, many of the indigenous people were treated little better than slaves). He travelled throughout the northern parts of the country and founded numerous towns and cities (hispanicised Vallenar in the Atacama region started life in 1789 as San Ambrosio de Ballenary). In Alaska, where Spain had a presence at this time, Vallenar Bay, Point Higgins and Port Higgins are on Revillagigedo and Gravina islands, in the southeast of the state. O'Higgins was known as 'the great viceroy'. He died in Lima on March 18, 1801.

6

Santiago's freezing weather and the hotel's miserable insulation ensure that my health shows no improvement. Next morning, I wake up feeling dreadful. I'm no better as the day goes on, and the remainder of my week drags by in an uncomfortable flu (*la gripe,* pronounced gree-pay). Most of my time is spent indoors, in Hotel Siberia, although it's difficult to tell if there's any difference between temperatures there and those outside.

During the week, in the broadsheet *La Tercera*, there's a tiny piece about Queen Elizabeth II. It reports that she's on a '*gira* (tour) *de Irlanda*'. I'm reminded of the near-equivalent Italian word, *giro,* and the Giro d'Italia cycle race. And now I can't rid myself of the image of the Queen zipping around Ireland bent over the handlebars of a racing bike, in full evening dress, wearing her crown. She has a grimace on her face and keeps just ahead of a peloton of reporters and photographers. For some reason, the photographers are from a black-and-white, Prohibition-era, US movie. They wear pinch-fronted fedora hats and long trench coats; cigarettes hang from the corners of their mouths. Their cameras come from the same era: those big, old ones, with large, popping flash bulbs. The Queen's previously unreported prowess on a racing bike allows her to escape her pursuers.

Disappointingly, my diminishing bank balance makes no improvement of its own accord, and it seems that I must make an effort. Avoiding pricier city centre alternatives, lunchtimes are spent at a café/restaurant around the corner from the hotel. For 2,800 pesos

(c. £3.50), Café San Francisco provides a decent three-course meal, albeit with relatively small portions.

One afternoon during the week, on day-release from Siberia, I notice that some cobbles on Calle Londres have been replaced with brass plates. The plates are outside No. 38 and two girls are on their knees polishing them. A plaque by the door explains that, in this building, from September 1973 to September 1974, 96 people, including two pregnant women, were detained, tortured, disappeared and executed (disappear, normally an intransitive verb, tends to have an alternative form when used in relation to those who were never seen again once they fell into the hands of the state: as in, 'they disappeared him'). Inscribed on each plate is the name and age of a victim. As I read the plaque, a passer-by says something I don't catch, and walks on. After a few steps, he turns to face me, makes a throat-slitting gesture complete with sound effect, and continues on his way.

In the aftermath of his coup d'état in September 1973, Pinochet was intent on eradicating socialism. He set up his own secret police, the DINA (*Dirección de Inteligencia Nacional*, Directorate of National Intelligence), an organisation with thousands of members and a broad network of informers. Those considered enemies of the regime were arrested. Some were executed, more were brought to detention centres for interrogation. Questioning uncovered links to others, and this, in turn, led to further arrests. Londres 38 was a detention centre. Here, up to 70 prisoners were held blindfolded in the living room before being taken for interrogation and torture. Often, in the early days of the regime, the DINA arrested not only those wanted for questioning, but also members of their families. At Londres 38, the latter were tortured and raped in front of prisoners in an effort to extract information.

Another infamous detention centre was the National Stadium in Santiago. In his book *Pinochet in Piccadilly*, Andy Beckett writes that beneath the stands 'was a labyrinth of corridors, entrances and exits, windowless changing rooms, concrete culs-de-sac – a whole architecture for controlling groups of people, already in place'. Here, prisoners were beaten and mauled. Some of those detained, but obviously innocent of anything even mildly offensive to the regime and about to be freed, were allowed to wander through the stands. On the pitch below, foreign journalists were invited to view the benign circumstances under which those arrested were being held.

Arrests continued well after the coup itself (it is estimated that approximately 130,000 were taken into custody in the first three years of Pinochet's rule). Sergio Rueda was one of those detained. A member of MIR (*Movimiento de Izquierda Revolucionaria*, Movement of the Revolutionary Left), Rueda was arrested and brought to Villa Grimaldi, a nineteenth-century house on the eastern outskirts of Santiago. First, his gaolers blindfolded him, and punched and beat him. Then, a mattress was removed from the metal frame of a bunk bed. Rueda was stripped, made to lie on the bed and strapped to it. Electrical leads were clipped to the straps, water thrown over him and the electric switch thrown. When the current was switched off, he was asked set questions, after which the process was repeated. This happened day after day. He was blindfolded for all of this time, and was moved from cells to rooms to cupboards. The strength of the electric current cracked his teeth. The electrodes damaged his face and his testicles. He had blackouts and temporarily lost feeling in his legs.

Doctors were on hand at the villa to revive patients so that questioning could continue. Some badly injured prisoners were released to serve as 'walking advertisements for the power of the secret police'. Rueda's torture continued. In early 1976, he was moved to a concentration camp, Tres Álamos, near Santiago. Here, despite being locked indoors night and day, prisoners were generally fortunate enough to be left alone.

Later that year, criticism from abroad led to the closure of Tres Álamos and Rueda was released. His wife had applied to the World University Service, which found student places for refugees. They were accepted, received a grant and moved to Britain. Many were not so lucky. It is estimated that 3,200 deaths occurred during Pinochet's military regime. Up to 30,000 people went into exile.

In a plebiscite in 1988, Pinochet was rejected by a majority of the electorate and in 1990 he was succeeded by the Christian Democrat, Patricio Aylwin. In late 2004, a commission investigating abuses during Pinochet's time in office published its findings. In response, the government announced that it would offer lifetime pensions to 28,000 victims of torture.

7

On Saturday, my body back in working order, I step out into another very cold morning. On the corner where Londres almost reaches the Alameda (they don't quite intersect), red and white graffiti has been sprayed on the windows of La Piccola Italia restaurant, leftovers from another demonstration. Last night, I had cut through a continuous stream of students as they made their way along the Alameda in the direction of the giant Chilean flag. The marchers were in good voice: '*sin re-pres-as*' (without dams), the chant repeatedly volleyed back in response to distant prompts of '*Pat-a-gonia*'.

Today, the Heineken Rugby Cup Final between Northampton and Leinster takes place at 5pm, Cardiff-time. That makes it noon in Santiago and a good excuse to visit Flannery's Geo Pub in Las Condes, further east in the city. I take the Metro to Tobalaba (from the Mapuche village, *Toblahua* – Place of Colourful Flowers), which exits on to a busy junction in a commercial and residential district. I'm early, and park myself at the second-floor window of a McDonald's, with a newspaper, coffee and a couple of *medialunas* (literally a half-moon, a *medialuna* is the same shape as a croissant, but smaller and heavier).

My newspaper provides more information on the demonstration last night. Although generally peaceful, there *was* more violence, some of it caught on video and shown on TV this morning. A policeman, isolated from his colleagues, was set upon by protesters. A passer-by took a two-handed hold of one end of his skateboard and swung it into the *carabinero*'s face (*Skater deja nocaut*, says the newspaper: 'skater delivers a knockout'). The policeman suffered a fractured cheekbone and nose and ended up in hospital where, later, he was visited by the president.

When I find it, Flannery's is closed. It doesn't open until 6pm on a Saturday; a glance at their website would have saved me a journey.

Back on the Alameda, a waiter with a car windscreen scraper is hard at work on the graffitied windows of La Piccola Italia. In my Siberian igloo, ESPN is showing the rugby. I switch on with fourteen minutes gone, just as Jonathan Sexton lands a penalty to reduce Leinster's deficit to 7–3. The Irish side make little impact in the first half, and a couple of tries later, Northampton head into the break with a commanding 22–6 lead.

Not long after the restart, and following two converted tries, Leinster are only two points behind. Sexton has a penalty to put them in front for the first time. '*Sí, Sí, Sí, Sí, Sí!*', the ESPN guy gets excited as the ball heads between the posts: 22–23! Northampton are stunned. Leinster's dominance continues. A penalty, another converted try and it's 22–33. Their opponents respond; an attack leads to the Leinster 22. Somehow the ball is stolen and thumped into touch down the field. Northampton momentum is quashed. Another penalty to the Irish team and then it's the end. Leinster are '*Campeones de Europa – campeonissimo!*'. Northampton look bewildered. '*Todo es azul, todo es felicidad!*' (Everything is blue, everything is happiness!).

The following evening, on a return trip to Tobalaba, Flannery's is open for business. A notice claims that it is the first real Irish pub in Chile, and it's a fine spot. Dimly lit, it has parquet flooring, wooden counters and thick wooden tables and chairs. Logs are piled high against the wall beside a blazing fire. Stained-glass windows are inlaid with Irish county and family crests. A framed page from the *Irish Times* of 1916 reports on the 'Sinn Féin Rebellion in Ireland'; another shows Michael Collins on the stump. And there's an indispensable 'Schedule of Tolls and Customs to be collected in the town of Ballinrobe'. Music is turned down low and the large, muted TV screens replay Real Madrid's 8–1 demolition of Almería, from earlier in the afternoon (unsurprisingly, Spanish, rather than English, football is the main draw here). I order the Tipperary Sandwich ('Tipery', says the waiter, confirming my order). It's pork loin pan-fried with Gouda cheese, tomato, jalapeño, guacamole and lettuce. Not, to my knowledge, a native Tipery dish, it comes with potato wedges and is quite tasty.

Returning from Flannery's, I stop off at Bellavista. On the way, the slightly curved, smoky glass in the Metro train door somehow throws back a slimline reflection. Unused to that image of late, I figure I should invest in some of that glass for mirrors in my flat in London. Over the bridge at Pío Nono, the Mapocho has shrunk further; it is now only puddles.

Dublin is on the fringe of patioBellavista with the back-to-front 'e'; it's not 'The Dublin Pub' or 'The Dublin Bar', just 'Dublin'. But it's packed, and I move on. I'm looking for a quiet, auld fella's pub, with a high stool and football on a TV in the corner. But tonight, Bellavista is busy with partying groups. I abandon the search for a peaceful pint, ramble back to the Metro and bask in my slimline reflection on my return to the city centre.

8

O'Higgins Square is a tiny space beside Richmond Bridge, in southwest London. I passed it often, on walks there, by the Thames. A bust in the square remembers Bernardo O'Higgins. He was the 'liberator of his country', according to an inscription on the plinth, beneath a quote: *'Vivir Con Honor o Morir Con Gloria'* (Live With Honour or Die With Glory). On occasion, wreaths and flowers appeared at the foot of the plinth; O'Higgins was not forgotten, it seems, even that far from home.

In Chile, it is difficult to stray far without a reminder of O'Higgins. On Calle Londres, Instituto O'Higginiano is dedicated to his life and works. I pass it every day on my way to Avenida Libertador Bernardo O'Higgins. West along the *avenida*, his remains lie in the Crypt of the Liberator, in front of La Moneda Palace. A glance at a map shows that, further afield, Bernardo O'Higgins National Park covers over 36,000 square kilometres of Patagonia; O'Higgins Lake there is the deepest in the Americas. It is near O'Higgins Glacier, and just to the south of Villa O'Higgins. The sports pages of newspapers report on O'Higgins FC of Rancagua, who play in Chile's *Primera División* (at one point in the '90s, their manager was Manuel Pellegrini, who, in 2013, took charge at Manchester City – coincidentally, both teams play in the same sky-blue colours. O'Higgins' main rivals are Rangers de Talca, a club named by a Scotsman, one of its founders). Bernardo O'Higgins was born in the city of Chillán, approximately 500 kilometres, and a morning's train ride, south of Santiago.

My Tuesday morning departure is at 7.30am. I wake up late, timing is tight, and not helped when I can't find the key to the lock for my bag. I dump the bag's just-packed contents on to the bed, but still can't find the key, quickly repack and run for a taxi. I make it to Estación Central with a minute to spare.

After the rush, it's a relief to fall into my seat. But it's difficult to relax just yet. Passing through the city, at the approach to every railway crossing, the driver sounds his horn repeatedly and at length (it's a safety measure; the crossings don't have gates). The train has three carriages and is well tended; drinks and snacks are served from a trolley, an attendant regularly collects rubbish, and every so often, another mops the aisle. The guards are two smartly dressed young women in pinstriped uniforms; their pony-tails fall from the back of blue, peaked caps. At some point on the journey, I find the key to the lock for my bag. It's in the small, zipped pouch in my daypack, exactly where it should be.

The train pulls into Chillán after midday. A short taxi ride brings me to Hostal Canadá, but I plump instead for Hotel Canadá Express, its upper-class relation around the block. Its tariff is beyond my self-imposed budget, but I can't face trudging further.

Hotel Canadá Express (complete with maple leaf logo) seems to be more of a motel than a hotel. On a residential street, a tall gate and security railings close off the narrow property at the footpath. Beyond a slightly unkempt front yard, the single-storey building stretches from reception to the rear of a long lot. A paved walkway keeps it company down its length. To the left of the walkway is fenced-in, well-tended greenery; to the right, the hotel has clean, cream walls and a red, tiled roof. A rag doll with a room number hangs on each of the eight bedroom doors. My room is small, modern and well decorated, and the bathroom is clean and fresh. But my enthusiasm is reserved for a small blow-heater. I'm excited about the prospect of getting my first, and well-needed, blast of artificial heat in South America.

Chillán seems a plain place. I've only just arrived, but am keen to find out when I can leave; I return to the station and note train times for a return north tomorrow. A railway guard provides directions to the town's museum, where I hope to find information about O'Higgins. It's on a side street, in the direction I've come, back towards the centre of town. On the way, a board on the footpath outside what looks like a terraced house lists the three courses of a single lunch option. Famished after my lengthy morning, I step into a small room. It has a stone floor and short lines of tables and benches that sit along bare walls. I take a pew and ask the hovering landlady for a menu. She giggles and points to the board on the footpath. OK, I say, nodding in its direction. Not quite sure what I've said OK to, I glance again at the board and recognise only the words *pan* (bread) and *fruta* (fruit). Soon a lamb stew arrives, loaded with potatoes. Dessert is the *fruta*, an unlikely-looking pear, hard, green and shaped like an apple. For 1,700 pesos (c. £1.70), the meal is tasty and filling and great value.

When eventually I find Museo Claudio Arrau, the doors are locked. '*Cerrado*' (closed), I say to the railway guard back at the station, when he asks if I was successful in my search. At the ticket office, I arrange my escape from Chillán, and book a seat on a train to Talca, 250 kilometres to the north, leaving early next morning.

Back in the city centre, the inevitable main plaza is nicely paved, with grass sections and tall trees. It is host to the equally inevitable posse of snoozing stray dogs (all cities seem to have their quota), pecking pigeons and smooching teenagers. In the middle of the square, the Libertador, Don Bernardo O'Higgins, stands tall on a plinth. Chubby-cheeked Bernardo assumes a statesmanlike, speechifying pose; his left hand clutches a lapel, his right arm is slightly outstretched. He is the '*Padre de la Patria*' and a '*Hijo Ilustre de Ñuble*' ('illustrious son of Ñuble', the province of which Chillán is the capital).

Bernardo O'Higgins was born in Chillán in 1778, the illegitimate son of Ambrose O'Higgins. At the time, O'Higgins Sr was a prominent figure in La Frontera (Chillán is c. 100 kilometres east of Concepción, in the Bío-Bío region). The year before, he had been camped nearby on land owned by Simón Riquelme, a member of the Chillán *cabildo*, and was in a relationship with Riqulem's eighteen-year-old daughter Isabel (O'Higgins was in his late fifties). The pair never married. O'Higgins soon left the area and never saw Isabel again.

O'Higgins also never met his son, although he did arrange his schooling. After spending his early years in the care of a family friend in Talca, Bernardo (he grew up as Bernardo Riquelme) was dispatched to Chillán, where he was taught by the Franciscans. Later, his education continued in Lima before, in his late teens, he travelled to London and studied at Richmond (which explains the bust by the Thames there). Ambrose O'Higgins died while his son was in Europe and he bequeathed him an estate, Las Canteras, a hacienda in La Frontera. Bernardo returned to Chile, took his father's surname and settled into life as a farmer near the place of his birth.

Around this time, at the start of the 1800s, relations between Spain and its colonies were unsettled. From the middle of the eighteenth century, the Bourbons (who had replaced the Hapsburgs on the Spanish throne in the early 1700s) had begun to introduce reforms aimed at increasing revenue for the Crown. In 1776, a new viceroyalty was created, the Viceroyalty of the Río de la Plata. It had its capital at Buenos Aires and incorporated the vast territories east of the Andes that had previously been under the jurisdiction of Lima (roughly modern-day Bolivia, Paraguay, Argentina and Uruguay). This shifted the economic emphasis of most of the continent away from Lima and the Pacific towards Buenos Aires and the Atlantic.

Along with the revision of territorial boundaries, Madrid was keen to enhance its control in the colonies. Judges, governors and tax officials were sent out from Spain to replace the *criollos* (*criollo/a*, anglicised as creole: any Spaniard, and descendants, born in the Americas), who had come to occupy these positions in the old Hapsburg bureaucracy. And in an attempt to improve the peninsular economy, the colonies were prohibited from producing certain goods (wheat and olive oil, among others), leaving an export outlet for Spanish producers.

Creoles weren't best pleased. Clearly, the changes were not in *their* interests. Trade was still dominated by merchants from the peninsula. In addition, creoles were continually being asked to contribute to the royal treasury to fund wars in Europe. The Bourbons also attacked the power of the Church, a force which bound together colonial societies otherwise riven by ethnic and regional divisions (many creoles were particularly bitter about the expulsion of the Jesuits from South America in 1767).

Edwin Williamson (*The Penguin History of Latin America*) writes: 'Under the Hapsburgs, the Crown had enjoyed a monopoly of legitimacy due principally to its compact with the Church'. In addition, 'the loyalty of the creole aristocracy had endured…because the economic enfeeblement of Spain had allowed the creole elites to satisfy in practice their two crucial aspirations: the exercise of power within their own societies and their participation in international trade through smuggling'. Bourbon 'reassertion of metropolitan power now threatened these two creole aspirations'.

Despite this, creoles still valued the Crown 'as a guarantor of law and order within their own racially divided societies'. And so, by the early 1800s, notwithstanding Bourbon reforms, imperial authority remained intact. Soon, however, events in Europe would change forever the relationship between Spain and its realms in the Americas.

In 1808, Napoleon invaded Spain. When he put his brother Joseph on the throne, revolts erupted throughout the country. A Supreme Junta was established in Seville, to rule in the name of the absent king, Ferdinand VII. In South America, creoles were unclear where authority lay: with Joseph Bonaparte, with the viceroys, or with the Supreme Junta. Eventually, they gave their allegiance to Seville.

Then, in 1810, Andalucía was taken by the French. The Supreme Junta retreated further south, to Cádiz. There, influenced by liberals, it called on delegates from the whole of the empire to assist in the drafting of a constitution. Once again, creoles were uncertain how to respond. Should they set up their own juntas to rule in the name of the king, or send delegates to Cádiz? In Chile, a junta was established on September 18, 1810 (celebrated as the country's Independence Day).

Tensions soon arose between Chilean royalists and those who favoured independence. Among the latter, there were further splits between factions based in Santiago (under the leadership of José Miguel Carrera) and those in Concepción (under Bernardo O'Higgins' mentor, Juan Martínez de Rozas, a former colleague of his father). O'Higgins had a minor military position under de Rozas, but ill health soon forced him to return to Las Canteras. From this point on, however, and from an initial position of little influence, Bernardo O'Higgins would grow ever more prominent in Chilean affairs to the extent that, by the end of the decade, he would be the leader of a newly independent country.

9

Next morning in Hotel Canadá, I wake to a warm, cosy bedroom. Last night, I had taken great pleasure in turning on the small blow-heater, and it remained on low through the night. As an added bonus, my bed has *two* duvets! I smile to myself as I dip beneath them; Hotel Siberia is but a shivering memory. Before I shower, I point the heater through the open door of the chilly bathroom and climb back under the covers to skim yesterday's *La Tercera*. It has a piece about President Obama in Ireland. They quote him: '*Mi nombre es Obama, de los Moneygall Obamas*'.

I leave my room at 6.15am, in plenty of time for the 6.45am train. But hotel reception is closed, and the front gate is locked; I can't get off the premises. I snake my hand through the gate's bars and ring the bell on the outside wall. Nothing. Back at reception, after a few loud knocks, a dozy head emerges from a window of the nearest bedroom. I hand my room-key to the owner of the dozy head and the double-gates slide open, released from within.

Nearby, the railway station is coming to life. Two women unbundle newspapers outside a small shop. Coffee is brewing at the just-opened café. A cup should clear the ridiculously early morning cobwebs. Winding between tables, bags hanging from both shoulders, I manage to spill the roasting drink over the back of my hand. It needs the attention of cold water, but the barrier at the station toilet won't accept my coins. Instead a chilled bottle of Diet Coke from the café fridge is put to cooling use.

The train originates here, at Chillán, and it stands ready at the platform. Over two hours up the track is Talca, where Bernardo

O'Higgins lived for a time as a child, and where, in 1818, he signed the Declaration of Independence. I'm hoping to find out more about the Libertador there than I did in Chillán.

On board, before departure, a guard gives a brief airline-style safety/facilities-on-offer spiel. In the bathroom, I run cold water over my hand, which helps, while in my seat, I continue to benefit from the previously unheralded medicinal properties of chilled Diet Coke. Later, the attendant in the on-board café provides ice cubes in a small plastic bag. The makeshift ice-pack soothes the throbbing, reddening blotch.

In Talca, the hotel is a short taxi ride from the station. It is still quite early on a freezing morning, and with check-in not until noon, I decamp to the town's central plaza. There, I join fully wrapped-up customers in a corner café. A hefty South American breakfast is a humungous meat sandwich: thick slices of beef with tomato, between toasted bread.

*

By 1813, and having recovered his health, Bernardo O'Higgins had joined pro-independence Chileans, now at war with royalists. The patriots were led by José Luis Carrera. After a number of defeats, the junta in Santiago removed Carrera, and replaced him with O'Higgins. He, in turn, appointed John Mackenna, his father's ex-colleague, as commandant general.

With both sides exhausted, a treaty in 1814 ended the fighting. Carrera opposed the treaty, again took control of the patriot side and exiled Mackenna. After a brief face-off between O'Higgins and

Carrera at the Battle of *Las Tres Acequias* (The Three Streams), where the former was defeated, the two joined forces to oppose the Spanish, who had decided to ignore the treaty. The royalists were victorious at the Battle of Rancagua, where a series of betrayals/misunderstandings (depending on who you believe) poisoned the already bitter relationship between the two Chilean leaders. After this victory (*La Reconquista*), the Spanish held control in the country for three years.

O'Higgins and Carrera, with other patriots, fled across the Andes to Mendoza in Argentina. From there, both men sent delegations to Buenos Aires to enlist the support of the government there. Luis Carrera represented his brother, José Miguel; John Mackenna travelled on behalf of O'Higgins. The enmity between the two Chilean leaders seems to have crossed the country with their emissaries; Carrera and Mackenna fought a duel in the Argentine capital. The Irishman was shot in the throat and killed.

At this time, Mendoza was governed by José de San Martín. Along with Simón Bolívar, San Martín is one of the two main figures of the independence struggles in South America. Born in Argentina in 1778 to Spanish parents, he returned with his family to Spain when he was six. He joined the army as a cadet and for more than twenty years fought for the Crown. In 1811, he applied to travel to Lima. Passing through Buenos Aires, he switched allegiance and joined the movement for independence there.

San Martín knew that the United Provinces of the Río de la Plata would always be at risk as long as Lima remained in royalist hands (the United Provinces of the Río de la Plata was the name of the entity that came into being after Buenos Aires established their breakaway *Primera Junta* in 1810; it comprised most of the former Viceroyalty of the Río de la Plata). He considered that it would be impossible to reach the city overland, through Upper Peru (Bolivia was at that time known as Alto Perú – Upper Peru). The only feasible option, he thought, was to cross to Chile and from there sail north. San Martín feigned ill health, was relieved of military duties and got himself appointed governor of the province of Cuyo, whose capital was Mendoza, at the eastern foot of the Andes.

It was here that he met O'Higgins. San Martín accepted O'Higgins as leader of the Chilean exiles. And, for his part, O'Higgins had no difficulty in acknowledging San Martín's overall command. Carrera, on the other hand, remained aloof, and kept a small army in a neighbourhood within the city.

In order to reach Chile, San Martín would have to cross the Andes with a fully equipped army, a monumental undertaking, successfully accomplished by the Ejército de los Andes (Army of the Andes) between January 18 and February 18, 1817. They went on to fight and beat royalists at Chacabuco, outside Santiago. The royalists scattered, some to Lima, others south to Bío-Bío.

San Martín was offered the governorship of Chile. He declined (his main aim was to take Lima); instead, O'Higgins became supreme director. Pockets of royalist resistance meant that the war was not yet over. In April 1818, however, San Martín won a decisive battle at Maipú, near the capital, which cemented Chilean independence.

In Talca, a plaque on the wall of the Museo O'Higginiano y de Bellas Artes states that, in this building in 1818, Bernardo O'Higgins signed his country's Declaration of Independence. The museum is just off the town's central plaza, not far from the café with the humungous meat sandwiches. It was once home to a Portuguese merchant and his wife who were also the Libertador's godparents. O'Higgins lived here for a time as a child before he was moved to Chillán to begin his education. Today, the museum is closed; not just temporarily closed, closed for lunch, or 'Back in 5 minutes' closed; it's a dust-gathering, cobwebs-in-the-corners closed. There's no sign of life.

I'm having very little success in my search for things O'Higgins-ish. Yesterday, the museum in Chillán was closed; today, Talca's museum is closed down. With little to keep me in the city, I decide to buy a ticket to return to Santiago in the morning. From outside the non-functioning *museo*, a *colectivo* drops me near the train station (common in many South American cities, *colectivos*, like buses, run fixed routes and have set fares). On our short spin, the driver informs me that the town's museum hasn't opened since an earthquake some years before.

Chile is situated on the Pacific Ring of Fire, a line that follows the rim of the Pacific Ocean and which is home to about 90% of the world's seismic activity. On February 27, 2010, an 8.8-magnitude earthquake struck off the coast here, its epicentre over 300 kilometres south of Santiago. Up to two million people were directly affected and tremors were felt as far away as Buenos Aires. Strict building regulations, in place since a 9.5-magnitude quake in 1960 (the largest ever recorded) and updated in the intervening period, were of limited help: approximately 400,000 homes were badly damaged. Offshore, the convergence of the South American and Nazca tectonic plates disturbed the sea floor and triggered a tsunami. Waves of up to fifteen metres hit the city of Constitución. They were three metres high and travelling at 725 kilometres per hour by the time they reached the Juan Fernández Islands, 675 kilometres offshore. Between them, the quake and tsunami claimed more than 500 lives.

*

Non-stop travelling and constantly moving from place to place means that sometimes it is easy to lose your bearings. Later that evening, I decide to visit the same restaurant as last night. I make it as far as the central plaza before I realise I'm no longer in the same city.

Once I determine that I am, in fact, in Talca, I find a small, homely restaurant in the lively city centre. Dinner is a rubbery, homemade burger, with rice, and a bread roll just out of the oven. But the highlight is a chilled bottle of Kunstmann Pale Ale. German settlers arrived in the Lake District of Chile (in the south of the country) in the second half of the nineteenth century and brought their traditions with them. Kunstmann of Valdivia holds a Bierfest every year, at the end of January. The shindig comprises four days of festivities, with a beer garden, German music, dancing, and drinking competitions. Superior drinking talent is rewarded with the title *Rey de la Cerveza* (King of Beer). This year, the reigning *Rey* is attempting to take the title for the fifth year in a row. He may well be successful. A very impressive ability to down a litre of beer in four seconds may once again be enough to see off allcomers. The *Reina de la Cerveza* (Queen of Beer) brings a civilising touch to proceedings. Grace and beauty are the determining factors in her election, in a kind of 'Lovely Fräuleins' competition.

*

After O'Higgins was made supreme director, he turned his attention to fighting royalists in the south of the country. Two Carrera brothers, Luis (who had killed John Mackenna) and Juan José, attempted to cross from Argentina to overthrow him. They were held at Mendoza, and tried and executed there. O'Higgins maintained that he had ordered their release, but that his orders had arrived too late.

José Miguel Carrera, O'Higgins' nemesis, did not cross the Andes with San Martín. He fought with federal forces in Argentina and was at the head of a party of Chilean soldiers who raided *estancias* (ranches) there. He was arrested in Mendoza and shot.

History has elevated the story of O'Higgins over that of his arch-rival. But it seems that memories are long in Chile. Sara Wheeler befriended a descendant of José Miguel Carrera on her travels in the country. On O'Higgins' birthday, 'his family used to go to the abattoir…and buy a bucket of blood to throw over his statue'. And sticking the O'Higgins postage stamp the right way up on their letters was always a no-no.

10

Next morning, it is time, once again, to pack my bags. After months of travelling, the process is now routine, and usually completed rapidly. Determined to travel light, I had brought with me to South America a shoulder bag, not a great deal larger than the type used for a long weekend. The idea of travelling light was good, but the choice of luggage was awful. After even a short walk, a heavy bag hanging from a single shoulder strap becomes a lead weight. And with each packing, the volume of baggage increases. The bag's side pockets are stuffed with leaflets and travel information, reminders of where I've been that I'm reluctant to fling away. A strategically placed knee is now needed to drag the bag's zip to its fullest extent. On 'moving days', my daypack, bought in Quito solely for tours and excursions, becomes a fully packed piece of travel luggage, and some of the many pockets of my *chaqueta* (jacket) now function as in-transit storage places.

It was another cold night. In bed, I wore my thermal gear (stretchy mountaineer-type base layers), socks, a woolly hat and a T-shirt. In the early morning, it is still freezing. Each breath is a mini-fog. On the way to the *estación*, the taxi seems to take a roundabout route. And the fare is quite a bit higher than that for yesterday's journey in the opposite direction. I protest to the driver. He points to the fare card, I splutter, but don't have the words, and in the end, stump up the full amount. Now, as well as being pissed off with him, I'm annoyed at myself for giving in and paying what he asked for.

It is a brief stop in Santiago; I'm on my way to Valparaíso, on the coast, 170 kilometres west of the capital. The city has been on my to-see list ever since I decided to stay on in South America. For at least one generation of Irish students, the mention of the city's name might dredge up the only snatch of Irish-language poetry retained from their schooldays. *Valparaíso* is a poem of longing for far-off places, and the possibilities of a life differently lived, a brief respite from Irish-language standards of national tragedy and loss.

Tháinig long ó Valparaíso,	A ship arrived from Valparaíso,
Scaoileadh téad a seol sa chuan,	Dropped its anchor in the bay,
Chuir a hainm dom i gcuimhne,	Her name reminded me of kingdoms,
Ríocht na Gréine, Tír na mBua.	Sunlit countries far away.

A German student in the window seat keeps me company for the two-hour bus journey. Herman plans to be in South America for a couple of months, he tells me. His first four weeks were spent in Argentina. The remainder of his stay will see him travel north to the Atacama Desert, then on through Bolivia to Cusco in Peru and Quito in Ecuador, before flying out of Bogotá, Colombia. Herman crossed the Andes by bus to Santiago. He will be in Valparaíso for only a day, he says; he wants to touch the Pacific Ocean.

Herman has exciting coffee news. It's about those Santiago cafés, the ones with the blacked-out windows and doors. It seems that the waitresses there wear only bikinis. Four times a day, these already scantily clad ladies divest themselves of their tops. There are no set times for these performances and punters must continue to top up their coffee in the hope that theirs is a timely visit. We speak about the recent demonstrations on the Alameda (O'Hidge-ins, he pronounces the name of the main thoroughfare). Apparently, the proposal for a

Patagonian hydro-electric scheme is old news; Herman had heard about it some years earlier.

Valparaíso is built around a crescent-shaped bay. By the sea, the land is flat on *el Plan* (level ground). Not far inland, it rises sharply in a series of *cerros* (hills). The city was founded in 1536. In colonial times, it was little more than a small port used for coastal trading, raided on numerous occasions by pirates, including, in 1578 by *El Draque*. In the nineteenth century, as the country opened up to international trade, Valparaíso became the preferred stopover for ships rounding Cape Horn. It developed into a major international banking centre. South America's first stock exchange was built here, as were the offices of the world's oldest surviving daily Spanish-language newspaper, *El Mercurio*. First printed in 1827, it was founded by Pedro Félix Vicuña, father of Benjamín Vicuña Mackenna.

Towards the end of the nineteenth century, as the hills above *el Plan* became more populated, access to them was facilitated by roads, sets of steps and famously, by *ascensores* (funicular railways). Little more than small carriages drawn by cable, the first of these was built in 1883. Where once there were 33, only about fifteen *ascensores* remain in use today.

The city declined with the opening of the Panama Canal in 1914. Also, prior to that, in 1912, a container port was built at San Antonio, 90 kilometres to the south. In time, this became the busiest port on the west coast of the continent. Valparaíso banks moved to Santiago and many of the middle classes shuffled off to the nearby resort town of Viña del Mar.

My accommodation is on one of the city's hills, Cerro Alegre. From the bus station, I make it on foot to its lower reaches. From there, a taxi delivers me uphill to La Luna Sonrisa, on steeply sloping

Calle Templeman. The efficient American girl at reception shows me around. The hostel is an old, colonial building, bright and clean, with high ceilings and bare, dark, varnished floorboards. The kitchen, communal bathroom and rest areas are spotless, and my single room is basic, but fine. *La chica americana* lets me know the house rules and goes on to highlight places of local interest on a photocopied map.

I drop my bags and, map in hand, wander downhill on Templeman. Directly ahead, and below, the bay lies fog-bound in the near-distance. One block to the right, El Desayunador (*desayunar* – to have breakfast) sits at the junction of Almirante Montt (parallel to Templeman), and Paseo (Promenade) Dimalow, which runs perpendicular to Montt on the other side. Here, I quieten my rumbling stomach with a *torta*, a sizeable slab of what looks like quiche, with bacon, spring onion and vegetable filling. It comes with small squares of lightly toasted bread and a side dish of salad and chopped tomato.

It is late afternoon, and I'm keen to visit the city's cemeteries, next door on Cerro Panteón. It seems that the easiest way to reach them is to descend to *el Plan* and make my way up Panteón from there. From El Desayunador, Paseo Dimalow leads to the upper landing stage of Ascensor Reina Victoria (Queen Victoria Funicular). Built in 1902, Queen Victoria climbs 40 metres from *el Plan* at a 57-degree gradient, in a car that holds seven passengers. The author of one guidebook claims that this is 'one of the city's most entertaining' *ascensores*. And it is, I guess, if your idea of entertainment involves swaying precariously in mid-air in a small wooden box. If so, then Queen Victoria is the *ascensor* for you, the one that puts the 'fun' into funicular. I watch this tiny, ancient, creaking contraption groaning its way up the slope before me and judge its entertainment value to be approximately nil. I plump instead for a regulation descent, via a nearby set of steep steps.

From *el Plan*, it's a winding road up Cerro Panteón (serpentines, Herman had called the twists and turns his bus had taken on its weaving way across the Andes to Santiago). Wooden shacks hang from the side of the hill, held in place by stilts. At cemetery No. 2, a sign says that the gates will be locked at 5pm. It is approaching that time now; I decide to defer my nosing around tombstones until another day. I return to *el Plan*. There, on the lower reaches of the hill beside Queen Victoria, an art studio called Hiperfocal sounds like a fast-speaking Gaeilgeoir (one for the Irish-language enthusiasts).

11

It is Saturday morning, and in a bulging El Desayunador, *porteños* – port dwellers, natives of Valparaíso – sip morning coffee and read the weekend papers. A roving newspaper seller stops at the door, barks something in incomprehensible newspaper-seller lingo and makes a sale.

This morning, I need to leave La Luna Sonrisa. I like the place and had wanted to stay on, but it's already fully booked for tonight. Online, I've reserved a room at Casa Fischer on Pasaje (Alley) Fischer, which my map tells me is nearby. Loaded with bags, I shuffle down Templeman and turn left on to Urriola. This leads straight on for a stretch, before curving right in a steep descent towards the bay. On the way, oil drums lie on their sides, held off the ground by a post at either end. A rectangular hole cut from the body of each drum converts them into rubbish bins. Soon, I reach *el Plan*, which means I've gone too far. Part-way back up Urriola, a Vegas-era image of Elvis has been stencilled on to a wall at the entrance to a passageway. I ask directions in a corner shop opposite Elvis and a girl points up the passageway steps. The climb is horrendously steep. At the top, through alleyways, and up more steps, I find myself back on Templeman. I've managed to walk in a full circle! By now, I am soaked in perspiration; the strap of my heavy bag is slicing into my shoulder. I retrace my steps. At the top of the steep passageway is the sign I've been looking for: 'Pasaje Fischer'. I suspect that Elvis and his quiff obscure the equivalent sign at the bottom of the climb. Half-way down is Casa Fischer; I had passed it fifteen sweaty minutes ago.

The Casa is an old, high-ceilinged, colonial house, not unlike La Luna Sonrisa. My comfortable double room faces the steps of the *pasaje*. The young *bean a' tí* provides me with the Wi-Fi password and tells me that the network name is 'Linda Evangelista', after her cat.

The Champions League Final between Barcelona and Manchester United is on at Wembley, at 2.45pm local time. I had planned to watch it in El Irlandés, a bar on Calle Blanco, near the waterfront, but its doors are closed. Luckily, Casa Fischer comes equipped with cable TV. It's a marvellous display by Barca (*una exhibitión*, says the Fox Sports guy) and in the end, an easy 3–1 win.

Later that night, I make a return visit to El Irlandés. The entrance to the bar is a pair of tall, mostly glass doors; on one is a large, stick-on transfer of a leprechaun; on the other, a harp. It's a narrow, dimly lit place. The counter runs down the left, small tables occupy the floor space to the right. On each table, a candle pokes from the neck of a wax-dripped bottle. Two sets of steps hug the right-hand wall, about half-way down. One set leads to a small raised platform towards the rear, the other to an upstairs seating area over the front door.

All tables are taken and I perch on a high stool at the bar. The counter is made of thick, varnished slabs of wood. The seats of the heavy bar stools are cut from similar beams, the same thickness, set on metal legs. Rock music plays in the background, not too loud, controlled from a computer by the till. On a wall near the door, a small glass cabinet holds Ireland-related books, key rings, playing cards and miscellaneous gumpf.

El Irlandés doesn't stock Kunstmann, the barman tells me. Instead, after a linguistic tussle, I'm offered a Kross Golden Ale (*Cerveza Ámbar*), a *cerveza independiente*. That the beer supplier is independent seems in keeping with the vibe of the place. This isn't an out-of-a-packet Irish-themed pub. It's raucous, my guidebook tells me. It's not that, not just now in any case, but it does have a good, lively feel about it.

I'm feeling very content in myself at this moment, settled on my bar stool, sipping my Kross. In fact, I can't remember when I last felt this at ease. This is surprising, I guess, as I'm in a bar on my own on the other side of the world. I think this 'at ease-ness' has to do with what Sara Wheeler refers to as 'the liberating sense of being alone without responsibilities'. I'm liberated from daily routine, free from the confinement of office life. And my responsibilities are minimal. Ahead, the biggest decision I have to make is where to travel next. Everyday cares and stresses no longer exist for me. Which is why I'm smiling inanely to myself on a high stool, and getting odd looks from the girl behind the counter.

In the background, ZZ Top's 'Sharp Dressed Man' plays over the sound system, followed by the Allman Brothers, with nifty guitar work. My mind wanders off to 'MT-USA' on teenage Sunday afternoons. But my very own 'Reeling in the Years' is soon disturbed by the arrival of a trumpeter who climbs on to the platform at the rear of the bar. His personal backing music replaces the rock soundtrack and he launches into easy-listening schmaltz. It's like lounge music from *The Fabulous Baker Boys*, but without the redeeming presence of Michelle Pfeiffer slithering over a grand piano. Time to move on.

To the left out of El Irlandés, groups of teenagers mooch about at a junction. Around the block, it's booming bars and discos. I make an escape, cut up a side street and end up back on Blanco. At the Rincón Bolivariano, the guy behind the counter runs his finger along a note at the bottom of a menu. He's letting me know there's a minimum spend of 5,000 pesos (over £5). With just a single beer in mind, I leave in search of another bar. But there's nothing nearby and I end up back at the Rincón. I order a small plate of chips to nudge my spending towards the lower limit. There's a good-size, lively crowd here, all locals it seems, and the air is thick with cigarette smoke. As I take my seat at the only free table, three guys step on to a tiny stage by the door. Behind them, a small handmade poster clings limply to the front window, held in place by a couple of strips of sellotape: '*Patagonia – sin represas*'. One of the musicians has a Spanish guitar, another, a pair of bongo drums, and the third plays what looks like a recorder but it has a sharper, Andean-pipe sound. My *chico* (small) portion of food arrives – it's a mountain of chips. I ask for a smaller plate, the *señorita* returns with a saucer, I shovel some chips on to it and send back the remainder.

Soon, a bearded guitarist replaces the three amigos on stage. He plays traditional songs, crowd favourites. Girls sway in their seats and everyone sings along. Two couples get up to dance. They pull out handkerchiefs, navy blue for the guys, bright red for the girls. The dancers weave around each other in slow, deliberate steps, waving the handkerchiefs above their heads. This may be a version of the *cueca*, the Chilean national dance, a parody of the mating ritual between a cockerel and a hen, the handkerchiefs symbolising the comb of the former and the feathers of the latter.

I demolish my hillock of chips and leave the Rincón. I'd like another beer, but it's after 1am now, and the choice of venue seems limited to disco bars. After a wander, I find a small café-type place. It's a kip, but it's quiet. A few shady types sit at a table by the wall. The barman tries to sell me a one-litre Escudo but I point instead to a smaller bottle, and sit and sip happily. Outside, couples, groups of blokes and posses of stray dogs wander past. Soon, even *el kip* must close for the night, and I aim for Elvis and the steep steps to Casa Fischer.

12

Before I left La Luna Sonrisa yesterday, I had already booked a room there for Sunday night. In the morning, I say farewell to Casa Fischer and Linda Evangelista, and work up a sweat trudging back up Templeman. On the way, Sunday morning organ music comes from Iglesia Anglicana San Pablo (St Paul's Anglican Church), where Templeman meets Pilcomayo. Built in 1858, the church is now a '*Monumento Histórico…en restauración*'. A replacement patch in silver is an island in the rusty brown corrugated-iron roof.

Unsurprisingly, St Paul's was built to serve the British community of Valparaíso, and Britain's link with the city is a lengthy one. In the early nineteenth century, after Chilean independence, Valparaíso was used as their southern Pacific base by British (as well as European and American) merchants. They began to populate the hills above the town, particularly here, on Cerro Alegre and next door, on Cerro Concepción. At this time, business was often conducted in English, with sterling the currency of trade. One resident of the time, quoted by Andy Beckett in *Pinochet in Piccadilly*, wrote: 'Retail shops for all sorts of European goods are nearly as common at Valparaíso as in any town of the same size in England. The English shops are more numerous than any. English tailors, shoemakers, saddlers, and inn-keepers, hang out their signs in every street. The number of piano-fortes brought from England is astonishing'. The same author 'went to dances…[and]…to picnics in the hills' and enjoyed 'London magazines, cricket matches…and local horse racing by British rules'.

At one point, between one-third and two-thirds of Chile's total exports went to Britain. And of their imports, between a third and a half came in the opposite direction. In Valparaíso, it became cheaper to import coal from Britain than from the country's own mines near Concepción, 600 kilometres to the south. By 1825, Britain had a consulate here, and the South American Squadron of the Royal Navy regularly patrolled offshore. Another writer quoted by Beckett found Chileans 'conservative and law-abiding…the English of the Pacific'. A likely relic of the British presence is the Chilean tradition of *onces*. Although taken in the afternoon, the translation, 'elevenses', is thought to derive from the English term for a mid-morning tea break.

My room at La Luna Sonrisa isn't ready; I drop my bags and head for morning coffee. I'm getting fond of El Desayunador; it's a quirky little spot. The tall, glass-panelled double doors are at the corner of the building. One of the double doors is bolted closed. The other, when half-way open, sticks against a slight rise in the tiled floor. Marooned in the doorway as you enter, it takes a moment to realise that it's OK to shove. Inside, on the left, a public phone sits on top of a small, red post box (*Correos Chile*). The phone is a black, push-button number with a coin slot on top, shaped like an old, ring-dial home phone but with a thicker base, where change is returned. Through the doors and on the right, a black-and-white mural covers a full wall. It's a caricature of Valparaíso life, stuffed with buildings and people.

Tables line the walls and occupy the central, open space. Two strips of velcro hang from each side of every table. I haven't seen them in use, but assume they're to loop through, and secure, the handles of handbags. Directly opposite the doorway is the serving area. Behind the counter, a set of steps leads to a tiny office. The office isn't on another floor but somehow clings to the top half of the wall of this high-ceilinged room.

Out back, the toilet is, well, basic. The cubicle has no door; in its place is a concertina-like cardboard 'shutter'. The shutter doesn't close properly and there's no lock. A card on the wall by the sink lists dates and times and signatures. I had assumed that the card detailed daily cleaning times. A closer look reveals that the dates are monthly. And the card displays likenesses of a mouse and a bug, all of which seems to indicate the frequency of a more industrial-strength cleansing.

After settling in at La Luna Sonrisa, I take a Sunday afternoon stroll down Templeman. For part of its length, the gable-ends of houses face on to the street. These have ended up as canvases for extravagant, garish murals. On side streets, artisan shops sell paintings, pottery, postcards, clothing and knick-knacks. Not far from Iglesia Anglicana San Pablo, a handsome church stands where Calle Abtao meets Pasaje Pastor Schmidt. Built in 1897, the Iglesia Luterana en Valparaíso de la Santa Cruz (Holy Cross) has lime-green walls and a dark-green roof. Like its anglican relation nearby, it too is undergoing '*Reparación y Manutención*'.

A cobbled walkway, Paseo Gervasoni, runs off to the left at the foot of Templeman. This short promenade is the upper landing stage for Ascensor Concepción. Built in 1883, this *ascensor* climbs 69 metres at a 45-degree gradient ('Fun' quotient – unknown). At weekends, visitors stroll between artisan stalls and enjoy views over the harbour from the Paseo's *mirador* (lookout/viewpoint). Today, a three-piece group has snagged a space between stalls. The trio is made up of a guitarist, a percussionist (he's not playing drums, but what looks like a wooden box that he strokes gently with brush drumsticks) and a girl who alternates between a small xylophone and a melodica. When played, a melodica is usually held to the lips. But the girl blows into a rubber pipe attached to the instrument's mouthpiece, and plays it horizontally in her lap, like a tiny piano.

13

The following afternoon, Tony, from New Zealand, joins me for a stroll along *el Plan*; Tony is also staying at La Luna Sonrisa. Now in his fifties, he had married youngish, divorced, and had expected to remarry but never did. He didn't take well to passing 40, he tells me, and packed in his management position in a construction firm. Now he drives a bus for a tour company and travels for three months every year. Originally from Birmingham, he left as soon as he could and wouldn't dream of going back. Tony has wind, gales of it. 'Gastric problem', he says, in between force-ten heaving belches. I'm not sure Tony is too keen on Valparaíso. 'It's a dump!', he tells me.

Today, at the foot of Templeman, Paseo Gervasoni is empty of stalls. From the *mirador*, the view of the bay below is dominated by the dock's sole lodger, the huge bulk of the *Dakota Princess*. We decide against using Ascensor Concepción and instead descend the steep steps past Casa Fischer, turn right at Elvis corner, and head down Urriola to *el Plan*. A short walk away is Plaza Sotomayor.

A large monument sits in the centre of the plaza. Ambling in its direction, we are surprised to find that what appears to be a pedestrianised, cobbled square is, in fact, open to traffic. Locals leaning heavily on car horns aren't slow to bring this to our attention. Nimble, traffic-dodging footwork leads us to the Monument of the Martyrs of the Battle of Iquique, an enormous memorial that holds the remains of heroes of the War of the Pacific.

Between 1879 and 1883, the *Guerra del Pacifico* was fought between Chile and the combined forces of Peru and Bolivia. The dispute that led to the war involved valuable nitrate deposits. Nitrates are used in the production of fertilisers for agriculture and in making explosives, and the largest natural supply of sodium nitrate in the world existed in the region of the Atacama Desert.

Prior to 1850, the extraction of sodium nitrate was a laborious process. Miners used sledgehammers to attack seams of deposits close to the surface. They broke off lumps, hammered them into fragments and brought these to local buyers. The buyers dissolved the pieces in boiling water, the water was left to evaporate and this left a usable product. Once a seam was worked, both miner and buyer moved on.

In the 1850s, the use of steam to dissolve nitrate made it profitable to work seams of lesser purity, and more permanent *oficinas* (mineworks) were built. Most of the mining in the region was conducted by Chilean companies; most of the finance was provided by British bankers in Valparaíso. Chileans migrated north and towns boomed. Antofagasta, at that time on Bolivia's coast, had a population approximately 90% Chilean. In the three years to 1871, Iquique, then in southern Peru, almost quadrupled in size.

In 1866, a boundary treaty set the frontier between Bolivia and Chile at the 24th parallel, just south of the city of Antofagasta. It was also agreed that Chile would share in the export tax revenues from mineral resources between the 23rd and 24th parallels, Bolivian territory.

Bolivia soon became unhappy with this arrangement. It was also wary of Chilean intentions in relation to its coastal territory (relatively sparsely populated, this region was separated from the rest of the country by the Andes). Peru had similar concerns about Chile's designs on *its* southern provinces. And so, Peru and Bolivia signed a secret treaty, assuring their mutual defence.

In 1874, Bolivia agreed not to raise taxes on Chilean businesses in its territory for 25 years. Four years later, it reneged on the agreement. When Chile protested, Bolivia threatened to confiscate the property of the Chilean Antofagasta Nitrate Company. In 1879, Chile's army occupied Antofagasta. Bolivia declared war and called on its ally Peru for assistance.

Chile easily occupied the Bolivian coastal region. The effective Peruvian navy put up a stern fight but was eventually overcome. With Chile in control of the seas, its army invaded Peru. Lima was occupied in January 1881. Peru continued its resistance for three years. In October 1883, the Treaty of Ancón ceded Peru's southernmost province, Tarapacá, to Chile. In addition, two provinces, Tacna and Arica, north of Tarapacá, were to be occupied by Chile for ten years. A plebiscite to be held after that time would decide on their final ownership. (Terms could not be agreed, however, and the situation dragged on until 1928. The US mediated: Chile kept Arica, and Tacna reverted to Peru, who also received concessions and $6m.)

A truce in 1884 meant that Chile also retained the Bolivian province of Antofagasta. And so, Bolivia lost its access to the sea, about which it remains unhappy today. The deal did mean that Chile had to build a railroad from La Paz to the now-Chilean coastal city of Arica, to facilitate Bolivian imports and exports.

One of the major figures of the War of the Pacific was Patricio Lynch, whose father, Estanislao Lynch y Roo, had crossed the Andes with San Martín and had settled in Chile. He was a descendant of Patrick Lynch, born in 1715 at Lydican Castle, County Galway. The Lynches were one of the fourteen tribes of Galway who were at the forefront of life there from the thirteenth to the late seventeenth century. Patrick Lynch had settled in Buenos Aires in 1749, married a wealthy heiress and became a successful merchant and landowner.

Patricio Lynch was born in Valparaíso in 1825. He went to sea at the age of twelve, and saw active service with the Royal Navy, where he reached the level of midshipman (the Chilean and British navies have a lengthy association, and it was not unusual for Chileans to serve apprenticeships on board British ships. Up to the 1970s, most of the country's naval vessels were of British origin).

In Chile, Lynch made lieutenant, and then, successively, maritime prefect of Valparaíso, colonel of the National Guard and minister of the marine. During the War of the Pacific, in what became known as Lynch's Expedition, between 2,000 and 3,000 men made raids along the Peruvian coast north of Callao (the port for Lima), extracting ransoms from businesses and landowners. Chinese slave labourers freed in these raids knew Lynch as the 'Red Prince', a reference to the colour of his hair. His service in victories at the subsequent battles of Chorrillos and Miraflores led to his appointment as military governor of Peru for the latter years of the war. In 1884, Lynch was appointed minister (ambassador) to Madrid. He died at sea two years later, returning to Chile.

*

On Plaza Sotomayor, the imposing, pale blue Armada (Navy) de Chile building sits landside of the Monument of the Martyrs of the Battle of Iquique, facing the square and the sea. By the dock, not far from a small statue of Cristóbal Colón (the Spanish name for Christopher Columbus), locals tout boat tours of the bay. Nearby is a *churro* stall. Fingers of waffle-like artery-cloggers, dipped in sugar, *churros* are fantastically tasty; I pay 500 pesos for four.

Strolling along the seafront, Tony suffers a gastric 'malfunction' and disappears into a university building to visit the bathroom. He's there for ages. When he reappears, we continue on to the bus station, where girls at the Information desk use us for English-language practice. Tony buys a ticket for the next stage of his trip, to La Serena, in the north of the country. Across the road from the station is Plaza O'Higgins. Here, the Libertador, seated on a rearing horse in the centre of the square, is a magnet for local pigeons, perching and pooping. Card tables line the paths that radiate outwards from O'Higgins. On the tables, a thin strap is tacked on to the green baize, parallel to, and centimetres from, each table edge. Cards slipped under the straps are safe from the wind: the actual wind, that is, not Tony's.

We get a nod from a card school guy and sit at one of their vacant tables. Coffee comes from an old lady at a nearby snack cart. It is bright and sunny and a little chilly on the plaza, and we pass an enjoyable fifteen minutes watching the world go by before returning towards the centre of town. There, Tony belches off in the direction of Viña del Mar, a short distance along the coast. Passing time before returning uphill to Cerro Alegre, I wander between secondhand bookstalls beside a *supermercado* in the centre of town. Opposite the entrance to the *supermercado* is a tall obelisk, erected to the memory of a British seaman, Lord Cochrane.

Although José de San Martín had won a decisive battle at Maipú in 1818, the Spanish still posed a threat to the newly declared republic. A royalist presence persisted in the south, and Spanish sea power remained a concern for a country with so lengthy a coastline. O'Higgins needed a navy and a man to lead it.

Thomas Cochrane came from an old Scottish family with a seat at Culross, on the Firth of Forth. He joined the navy at seventeen and within a decade had become famous for his exploits in battle. In particular, he gained a reputation for an unconventional approach to naval warfare and for overturning impossible odds. In 1799, off Gibraltar, he single-handedly boarded a pirate ship. Two years later, he captured a Spanish frigate many times the size of his own vessel; and in a ten-week spell in 1805, his success against a string of Spanish treasure ships meant that his personal share of the prize money was £75,000.

Cochrane's reputation for achieving victory against superior forces encouraged O'Higgins to instruct his representative in London to approach him. In fact, the Scotsman had already rebuffed the Spanish, who had asked him to help *them* put down the South American rebellions. By late November 1818, Cochrane was in Valparaíso. O'Higgins was there to meet him and awarded him the rank 'Vice-Admiral of Chili (sic), Admiral and Commander in Chief of the Naval Forces of the Republic'. With this impressive title, Cochrane took charge of half a dozen ships.

At the beginning of the new year, the Admiral and Commander in Chief took his small fleet north to attack Callao. There, he sailed into a thick fog. When the fog lifted, he found that he was exposed to the 160 cannon that defended the harbour. He beat a hasty retreat. Next, reprising a previously successful tactic, he organised for a boat packed with explosives to be floated towards shore. The Spanish sank it before it could pose a threat. Cochrane finally achieved a minor success. Having organised informers on land, he received information that led to the capture of two ships carrying servicemen's pay. Cochrane was well received on his return to Chile, his mishaps at Callao somehow spun as heroic failure.

Valdivia, almost 1,000 kilometres south of Valparaíso, was Spain's other great port on the Pacific coast. It was the 'Gibraltar of the southern hemisphere' and the base from which Spain hoped to regain Chile. The town itself, over 30 kilometres inland, was guarded by earthworks and towers, its approach from the sea via a long estuary lined with thick-walled, star-shaped forts, guarded by cannon at every turn.

Early in February 1820, Cochrane disembarked his forces on a beach beneath one of the estuary's forts. When darkness came, the troops split into two groups. One group climbed silently into the fort and started firing; the other made a noisy, frontal approach across open ground. Thinking they were being attacked by larger numbers than was actually the case, the Spanish fled. Panic spread and the remaining forts surrendered in turn, each thinking they faced insurmountable odds. By 8am the next morning, the town was won. Cochrane had more or less guaranteed the safety of the republic. He was now a public hero.

Meanwhile, after his victory at Maipú in 1818, José de San Martín had been waiting to implement the next stage of his plan for the liberation of the continent: to sail north, and take royalist Lima. In August 1820, he left Valparaíso in a fleet commanded by Cochrane. With the port of Callao under blockade, he disembarked his troops at Pisco, further south. For almost a year, San Martín resisted attacking Lima, at which point, the royalists, not receiving the help they had expected from Spain, withdrew to the mountains. San Martín entered Lima, and declared the independence of the country on July 28, 1821.

Once he had liberated Peru, San Martín arranged for the flags of his defeated enemies to be presented to the government in Buenos Aires. The man he chose to deliver them was John Thomond O'Brien.

O'Brien was born in Baltinglass, County Wicklow in 1786. He arrived in Buenos Aires in 1812, joined the army there and soon made lieutenant. He crossed the Andes with the *Ejército de los Andes* and fought in the independence wars in Chile. Promoted to captain after the Battle of Chacabuco, O'Brien became San Martín's aide-de-camp and continued with him to Peru, where he was promoted to colonel.

In Peru, O'Brien turned his hand to business. He operated a mine near Puno, on Lake Titicaca. To facilitate his mining work, he arranged for a stripped-down boat to be transported across the Andes from Arica on the coast. It took two years for the boat to reach Lake Titicaca. Soon after its arrival, it was wrecked in a storm. The mining venture ended in failure.

A general by 1835, O'Brien fell foul of the Argentine dictator Juan Manuel de Rosas and was thrown in jail. British diplomacy and the intercession of Rosas' daughter combined to ensure his eventual release. In 1848, he was appointed Uruguay's special envoy to Britain.

O'Brien died in Lisbon in 1861, returning from Ireland to South America. Later, his biography, *El Jeneral O'Brien*, was written by Benjamín Vicuña Mackenna. In the *partido* (county) of Bragado in Buenos Aires province, a railway station is named after John Thomond O'Brien. When the railway arrived in the area, the owner of the land on which the station stood decided it should be named for a hero. Oddly enough, the town which the station services is also named O'Brien (patron saint: St Patrick), after a Wexford man, Eduardo O'Brien, who donated the land on which the town's first buildings were built.

Returning to La Luna Sonrisa from the bookstalls near Cochrane's obelisk, the prospect of the steep steps at Elvis corner is too much. Instead, Ascensor Concepción delivers me to Paseo Gervasoni. In the *ascensor*, a typed page notes that *manutención preventiva* (preventative maintenance) is scheduled for May 3, 7, 10, 17, 24 and 31. I'm not sure whether to be comforted or alarmed. Clearly, care is taken to maintain the *ascensor*. But what kind of contraption needs to be serviced six times in a month?! The car takes off with a judder and clacks up the slope. I jump out quickly at the top.

14

Next morning, I finally get to visit the city's cemeteries (there are three of them) on Cerro Panteón, next door to Cerro Alegre. From *el Plan*, an exhausting climb leads to the main gate of Catholic Cementerio No. 2. Through the gates, the lengthy main avenue is lined with well-tended mausoleums. Elsewhere in the yard, gravestones are more discreet; quite a few that date from the nineteenth century are crumbling and broken. Names on the gravestones are mostly Spanish, but some are German, east European, English and Irish (Kelly, MacAuliffe...).

Next door, the sign on the wall of the Protestant cemetery (*Cementerio de Disidentes*) has a Celtic cross design (when referring to religion, *disidente* translates as non-conformist). Inside the gate, a memorial is dedicated to those '*que perecieron a bordo de la Fragata Essex de los E.E.U.U. en la guerra de 1812*' (those who died on board the frigate USS *Essex* in the War of 1812). Out of a crew of 255, it says, 58 died, 31 went missing and 65 were wounded. Among the missing were Farrell, Bolger, McCarty (sic), Mahoney and Carroll.

The USS *Essex* is one of the most famous ships in early US naval history. Built in 1799 by the people of Essex county in Massachusetts, it was presented by them to the US navy (with the young republic short of cash, some American naval vessels at the time were paid for by the public). In the following year, it became the first US military vessel to cross the Equator.

In June 1812, America declared war on Britain. At this time, the *Essex* was captained by David Porter (he would later become commander-in-chief of the Mexican navy). In the course of the following year, Porter disrupted British commercial shipping in the Pacific, capturing over a dozen whalers. In January 1814, the *Essex* and the *Essex Junior* sailed into neutral Valparaíso. Ships dispatched by the British, the frigate *Phoebe* and the sloop *Cherub*, trapped them in the harbour for six weeks. Towards the end of March, the *Essex* made to escape, lost a topmast in a squall and headed for a small bay north of the city. The British ships closed in. On board, the *Essex* had short-range cannon only (*carronades*) with which to defend itself. The *Phoebe* stayed out of reach and bombarded the *Essex* with long-range guns. The Americans had little hope, and in time, they surrendered.

The captured ship was towed to Plymouth in England. In 1824, she was moved to Kingstown (Dún Laoghaire) near Dublin, and her masts removed. Used as a prison hulk, she held between 200 and 300 prisoners, most awaiting transportation to Australia. In 1836, inmates were transferred to prisons onshore, and in the following year, the ship was sold at public auction. Over a century and a half later, in November 2004, work commenced on resurfacing the east pier at Dún Laoghaire harbour. An anchor uncovered there, which had been adapted for permanent mooring, is thought to have belonged to the *Essex*.

The *Cementerio de Disidentes* is small and compact. As well as the expected English, Scottish and German names, a sizeable number are of Spanish origin, some are east European, and some are Irish (Murphy, McLaughlin…). A Royal Naval vault commemorates those 'who lost their lives on active service off the coast of Chile'. In the centre of the cemetery, the Immigrant's Memorial Square has a tiny, neat garden. At the rear of the garden, on a memorial slab, lines are written in memory of the city's immigrants:

They arrived from the sea…
like fresh waves and new breezes…
To the immigrants who stayed,
To the transient immigrant,
And also to the abandoned immigrants
Immigrant, your stamp
Lives to our days

'Valparaíso, the port and the land of the immigrants'

Catholic Cementerio No. 1 is opposite the *Cementerio de Disidentes*. I'm tempted to venture a look, but I figure I've seen enough gravestones for one day. Any lingering inclination to investigate further is quashed when, inside the yard, a toothy, howling dog flings itself against the bars of the gate as I pass.

Back on *el Plan*, I cast a weary eye up the steep steps that lead to Paseo Dimalow, near El Desayunador. I can't face another climb. Which means that I must tangle with Ascensor Reina Victoria, the 'fun' funicular. Creaky Queen Victoria sets off with a jerk and shudders her way to the top. If the frequency of Ascensor Concepción's maintenance made me nervous yesterday, the lack of any similar plans for Victoria jangles my nerves today. It's 100 pesos for this trip, Ascensor Concepción's more popular route costing three times as much.

In the afternoon, I take the short spin to Viña del Mar, less than ten kilometres up the coast. The train leaves from Plaza Sotomayor. At the foot of Templeman, I pause at the *mirador* on Paseo Gervasoni. The *Dakota Princess* has departed, its place at the dock taken by a large black ship whose name I'm unable to make out. Four on-board cranes linger over its open hold doors, only one in operation just now, dipping in and out of the ship's bowels.

Today is one of Ascensor Concepción's many maintenance days. So it's downhill on foot to Elvis corner and onwards to Plaza Sotomayor, where I get a closer look at the moored ship, the *SPOT*. Its huge bulk is red below the water line. Thick steel ropes fasten it to the dock. A massive, rusty anchor is weighed at the prow. On board, another crane is now at work. But it seems that I've wandered into a restricted area. I plead ignorance to the guard; he smiles and directs me across the road to the train station. With difficulty, I ignore the nearby *churro* stall. Instead, I quieten my grumbling stomach with a healthy, boring, apple from my daypack.

It's a short trip to Viña del Mar, but I exit at the wrong station and end up in the centre of town instead of at the waterfront. Here, Plaza José Francisco Vergara commemorates the guy who founded this young city in 1878. José himself looks out from a plinth in the centre of the square. His plaza is well tended. A six-man team wearing blue-and-yellow fleeces sweep, fork flower beds and rake yellow leaves.

I find my meandering way to the ocean. Here, a long line of huge stone blocks protects the shore. Water laps gently against them. I'm reminded of Herman and wonder if he managed to dip his hand in the Pacific. A broad footpath lines the shore behind the blocks; horse buggies carrying tourists trot by on the road. At points along the path, viewing platforms nudge into the sea. In the distance to the right, a beach curves almost to the point of a headland. To the left, beyond the blocks, is a small promontory. At its head, a crenellated tower pokes into the water.

Biblical quotes are neatly painted on the stone blocks. They come from *Proverbios* 23:19, *Corintios* 8:3 and others. Beside a food stall, men sitting on the sea wall play cards on a chessboard. Posters on lampposts advertise a casino; there have been '*250 Millonarios*', and '*tu puedes ser uno*' (you could be one)! Further left, the tower on the small promontory belongs to Castle Wulff, a National Historical Monument and headquarters of the Viña del Mar City Hall Patrimony Unit.

I follow the road, over a bridge, and return towards town. A sign states that this route is a '*via de evacuación*' and shows a running man, a huge wave towering over him; instinctively, I pick up my walking pace. Near the town centre, on Viana, a broad set of steps leads to the entrance of a low building, 'EVERTON' in tall letters above the open doorway. In 1909, English immigrants founded Everton Football Club on Cerro Alegre in Valparaíso. They took their name from the English team of the same name who were touring Argentina at the time. In 1950, they were renamed Everton de Viña del Mar (they had moved to the city in the 1940s). *Los Ruleteros* (the roulette players – the city is a well-known gambling resort) have four national titles, and are the country's sixth most successful team. Their local rivals are Santiago Wanderers, of Valparaíso, with whom they contest the *Clásico del Puerto* (the Seaport Derby). The Viña del Mar team have the upper hand, with 55 victories to 45 losses. In 2010, they played Everton of England at Goodison Park for the *Copa Hermandad* (the Brotherhood Trophy). The home side ran out 2–0 winners in the first meeting between the teams.

At a nearby station, I catch a return train to Valparaíso for my last night in La Luna Sonrisa. My time in Chile is coming to an end. Tomorrow, I return to Santiago, from where I plan to cross the Andes to Argentina, and make my lengthy way cross-country to Buenos Aires.

*

After San Martín travelled north to Peru with Cochrane, Bernardo O'Higgins continued in his role as supreme director of Chile. He made initial progress. He founded a Military Academy and a Naval School, and he brought about improvements in agriculture. But the finances of the new republic were in a perilous state. Also, attempted liberal reforms made him unpopular with the country's elite and with the Church. Soon, his enemies lined up against him. Civil war threatened. In January 1823, O'Higgins resigned and was banished by his erstwhile second-in-command, Ramón Freire. He left for Peru with his mother and half-sister (he never married but briefly had a lover with whom he had a son, Demetrio). After almost twenty years in exile, O'Higgins was informed that he could return to Chile. But the Libertador never made it home. Preparing to leave, he fell ill and died, at Callao, in October 1842.

15

At almost 7,000 metres, Mount Aconcagua is the highest point in the Andes and one of the Seven Summits (the tallest peaks on each of the continents – in the US, North and South America are treated as separate continents). When approached from the north, it is considered, in mountaineering terms, a relatively straightforward climb. Despite this, the ascent has claimed over 100 lives. In 1940, Adrienne Bance from France became the first woman to reach the summit. She was joined on the climb by her dog Fifi (presumably, Fifi became the first dog to achieve the same feat) and her husband George. Afterwards George would show fellow mountaineers a jar of what he called Aconcagua mushrooms. These were, in fact, eight of his toes, removed with scissors when frostbite had left them useless. Some years later, the couple attempted another ascent of Aconcagua. On that occasion, they lost their lives, just short of the summit, at 6,000 metres.

One hundred kilometres east of Aconcagua, the city of Mendoza is at the foot of the Andes. It was to Mendoza that Bernardo O'Higgins fled in 1814, after defeat by royalists at the Battle of Rancagua. Here, he joined with José de San Martín, and together they made plans to return across the mountains to Chile. In January 1817, they made their way through Los Patos Pass with 3,000 men. It is said that San Martín deliberately camped for a night at the highest point of his journey, looking up at Aconcagua.

As San Martín travelled through Los Patos, another section of his army trekked through the Uspallata Pass, further south. Almost 100 years later, the village of Uspallata witnessed another Andes crossing.

In 1916, Eduardo Bradley landed there in an aerostat (hot-air balloon) and became the first person to cross the mountain range in this type of craft. Bradley was the son of Tomás Bradley Sutton (whose own father had arrived in Argentina from Massachusetts), and Mary Hayes O'Callaghan, daughter of Daniel Hayes from Cork and his wife Mary O'Callaghan. Fuelled by coal gas, the aerostat, manned by Bradley and co-pilot Ángel María Zuloaga, climbed to a height of more than 8,000 metres and hit temperature lows of minus 30 degrees celsius. Their three-and-a-half-hour journey made them national heroes.

My own Andes crossing was a more leisurely eight hours, in a weaving bus from Santiago. In Mendoza, my rambling accommodation is on a street parallel to a main thoroughfare, Avenida Villanueva (at some point on the short walk to the centre of town, Villanueva seems to morph into Avenida Colón). Last night, temperatures didn't quite plummet to the lows suffered by Bradley in his aerostat, but my room was freezing, and I slept wearing a beanie, thermals, socks and a jacket. This morning, it is not a great deal warmer. A few moments exposed to the chill wind blowing across the wide, red-tiled *terraza* on the hotel roof is enough to send me scuttling indoors.

Downstairs, A4 head-shots of beauty queens cover a wall of the breakfast room. These are participants in a pageant that is part of the *Fiesta Nacional de la Vendimia* (The National Grape Harvest Festival – the area around Mendoza is the largest wine-producing region in Latin America). The pageant takes place in March each year, with a contestant from seventeen of the eighteen *departamentos* that make up the province of Mendoza (the representative from the Mendoza city department acts as hostess). And so, Jennifer from Maipú and Gabriela from Godoy Cruz watch over me as I tuck into a tasty pastry and a bread roll that once was fresh.

After breakfast, a stroll towards town involves tangling with a major intersection, where the broad Avenida Villanueva/Colón meets the four lanes of Avenida Belgrano. Crossing the road here, as on much of the continent, is a lottery. The junction has no traffic lights. It does, however, have pedestrian crossings. But these work in the South American way. They *are* where pedestrians cross, but not necessarily where cars stop; they stop if they feel like it. Successful negotiation of this Death Junction requires eyes in the back of your head and a rapid turn of foot.

A well-timed sprint leads me down Colón to a trendy part of town, where clothes shops sell polo fashion and morning coffee comes in at a hefty 20 pesos (almost £3). En route, I get an unreasonable amount of satisfaction when a skateboarder lands on his backside negotiating the step up from the road to the footpath.

Later, at the hotel, my bedroom is cosy and warm. Unseen by me, a heater lurks on the wall, behind the television. The cleaner switched it on in my absence. Last night, I froze for no reason.

16

San Martín's crossing of the Andes is an iconic event in the history of the South American wars of independence. In Mendoza, a famous memorial celebrates it, in a park on the western side of town.

Parque San Martín covers over 390 hectares. Within it, there is another park, a museum, lake, university campus, zoo, theatre, football stadium, velodrome and the Cerro de la Gloria. On top of this small hill, a monument was built to commemorate the 100th anniversary of Argentine independence and to honour the Army of the Andes.

At the park entrance, a short length of railing sits on either side of massive black- and gold-painted iron gates. An ornate arch spans the gates, a condor perched on top of the arch at its centre point, wings spread wide. These magnificent gates were made at the MacFarlane Iron Works in Glasgow. It is said that they were commissioned by the Red Sultan of Turkey, but that the deal fell through when the Sultan died. The foundry advertised them, and they were bought by the Argentine authorities and placed here in 1907. MacFarlane's was famous for its ornamental ironwork. Established in 1850, they specialised in, among other things, the production of bandstands and drinking fountains. They are no longer in business (after various takeovers, production finally ceased in 1967), but their work can still be seen, mostly in the UK, but also further afield. They made the verandas of the Raffles hotel in Singapore and, at the end of the nineteenth century, the canopy outside the Olympia Theatre in Dublin.

From the gates, Avenida Libertador leads on through the Parque. An earthen path runs alongside the *avenida*. Between the two is a line of tall, thin trees and a broad trench (similar trenches can be seen throughout Mendoza. Nicknamed 'yanqi traps', they form part of an irrigation system that allows for the watering of trees on the city's streets). The afternoon has warmed up. En route, my daypack seems to gain in weight and it clings to my saturated back.

After a longer-than-anticipated walk, I reach the foot of Cerro de la Gloria. From here, I follow a steep uphill path. The Malvinas Argentinas Stadium is visible from part-way up the climb. Built for the 1978 Football World Cup, and originally called the *Ciudad de Mendoza* (City of Mendoza), it was renamed after the Falklands/Malvinas War. On the approach to the summit, walls lining the path are studded with bronze plaques. These have been dedicated by various societies and associations in Argentina and elsewhere, in tribute to San Martín and his army. Past the walls, and on the top of the hill, an enormous monument sits beyond a small car park. Fourteen tonnes in weight, the *Monumento al Ejército Libertador* (Monument to the Army of the Liberator) was created by a Uruguayan sculptor, Juan Ferrari. Towards the front, a dedication is chiselled in rock: '*La Patria Al Ejército de los Andes*' (From the Fatherland to the Army of the Andes). Above that, San Martín sits on horseback. To the rear, a tall strip of bronze wraps around an enormous rock base. Depicted on the strip are scenes relating to the Andes crossing: a friar directs workers in the making of gun carriages, high-society Mendozan ladies hand over jewels to fund the army (apparently, they did not do this all that willingly at the time), people donate food, women say farewell to their menfolk. Rising from this base is a jagged, rocky plinth. And on top of that, surrounded by dashing cavalry figures, the main feature is a massive bronze, Lady Liberty. Manacles with broken chains hang from the wrists of her outstretched arms. This is the highest point of

Parque San Martín. Visitors circle the monument, linger in the car park, and take in the views over the dry, flat land that stretches to the misty Andes in the near-distance.

Back at the hotel, my sweaty, Parque ramblings have brought on a thirst. In the lobby, a flyer advertises the 'Believe Irish Pub'. As Irish pub names go, I think, this is pretty rubbish. I dice with Death Junction and aim for the centre of town. Part-way down Colón, a Celtic symbol, a triskele, sits between 'Irish Pub' and 'Pub Irlandés' on a sign over the door of a narrow building (a triskele, with its three conjoined spirals, looks not unlike an ampersand). Numerous translations of beer-related words (bier, cerveza, ól…) are painted on a wooden strip that runs the width of the premises. Inside, a horseshoe counter reaches from the rear wall. Tables and chairs occupy most of the floor space, Guinness posters and framed photographs cover the walls. Football jerseys hang from pegs near the ceiling, a single Kerry Gaelic football shirt nestled among its soccer and rugby cousins. Two large screens show the Argentine national rugby team (the Pumas) playing the French Barbarians. I was unaware even of the existence of the French Barbarians, who don't play in traditional Barbarian black and white, but in sky, navy and royal blue hoops.

I take a seat and from an extensive menu of beers, choose a bottle of Argentinian Golden Ale, an OtroMundo, from the OtroMundo Brewing Company; it arrives with a chilled glass. A couple of table servers wearing 'Believe Irish Pub' T-shirts stand outside the counter folding a mountain of napkins. Beside them is an almost-life-size wooden carving of an old guy perched on a high stool, with a tall green hat, green scarf and large glasses. His right arm is folded across his stomach, a pint of stout raised chest-high in his left hand: an Irish bar sage.

The OtroMundo Golden Ale is nice. The blurb on the label says that it goes well with light meals, hors d'oeuvers (sic) and Spanish tapas. Or with another helping of OtroMundo Golden Ale, I suspect, and I order another. It is almost eleven o'clock now, and as the pub begins to fill, I finish off my beer and return to the hotel. Through the windows of restaurants on Colón, diners are tucking into late evening meals. A stall-holder in a traffic island puts together supplements for the Sunday papers. Further on, and after a couple of OtroMundos, Death Junction is a doddle.

17

Sunday is lost in a very dull twelve-hour bus journey from Mendoza to Córdoba, in the heart of Argentina, the next stop on my lengthy trek to Buenos Aires. From a manic bus station there, a taxi delivers me to Hostel Babilonia, on Simón Bolívar, near the centre of town.

Occasionally while travelling, usually over a coffee, I pass time paging through a Spanish-language newspaper. The content is beyond me, but sometimes, when I work up the enthusiasm, I plough through an article armed with my pocket Spanish–English dictionary; newly discovered words are stashed in the back of a notebook. Almost always, the article comes from the football pages. It seems that football-speak in Spanish-language newspapers differs little from that used in English-language equivalents. And so, I discover that Birmingham City's poor form means they *despedirse de la máxima categoria* (say goodbye to the top flight), in the recent Champions League final, Scholes and Giggs are *sobrevivientes* (the sole survivors) of United's Champions League win of 1999 and Alexis Sánchez, about to be transferred from Udinese to Barcelona, is *el niño maravilla* (the boy wonder).

In the sports pages of Argentina's newspapers, it is difficult not to notice the name of Vélez Sarsfield. One of the country's leading football clubs, they are currently top of the national league. They take their name directly from a railway station in Buenos Aires (the club grew up beside it) and indirectly from Dalmacio Vélez Sarsfield, a leading figure in nineteenth-century Argentina. Dalmacio Vélez Sarsfield was born in the small town of Amboy, in Córdoba province. I'm hoping to find out more about him while I'm here, and to discover if he has any connection to Patrick Sarsfield, the famous Irish general of the Williamite War. In the meantime, I also plan to take in some sights.

Up to now, the most noteworthy thing about my sightseeing in South America is how spectacularly unsuccessful it has been. Museums I visit are closed, or closed down. In Santiago, a bookshop I was looking forward to browsing around no longer exists. Often I never reach the sights I set out to see. En route to city attractions, I get distracted easily and regularly lose my way.

In an effort to lessen the time given over to aimless wandering, more planning is required. This morning, before leaving to see a statue of Vélez Sarsfield en route to the Palacio de Justicia, I carefully study a map of the town. I highlight my route, mark junctions and note street names. Ready to set off, I check my map again. Pleased with my thoroughness, I stride from the hostel. Two minutes later, I'm lost. I've marked the hostel in the wrong place on the map. My in-depth preparations have resulted only in my losing my way more quickly than usual. Ten minutes after I had left, I shuffle sheepishly past the hostel entrance, now heading in the opposite direction.

After this organisational debacle, I decide to abandon my visit to the statue of Vélez Sarsfield and instead go directly to the Palacio de Justicia. The building is on the same lengthy road as the hostel; this radically increases my chances of actually finding it.

Plaza de la Intendencia, opposite the Palacio, is relatively unattractive. A low, dark-glass building sits at its centre; a small maintenance team brushes leaves from the paved area that surrounds it. Two quadrants of the square are concreted over, the others are burnt-brown grass. Children play football on a miniature, purpose-built concrete pitch. In one corner of the plaza, bronze soldiers help raise a flag in a monument dedicated to Argentines who fought in the Falklands/Malvinas War. It is not unlike the famous Iwo Jima memorial near Arlington Cemetery in Washington. A sign states that this *Monumento Héroes de Malvinas* is 2,259 kilometres from Puerto Argentino (the Argentine name for Port Stanley, capital of the Falklands).

The Palacio de Justicia runs the length of one block on Simón Bolívar. Broad steps rise from the footpath to its foyer. From there, a central corridor runs through the building to an exit on the next block. The corridor is lined with filing rooms, where attendants retrieve documents for customers waiting at marble-topped counters. Halfway down the corridor and to the right, the spacious *Salón de los Pasos Perdidos* (Hall of Lost Steps) has a high, domed ceiling. Here, in a small, glass-walled room, where hall meets corridor, an urn holds the remains of Dr Dalmacio Vélez Sarsfield.

Vélez Sarsfield's mother was Rosa Sarsfield Palacios. Her Irish antecedents were linked to the Argentine military of the eighteenth century. Disappointingly, I was unable to discover if she was related to Patrick Sarsfield, hero of the Siege of Limerick in 1690. Patrick Sarsfield left Ireland in late 1691, fought in the army of Louis XIV of France and died in Flanders in 1693.

Born in 1800, Dalmacio Vélez Sarsfield attended university in Córdoba. In 1826, he became the youngest speaker of the house in the Chamber of Deputies (the Argentine lower house). In the same year, he was appointed professor of economics at the University of Buenos Aires. At one point, he fell out with the dictator Rosas and was forced into exile in Montevideo. Later, in Argentina, he became an ally of future president Bartolomé Mitre. In 1854, after the province of Buenos Aires seceded, he drafted the constitution of the state of Buenos Aires. When Mitré became president of the reunified country in 1862, Vélez Sarsfield became its first finance minister. Soon after, he began work on the civil code of Argentina, the basis of civil law in the country, which came into effect on January 1, 1871. With modifications over time, it remained in place until 2015. Vélez Sarsfield died in 1875.

Having managed to walk the straight line from the hostel to the Palacio de Justicia without the time-consuming business of getting lost, it means that my afternoon is free for a ramble around the centre of Córdoba. The city is the second-largest in Argentina (population c. 1.3m), and also one of the oldest, founded in 1573. A statue of *el fundador* (the founder), Jerónimo Luis de Cabrera, stands in a *plazoleta* named for him. A short stroll away, the town's main central space is Plaza General San Martín. Here, the Libertador, seated on a rearing horse, faces Córdoba Cathedral on the western side of the square, the oldest cathedral in the country. Nearby, the *Manzana Jesuítica* (Jesuit Block), is on Calle Obispo Trejo. This dates from 1613, and holds the Catholic University of Córdoba (Vélez Sarsfield's alma mater, and the oldest university in the country), a private chapel and the National College of Monserrat (a secondary school).

Further along Trejo, I dip into the less antiquated surroundings of Bar Monserrat. The café's patrons pore over newspapers spread open on small, wooden tables. The tables have protective glass tops inscribed with black lettering: '*una esquina con historia*' (a corner with history). The café is busy just now and I take a seat at the only unoccupied table. A waitress delivers coffee in a small cup for a very reasonable 11 pesos. Bar Monserrat is an atmospheric little place, a traditional coffee shop with an academic/student feel. I take to it immediately, my fondness for it not lessened by the steady stream of pretty Latin women passing by outside, to and from the nearby university.

18

I've booked a place on a tour, leaving tomorrow morning, to visit the house in which Che Guevara grew up. Guevara was raised in the small city of Alta Gracia, 36 kilometres southwest of Córdoba. He was born in Rosario, further east, but when he was diagnosed with asthma as an infant, the family moved west to the clear air of the Sierra Chicas.

Che Guevara's father was Ernesto Guevara Lynch. He once said that 'the first thing to note is that in my son's veins flowed the blood of the Irish rebels'. It is said that Guevara was a descendant of Patrick Lynch, of Lydican Castle, County Galway, the same Patrick Lynch whose grandson Patricio Lynch, the 'Red Prince' of the Chilean navy, fought in the *Guerra del Pacífico*.

Although conscious of his distant heritage, there is, unsurprisingly, nothing to indicate that Guevara identified with Irishness. He did, however, have a few pints in Limerick once. On March 13, 1965, on a flight from Prague to Havana, Guevara stopped over at Shannon. After an interview with local journalist Arthur Quinlan, he visited Hanratty's Hotel on Glentworth St. Quinlan reckons that Guevara was 'three sheets to the wind when he got back to the airport' and that he was 'festooned in shamrock, as it was coming up for St Patrick's Day'. He may have enjoyed some Limerick rugby chat. Despite his asthma, he was a keen player, a fly-half for Club Universitario de Buenos Aires. He played with an aggression that earned him the nickname Fuser, from the term 'El *Fu*ribundo' (raging), and his mother's surname 'de la *Ser*na'. (The city of Córdoba is itself a major centre of Argentinian rugby.)

And it was Jim Fitzpatrick, designer of Thin Lizzy album covers, who produced the Che Guevara poster that became the iconic image of student protest in the 1960s and '70s. The poster was generated from an original photograph by Alberto Korda. Korda was Fidel Castro's official photographer and he took the photo of Guevara at a funeral in Havana, on March 5, 1960. Fitzpatrick saw it in the German weekly, *Stern*. Months later, he was sent an original copy by a Dutch anarchist. And it was from this that he produced his famous impression.

Although popular in student bedsits, Fitzpatrick's poster (according to his website) wasn't to everyone's liking. In Spain, his distributor was 'arrested by Franco's secret police'. In Ireland, 'every shop that stocked the poster was threatened or harassed: in the very fashionable Brown Thomas on Grafton Street, which sold cards and posters at the time…a well turned-out lady bought the entire stock, tore them all to pieces in front of the astonished staff and walked out'.

*

At 9.30 the next morning, the tour-meister calls to the hostel. Hector gives me a gap-toothed smile and sticks out his hand.

'I was expecting a girl', he says. 'Michelle.' He pronounces it *Mee*-tchel.

'I'm sorry to disappoint you.'

He lets out a guffaw, throws a friendly arm around my shoulder and leads me across the road to a waiting minibus.

There's a stop-off on the way to Che's house, at a Jesuit *estancia* in Alta Gracia. The main *estancia* building is now El Museo de la Estancia Jesuítica de Alta Gracia. The land on which it is built had originally been granted to a Juan Nieto in 1588. According to the museum blurb, Nieto was the co-founder of Córdoba. This may be news to Jerónimo, who was taking sole credit for this in his *plazoleta* yesterday.

The *Manzana Jesuítica* in Córdoba was supported by income from *estancias*. One of six in the region, the Alta Gracia Estancia had a main residence, church, workshop, reservoir and slave-dwelling. Water from the reservoir irrigated orchards and powered mills; furnaces were used to make bricks and tiles, looms to make simple garments. Three priests ran the *estancia* and taught the different crafts. Approximately 300 black slaves were used in the forge, workshop, mills, orchards and in outposts in the hills. Cattle were the main source of income. Also, mules bred here were sold for use in the mines at Potosí in Alto Perú. In 2000, the Alta Gracia Estancia, as part of the Jesuit system of Córdoba, was awarded UNESCO World Heritage status.

Hector was a fan of the Jesuits. 'Very clever', he thought them. He showed us purpose-made holes, no more than fifteen centimetres square, in the thick walls that surround the main *estancia* dwelling. According to folk legend, the holes were there so that the Jesuits could poke rifles through them, and shoot the indigenous people. But the gaps provided ventilation for the walls, Hector says, and they remain in good repair.

From the *estancia*, it's a short spin to Che's house, a bungalow on a residential, suburban street. A bronze figure seated on an outside wall is the revolutionary as a young boy. Inside are photos of him at various stages of his life. In his youth, he rode around South America on a motorbike; the bike sits in the living room, the route he took is displayed on a wall map. In another room are his diaries and various passports. His trademark fatigues hang in a glass case on a wall by the bathroom. Hugo Chávez and Fidel Castro made a joint visit here some years back; photos and autographs mark the occasion. '*Patria o Muerte*' (Fatherland or Death, the motto of Cuba), wrote one, and '*Hasta la Victoria Siempre*' ('Ever Onward to Victory', a well-known Guevara saying). It is a small house, and the next tour is close behind. Hector herds us up and moves us on.

There are two more stops on Hector's tour, but I ask him to drop me at the bus station.

'I'd like to visit Villa General Belgrano', I explain.

'Good choice', he tells me.

In the 1930s, two German land speculators founded Villa General Belgrano, 55 kilometres south of Alta Gracia. In time, they were joined by more German migrants, including survivors from the battleship *Graf Spee*, sunk off Montevideo in 1939. I was keen to see what the town's website calls 'a central European town in Córdoba'.

At the bus station in Alta Gracia, the Information Lady delivers a rapid spiel when I ask how to get to Villa General Belgrano. My resultant gormless expression accurately conveys that I haven't understood a word; she leaves her desk and leads me to the departure bays. There, she speaks to the driver of an idling bus who beckons me on board and delivers me to a stop by a roundabout on the outskirts of town. After a lengthy wait, another bus arrives and follows a mostly uphill route through bare hills. Towards the end of the journey, a large sign by the roadside advertises 'Hotel Edelweiss'. The sign, in varnished wood, with its mid-European moniker, offers a foretaste of what is soon to come.

From the bus station at Villa General Belgrano, it is a short stroll to the town's small central plaza. Here, Germanic lettering on an oversized wooden keg advertises the town's Oktoberfest. Nearby are wooden benches, wooden litter bins and a large, varnished wooden signpost. Through the plaza, on the main street, there are wooden houses, wooden benches, wooden shop signs and more wooden signposts. There's a lot of wood.

A brief wander leaves little doubt as to the townspeople's central European origins. The orthodontist Cecilia Hoffman looks after local dental needs. A bed awaits the weary traveller at Hotel Tirol D'Andrea. *Pan dulce alemán* (sweet German bread) is on offer at Stollen's, ice cream and tourist tat at Helados Artesanales Swiza (Swiss Artisan Ice Creams, with a Swiss cross for added emphasis). Spreewald Regalos (presents) is the place to go for gifts for the folks back home. The window display at Spreewald's is tat-heaven: beer steins, egg cups, saucers, key rings, magnets, aprons, tea towels and more, all Oktoberfest-related gumpf. The Alter Zeppelin seems like a good place for coffee and a snack. And for something stronger, there's cerveza Fritz (*cerveza artesenal*) or one of the 200 or so other beers Hector said were available here. If one overindulges on sweet bread, ice cream or beer, a remedy is at hand. On the footpath outside the farmacia is a life-size carving of a roly-poly Alpine bloke, complete with lederhosen, braces, Tyrolean hat and twirly moustache. He holds a plate-size Bayer tablet in an outstretched hand, a panacea for your ills.

I escape the mid-European onslaught and slip indoors, to Café Rissen. Here, two hands are needed to manoeuvre the café's dense, wooden chairs. It is after 3.30 now and I've been in town for less than half an hour. I had planned to stay for the afternoon before catching an early-evening return to Córdoba. But already, I'm worn out by things Alpine; I rush to the station for the 4pm bus.

Recovery from the wood-fest is aided by late-afternoon coffee at Bar Monserrat. A hard, crescent-shaped biscuit slots snugly against the base of the seated cup. On the pedestrianised street, tables and chairs sit under the bar's canopy. At one table, an unknowing woman stares directly at me, fixing her hair in the window that acts as a mirror in the half-light.

19

Rosario (population approximately 1.1m), capital of the province of Santa Fe, is the third-largest city in Argentina. It is over 400 kilometres east of Córdoba, and ideally situated for a brief overnight stop en route to Buenos Aires, a further 300 kilometres to the southeast.

Before leaving Córdoba, the hostel owner there had recommended accommodation in Rosario. It is early evening when I arrive at La Lechuga and it seems that I'm the only guest. The girl at the desk asks me to sign in, but she can't find the register. 'Later', she says, and leads me to a double room at the end of a rooftop path. I return to reception to get the Wi-Fi password. Back in my room, the password doesn't work. Several visits to reception result in more, non-working passwords. In the end, she rings the manager.

I need to find a place to eat. She has a map she can give me... somewhere. She can't find it. Instead, she offers directions.

'Is it safe around here?' I ask.

'It's not *really* dangerous', she tells me. 'You *should* be OK.'

Hostel Girl is a bundle of efficiency and reassurance.

I've been in contact with the letting agency looking after my flat in London. They tell me that the management company of the block my flat is in has fined me for late payment of the annual maintenance charge. The fine isn't a large amount, but I'm a bit miffed; I had left instructions with the agency to pay the charge on my behalf. They had tried to contact me by email, they tell me, but had gotten no response; it seems they had used an incorrect email address. They insist that the email address I had provided on the original tenancy agreement is unclear; it seems perfectly legible on the scanned copy I'd asked them to forward. So there's a minor transatlantic barney in progress as we thrash it out. Emails representing the latest instalment of this mini-saga are waiting when Hostel Girl eventually unearths a Wi-Fi password that works.

Che Guevara spent the early years of his life in Rosario, and next morning I search for the place where his family lived before they moved west to Alta Gracia. By chance, it is close by. Several blocks away, a handsome grey building curves gently around the corner where Entre Ríos meets Urquiza. It has six storeys, at least some of which are used as offices by an insurance company; their red signs are over the door and windows at ground level. The building's roof has elegant black slatework; its shuttered windows are guarded by low, black, metal railings. On Entre Ríos, Argentine colours are woven through the railings at a window on the fourth floor. I consult my guidebook. This seems to be it. I look for confirmation from the waiter at a café on the corner. 'Che Guevara?', I ask, pointing towards the colours. He looks and nods. It's all very understated. I had been hoping for a nosey around. But it seems that this low-key display of Argentine blue and white is the only evidence that this was once home to one of the continent's most famous men, and probably its most famous of Irish extraction.

This morning I had also hoped to visit Newell's Old Boys football stadium. Originally made up of ex-pupils from the English high school in the city, the club is named for an Englishman, Isaac Newell, who founded both the school and the club. The team are known as *los leprosos* (the lepers), a name given them in the 1920s when they played a charity match to raise funds for a leprosy clinic. Their local rivals, Rosario Central, founded by English railway workers, are *los canallas* (the scoundrels), because they wouldn't take part in that match. Newell's ex-players include Argentina internationals Gabriel Batistuta, Gabriel Heinze and Lionel Messi. But plans for a stadium visit are shelved. I'm running late and need to get to the bus station. I also need to visit an ATM. Returning to the hostel, I nip into a greengrocer's and ask the man behind the counter where I can find *el banco* (bank). The guy picks up a fruit and offers it to me. I look at the fruit in his hand, then at the greengrocer. I look again at the fruit. He thinks I've asked for a mango. Eventually, we work it out. There's a mango, oops, *banco*, two blocks further along. I withdraw cash, gather my bags and grab a taxi to the station for the four-hour trip to Buenos Aires.

20

The lock on my bedroom door is infuriating. Unusually, it's a sliding door; it opens and shuts like a patio. When the key is turned in the lock, a bolt slips out from the side. On the bolt, a 'hook' pops out from the top, and another from the bottom. So you close the door, turn the key, the bolt slides out, one hook flips up, the other flips down, and the hooks catch in the receiving piece of the door frame and lock the door. But, only if you're lucky. More often than not, the hooks refuse to show themselves. They shelter inside the lock's bolt and leave you standing outside the room, continually sliding the door open and shut and turning the key, to no effect. At a randomly chosen moment, the hooks poke themselves out and the door locks. At which point, I heave a sigh of relief and clear off while the going is good.

This is Che Lulu, in the Palermo district of Buenos Aires. Advertised as a hotel, Che Lulu is more of a guesthouse really. But it is fine…apart from the door. And its name sounds a lot better when the girl with the nose-ring at reception says it. It's less Looloo and more L'lu, French-sounding. Lulu is on a quiet side street off Calle Fray Justo Santa María de Oro, which links busy Avenida Santa Fe and fashionable Plaza Serrano, with its bars and restaurants. For the past couple of weeks I've been knocking around Palermo with Kathy, from Oregon; we met in Córdoba and caught up again in Buenos Aires. Kathy has returned to the States now; it is time to see more of the city.

The transcontinental shemozzle with my letting agency has come to an end. The agency offered to pay the fine imposed by the management company. When I say that 'they offered to pay', what I really mean of course is that I had to drag it out of them. But it's done now.

The nearest Subte (underground) station to Lulu, Plaza Italia, is on Avenida Santa Fe. Every day, a small guy sits on a high stool outside a shop near the Subte entrance; beside him, a pair of crutches lean against the wall. An irregular, shrill, nasal shriek never fails to make me jump, and alerts passers-by to the lottery tickets fanned out in his hand. Plaza Italia Subte is on Line D, at one end of which is Catedral, the stop for Plaza de Mayo (May Square), the historic centre of Buenos Aires.

In 1536, the conquistador Pedro de Mendoza landed on the shores of the Río de la Plata. He formed a settlement and named it Nuestra Señora Santa María del Buen Ayre (Our Lady St Mary of the Fair Winds). There's a shrine to the Virgin Mary on the hill of Buen Ayre in Sardinia. The expedition's chaplain, a devotee of the Virgin, chose the name. The local population was none too pleased about the arrival of strangers in their midst, and five years later, after continual attacks, the Spanish abandoned the site. In 1580, a permanent colony was founded when Juan de Garay sailed down the Paraná from Asunción, in modern-day Paraguay. The site of de Garay's settlement was in the vicinity of Plaza de Mayo.

As you approach the plaza from the Catedral Subte, the imposing Casa Rosada (Rose House) sits off the far end of the square. Not quite red, not quite pink, but somewhere in between, the building is the workplace of the president. From the Casa's northern balcony, Eva Perón once addressed crowds of adoring followers. Madonna replicated those scenes from the same balcony in her 1996 movie, *Evita*. And it was from there, in 1982, that General Galtieri declared war on the UK over the Falkland Islands (Las Islas Malvinas). Railings and a tall gate close off the Casa from a narrow road that runs in front of the building; bollards at each end block the road off to traffic.

At the head of the plaza, directly opposite and sideways to the Casa gates, a large bronze portrays General Belgrano on a rearing horse; a flag is raised in an outstretched hand. A lawyer, politician and military leader, Belgrano is a hero of his country's independence. *'Al Creador de la Bandera Nacional'* (To the Creator of the National Flag) reads a plaque from *La Asociación Patriotica Estudiante* (Belgrano came up with the flag's design). From here, a well-tended lawn sits on either side of a broad path that leads towards metal barriers that run the width of the square. Beyond the barriers, the centre of the plaza is a circular, paved area, the mid-point of which is the *Pirámide de Mayo* (Pyramid of May). Dated May 25, 1810, this tall, gently narrowing, stone structure is approximately eighteen metres high and commemorates the May Revolution, when the Spanish viceroy was removed and the first local government (*Primera Junta*) was formed (the May Revolution is seen as the start of the Argentine wars of independence). The layout of the remainder of the square mirrors its other half.

The handsome Cabildo is opposite the Casa Rosada, off the other end of the plaza. This small, white building dates back to colonial times and was the original seat of government. Its two storeys have a series of five tall arches on each level; a bell tower reaches upwards from its centre point. Early paintings show a building with eleven arches, but a number at each end were demolished to accommodate new roads. Today, it houses the National Museum of the Cabildo and the May Revolution.

Tall columns line the front of the nearby Metropolitan Cathedral. Hanging over the centre columns, from roof to above head-height, and held in place by scaffolding, a massive print of a smiling Pope John Paul II tells us to *'Abran las puertas a Cristo'* (open the doors to Christ). A papal tiara and crossed keys, symbol of the Vatican City, sit on the cathedral's front wall. Here, also, is the eternal flame, in memory of the unknown soldier of Argentine independence, a popular backdrop for photographs.

Inside the cathedral, the main pews are flanked by side-aisles. Off these are altars and small chapels. Half-way down the side-aisle on the right, behind a tall gate, a black, marble sarcophagus sits high on a plinth, the Argentine colours draped down one side. This holds the remains of General José de San Martín. A group of schoolchildren face the general from across the aisle. Their teacher speaks softly to them and they are incredibly well behaved. This may not have been the first visit for another teacher in the group. She seems less than enthralled and files her nails in front of the Father of the Nation.

Further along, a tiny chapel sits off the side-aisle; I take a seat in a pew facing its entrance. In a glass case to my left, the child Jesus lies cradled in the arms of a monk. People line up before the statue, stop for a moment, drop coins in a collection box, touch the glass case, and move on. To my right, an old guy has nodded off. He droops over, his head almost touching the pew in front, but somehow he stays in his seat. Inside the chapel, twirling pillars support the roof of a small, ornate altar; a spread-eagle lectern is front-right. A sprinkling of the faithful kneel in the pews. A sign outside the chapel asks for *'Silencio'*; this is a *'Lugar reservado únicamente a la oración'* (a place reserved solely for prayer).

On the other side of the cathedral is *Santo Cristo del Gran Amor* (Holy Christ of Great Love), a Hispanic Jesus in a pure white robe. In the 1970s, the family of an Argentinian soccer player was disappeared.

The footballer had promised to donate a statue if they were found and he was fortunate enough to be able to follow through on his pledge. As I complete my circuit of the cathedral, the next batch of schoolchildren is being shushed at the entrance.

From the Cabildo end of the square, the Avenida de Mayo runs straight for 1.5 kilometres towards the Congressional Plaza (it was to accommodate this avenue that one end of the Cabildo was demolished). Part-way down the *avenida*, Café Tortoni has, according to one guidebook, 'served as the artistic and intellectual capital of Buenos Aires since 1858'.

The café is spacious, broad and long; lines of tables and chairs stretch to the rear wall. Waiters wear tuxedos and black aprons; each carries a silver tray and has a white tea towel folded lengthways over the left forearm. There are photos on the walls and in display cases. Gabriela Sabatini, Hillary Clinton and Francis Ford Coppola have signed theirs, as have a host of others unknown to me. My coffee, a medium-size, slightly bitter cup, expensive at 21 pesos (c. £2.80; £1 = c. 7.5ARS), comes with a treat, a sticky-topped *medialuna*.

Before I leave, I notice three rooms at the rear of the café. One, on the right, is closed off. In the centre is what used to be a *peluquería* (barber's); today, it is full of photos and stuffed bookcases. And on the left, behind a partition, a door leads to a dimly lit room with a tiny stage set against the back wall. It feels like an illicit speakeasy, tucked away here in a hidden corner off the main café. It is easy to imagine it in an earlier time, tango music playing, sharply dressed men and classy Latin women crowded around small tables clouded in cigarette smoke.

From Café Tortoni, I continue on to the end of Avenida de Mayo. The *medialuna* has done little to fend off my hunger and I stop for late lunch at an Italian restaurant. Here, I scrape dollops of cheese from the top of a pizza. This reduces the cheese coating from mountainous to merely excessive, and hours later, it remains lodged in my stomach.

21

On my return to Plaza de Mayo, a politician is 'meeting and greeting' at a junction where Avenida de Mayo meets Perú; his sidekicks hand out leaflets. The poster beside him announces that this is Ricardo López Murphy.

I shuffle up to him and point to the poster.

'*Es un nombre irlandés*', I say, stating the obvious, before going on to apologise for my poor Spanish.

'It's OK, I can speak English.'

He has been to Ireland many times, he tells me. His grandfather had emigrated from Roscommon at the end of the nineteenth century. We have barely begun to chat when one of his sidekicks points at my camera and suggests a photo. This done, and in what I suspect is a well-practised move to prevent monopolisation of her boss's time, she leads him off to meet another passer-by.

I was keen to know more about Señor López Murphy. Disappointingly, I could find out nothing about his Irish connection. But he did have a role to play in an interesting period of Argentine history.

López Murphy was born in the small city of Adrogué, 23 kilometres south of Buenos Aires. He followed up a degree in economics from the National University of La Plata with a Masters from the University of Chicago. He taught economics at universities in Argentina and Uruguay, served as an advisor to the central banks of both countries and was employed as a consultant by the IMF and the World Bank, among others. He entered politics in 1999 and was appointed minister for defence before being transferred to Finance two years later. At this time, Argentina was deep in the financial mire, a situation that had been some time in the making.

In the early 1990s, in a bid to end hyperinflation, Argentina's peso was pegged to the US dollar. Over the decade, as the value of the dollar rose, so the country's exports became expensive. Argentine output declined, and unemployment increased. Privatisation undertaken in this period resulted in a further lengthening of dole queues. All this time, the government spent freely and ran up an enormous debt.

On March 2, 2001, with an ongoing recession and an ever-growing deficit, Ricardo López Murphy stepped into the Finance hot seat. His reputation ensured that his appointment was welcomed by economists at home and abroad. Two weeks later, he proposed a tough austerity programme which included severe cuts in education. In protest, six officials resigned from a junior party of the governing coalition. On March 19, less than three weeks into the job, and having lost the support of the president, López Murphy resigned. By July, Argentine stocks had fallen to a 28-month low. The country's credit ratings were slashed. By the end of that month, an austerity budget was passed, cutting state salaries and pensions. The IMF recommended an increase of $8bn in Argentina's existing $14bn standby loan agreement. On November 30, Argentines withdrew $1.3bn from personal bank accounts. The next day, to halt a run on the banks, a monthly limit was placed on individual cash withdrawals. At the start of December, unhappy with what it considered inadequate austerity measures, the IMF refused to sign off on the next $1.3bn tranche of aid. Unemployment hit nearly 20% and unions called a national strike. Twenty-two people were killed as protests and riots spread nationwide. At the end of the month, both the president and the minister for finance resigned. In 2002, the Argentine government formally defaulted on $132bn of debt, the largest default in history.

As head of his own party, Recreate for Growth, López Murphy went on to contest the presidential election of April 2003. He came in third behind Carlos Menem and Néstor Kirchner, with a very respectable 18% of the vote. As part of a new centre-right coalition in 2007, his next bid for the presidency did not fare so well. Just over 1% of the voting population supported him. López Murphy is known as the Bulldog, a nickname that doesn't displease him. His online presence includes a 'Bullblog'.

Today, Ricardo López Murphy is canvassing for the upcoming election of the mayor of Buenos Aires. Later in the week, a televised mayoral debate involves him (Moorphy, according to the mediator) and two other candidates. At the end of the debate, each is given two minutes to sum up. Moorphy is impassioned, the second guy is measured. The third passes a dog muzzle to each of his fellow panellists.

Murphy is unsuccessful in his bid for the mayoralty. Mauricio Macri, former president of the Boca Juniors football club, and recently possessed of a dog muzzle, retains his position.

22

It's an overcast and very chilly Thursday afternoon, and I'm back at Plaza de Mayo. As I approach the centre of the square from the Cabildo end, the Pyramide de Mayo is ahead, shielded by waist-high railings around its base.

I hadn't noticed on my previous visit, but a white circle is painted around the Pyramide, at the outer edge of the broad, paved area that surrounds it; white radii run from the railings to the circle's circumference. White, knotted headscarves are painted on the ground within each resulting segment. The white headscarf is the symbol of the *Madres de la Plaza* (Mothers of the Plaza).

In 1976, amid soaring inflation and economic difficulties, military officers deposed President Isabel Perón. (The world's first woman president, she was the third wife of the by-now deceased former president Juan Perón. Juan Perón had begun his first term as the country's leader in 1946, when he succeeded Edelmiro Julián Farrell, grandson of a Matthew Farrell from County Longford.) For some time prior to the coup, the country had been plagued by armed violence. Far-left groups were involved in bombings, kidnappings and assassinations. They were opposed by a right-wing paramilitary organisation, the Argentine Anticommunist Alliance (the Triple A), which operated with discreet government support. During the brief Perón regime (1974–76), levels of violence soared. After the coup, the military appointed Lieutenant-General Jorge Videla as president. Congress was closed, trade unions were outlawed and the press was censored. Videla started the Process of National Reorganisation, later known as the *Guerra Sucia* (the

Dirty War), directing his attention not only against active, left-wing guerillas, but also against the communities from which they sprang. Figures are disputed, but it is estimated that between 10,000 and 30,000 people were killed. Victims were routinely tortured. The *Guerra Sucia* continued into the early 1980s. A civilian government regained control only in 1983, after the failure of the military's attempts to take control of the Falkland Islands. In 1977, the *Madres de la Plaza* had brought worldwide attention to the human rights abuses of the state by holding a vigil in Plaza de Mayo, in an attempt to discover the fate of disappeared relatives, *los desaparecidos*. For over 30 years, they have continued with their weekly demonstration.

As I enter the centre of the plaza, large portrait paintings of the disappeared are being set up on the right, around the outer edge of the area that circles the Pyramide. To the left, a stall-holder sells peanuts slathered in a sugary coating; the concoction, sizzling on the stall's hotplate, gives the air a sweet smell. Beyond the peanut stall, a white headscarf is imprinted on the pointed roof of a small, blue and clear plastic tent. Inside, three women sell books and mementos for the *Asociación Madres de la Plaza*. Two of the women are quite elderly and wear white headscarves. A girl beside me makes a purchase. '*Suerte!*' (best of luck!), she says to one Madre, and they clasp hands, a footballer's clasp, thumbs entwined. Two small vans on the far side of the tent belong to the *Asociación*. From the back of one, a guy takes a bundle of small, blue plastic flags and hands them out to the crowd milling in front of the tent. *Ni un paso atrás!* (not one backward step!), declare the flags. By the side of the plaza, a TV van has a satellite dish and a camera on the roof; at ground level, a technician extends a cable. Tied to the barriers that run across the square, a white blimp with blue tail fins floats higher than the Pyramide.

Somewhere, a bell tolls for 3.30. A minibus arrives through the Pyramide circle and parks beside the *Asociación*'s two small vans. White headscarves are visible through the windows.

The frail Madres climb from the minibus and, led by young helpers, walk slowly towards the centre of the plaza. Supporters gather round and offer hugs and kisses; others start up a rhythmic clapping and chanting. A broad banner is raised on four tall poles: *Siempre con Las Madres* (Always with the Mothers). The Madres stretch out in a line the length of a radius of the Pyramide circle and proceed around the monument, followed by their chanting followers.

Unseen by me, a number of Madres had begun a separate walk before the main group. First around the Pyramide, three of them hold a banner waist-high, its message obscured by photographers walking backwards in front of them. A small, silent crowd follows these Madres; placards raised above their heads show the forever-young faces of the disappeared: César, Luis, Alejandro...

After three laps of the Pyramide, one of the barriers that stretch across the width of the square is moved aside and the Madres make their way towards the Casa Rosada. They stop at the statue of Belgrano and line up in a row on a single step of the plinth. I count fourteen of them. The head Madre makes a short speech. The crowd is attentive and clap at various points. TV cameras record the goings-on and tourists snap photos. The speech is followed by more chanting and clapping. It is now 4pm; the Madres turn left, step from the plinth in single file and make their way back towards the Pyramide. It's an unhurried return; they stop for conversations, words of encouragement, and hugs and kisses. On the minibus, one Madre touches her palm to a window; on the other side of the glass, a well-wisher meets it with her own. TV cameras poke in the side door. As the final Madre steps on board, there's a sustained round of applause and the minibus leaves the plaza in the opposite direction from which it had arrived.

After the departure of the Madres, a crowd dawdles in the centre of the square. The plastic souvenir tent continues to do good business; the TV guy winds up his cable. An American tour guide informs her group about what they've just seen. The portraits have been moved from the outer edge of the Pyramide circle and now lie against the railings that shield the Pyramide's base. One portrait, the tallest among them, shows the bespectacled figure of journalist and author, Rodolfo Walsh.

Rodolfo Walsh was born in 1927 in the province of Río Negro (south-central Argentina). He spent most of his adult life in Buenos Aires, and a square in the city is named for him. It's not far from Plaza de Mayo, a small, cobbled space, at the intersection of two city centre streets, where a couple of terraced houses might once have stood. Despite its minute size, Plaza Rodolfo Walsh manages to squeeze in trees and benches. On my visit, a pair of dishevelled guys sit on one of the benches, wine bottles clutched tightly. The gable ends of houses form two sides of the square; one of them is covered in murals. As I examine the murals, a wine drinker approaches; he forms a gun with a thumb and two fingers, simulates firing it and points at the gable end. High on the wall, a life-size statue of Rodolfo Walsh stands on a balcony, bullet holes showing clearly in a perforated pullover.

Rodolfo was the son of Miguel Walsh and Dora Gill, and descended from a long line of Irish-Argentines on both sides of the family (please note, if you're Googling him; the following does not refer to Rodolfo Walsh, the Guatemalan wedding photographer). As a boy, he attended the Irish school in Capilla del Señor in Buenos Aires province, and later, the Fahy Institute in Moreno (less than 50 kilometres west of the city). He dropped out of university, became a proofreader and, by his mid-twenties, was a full-time writer. In 1959, he went to Cuba, where, with Gabriel García Márquez, he was one of the first journalists to work for Prensa Latina, the state news agency. On his return to Argentina, Walsh became involved with the Montoneros, a left-wing guerilla group, reportedly acting as their intelligence agent.

After the military coup of 1976, Walsh founded his own news agency in response to the clampdown on the press. That same year, his daughter Victoria, also a member of the Montoneros, was involved in a shoot-out with the army. She committed suicide on the terrace of her house rather than surrender to her attackers, who had the house surrounded and from whom there was no escape.

On March 24, 1977, exactly a year after the military coup, Walsh wrote an accusatory '*Carta Abierta*' (Open Letter) to the ruling junta. The following day, army tanks demolished his home in the suburbs of Buenos Aires. In the city, a military death squad tried to take him into custody. Walsh pulled a gun to defend himself and was killed. His body was thrown into the boot of a car and was never seen again.

An influential writer, Walsh was considered a pioneer of investigative journalism in Argentina. The Rodolfo Walsh Prize is awarded annually by the National University of La Plata to those who have advanced the cause of press freedom.

23

On Saturday, Paula calls for me at Lulu. Paula is in her thirties, trim and tanned. She wears denim jeans and a jacket, has a stud through her right eyebrow and a wide hairband pulled back off her forehead. I hand Paula 350 pesos (over £50) and in return, she passes me a match ticket for River Plate vs Lanús. This expensive fee also gets me a lift in a minibus waiting nearby; its only remaining seat, second from back, places me in a mini German-speaking enclave.

River Plate are one of the top two football clubs in Argentina. The other, Boca Juniors, are their fiercest rivals. Local derbies in Latin America are *clásicos*, but the papers say that River Plate vs Boca Juniors is a *superclásico*, and attendance at that fixture is top of the '50 sporting things you must do before you die', according to *The Observer*. Both clubs originate in the docklands barrio of La Boca in southeast Buenos Aires – the barrio sits at the *boca* (mouth) of the Riachuelo. In 1925, River moved to affluent Belgrano, in the northeast of the city. In the following decade, a huge outlay on player transfers gave them the nickname *Los Millonarios*. Not surprisingly, relations between rival fans can be strained. To River supporters, their rivals are *los chanchitos* (little pigs), a reference to the supposed smell from Boca's stadium. Boca fans call their River counterparts *gallinas* (chickens). They suspect that River players lack *cojones*. River's 'bottle' will be put to the test against Lanús today. It is the final League game of the regular season and they are in danger of being relegated for the first time in their history.

The minibus deposits us a short distance from River's stadium, *El Monumental*. A stroll through ever-more thronged streets brings us to a crowded, gated entrance. Here, stewards randomly pull aside those they want to search and herd us through the gates into the stadium grounds. *El Monumental* is a bowl with two levels, and our seats are behind a corner flag, at the back of the lower tier; the bottom lip of the upper stand stretches out above us.

Despite the potentially duff seats, the view from the back of the stand is fine. The white, wooden slat benches are muddy-brown from punters sitting on seat-backs and resting their feet in front of them. Behind us is a broad, concrete concourse. The toilets are here. For the toilets, imagine Croke Park, circa 1895. This may also have been the last time they were cleaned. To our right, at the back of the stand, is a reinforced-glass, private box. The bottom half of the glass is frosted; through the clear glass above that, TV pictures are visible on a screen on the far wall. On the pitch, Lanús are already limbering up as River run out from a far corner of the stadium. The visitors play in maroon shirts, River are all in white, a diagonal red stripe on the shirt, front and back (imagine Galway vs, er…Peru).

The stands are covered in red and white, on shirts and scarves, on banners hanging from the upper tier and on those draped over the hoarding at ground level. As the game kicks off, the crowd are in good fettle, chanting and clapping. On my left, Paula is nervous. She's smoking a cigarette and she can't keep still. Paula supports Boca Juniors and she desperately wants Lanús to win. But, here among the River fans, she must keep her enthusiasm for the visitors in check. There's a head-case near us, standing and roaring, pointing and ranting, spitting with rage. The guy has his young son with him, a psycho-in-training for the next generation.

In the 30th minute, Lanús score. There's silence for several moments before River fans start roaring and urging their side on. The team respond and try harder, but Lanús are slicker and have the upper hand. A River fan on my right takes an interest in the game on the TV inside the private box. In good English, he tells me that it's Quilmes vs Olimpo. The result of that match, he says, might be more important than this one. If Olimpo lose or draw, River are safe from relegation. Olimpo are one–nil up. Paula is thrilled. She quickly puts a clamp on a broad grin and pulls out another cigarette.

Two minutes after half-time, River equalise. The chanting of the crowd rises a notch. The head-case is apoplectic. Paula is now chain-smoking. Others sitting nearby have picked up on the TV in the private box, and during breaks in play, nervous heads turn to get the latest from above the frosted glass.

River are a different team in this half. Their hard work is overpowering Lanús. One clear chance on goal should have wrapped it up, but the striker duffed it from less than five metres. The head-case rants and rages, Paula lets out a relieved sigh. River dominate the second half, and, as is often the way, they fall to a late sucker punch. Two minutes into injury time, Lanús score the winning goal. The match is over. Lanús have won, Olimpo have won, and River are in a relegation play-off. As the players leave the pitch, the crowd pelts them with plastic bottles. Paula bounces out of the stadium in a happy trail of smoke. On the minibus, she entertains us with football chants, something about River and relegation that needs no translation.

24

Argentina is the only South American (and, interestingly, the only mainly Catholic) country to which the Irish emigrated in any great numbers. Most arrived after 1830 and by the time Ricardo López Murphy's grandfather had left Roscommon at the end of the nineteenth century, the emigrant stream was down to a trickle. It is difficult to be exact about the extent of the migration (in official documentation, all arrivals from the British Isles formed a single category and Irish figures are not easy to isolate). One commentator says that 45,000 came to the country in the period from 1830 to 1930, the majority arriving before 1880.

In Ireland, just three counties provided most of the emigrants. Approximately two-thirds came from Westmeath and Longford, with about 15% from the Forth and Bargy area of Wexford (the southeastern tip of the county). In the late 1820s, John Thomond O'Brien had been engaged by the government in Buenos Aires to travel to Europe and encourage emigration to Argentina. The scheme was not a success, but O'Brien did persuade a Thomas Mooney from Streamstown, County Westmeath, and his brother-in-law, Patrick Bookey, to return with him. Patrick McKenna, writing in *Patterns of Migration*, mentions these early migrants, as well as a Browne from Wexford, as being originally responsible for enticing settlers from their home areas.

Those who travelled, McKenna says, were often 'the younger, non-inheriting sons, and later daughters, of the larger tenant farmers and leaseholders'. The fare for the three-month journey was £16, four times the price of a pre-Famine ticket to the United States, and roughly the annual wage of a mid-nineteenth-century Irish labourer. Often, this would have been paid by relatives already in Argentina or by prospective employers there.

According to Helen Kelly in her book *Irish 'Ingleses'*, the arrival of the Irish coincided with 'the exceptional growth' of sheep farming in Argentina. In a sector that was to become an important part of the economy, its 'early domination…belonged to the Irish'. Its expansion meant that 'labourers received handsome recompense for their toil, in turn accumulating significant capital'. After mid-century, 'in terms of land, stock and capital accumulation, the Irish [had become] unassailable'. In the 1870s, the British Consul wrote that 'the progress of Buenos Aires is mainly due to the industrious Irish sheep-farmers'.

The success of some Irish was an encouragement to those from their home areas in Ireland. Immigrant letters recounted tales of wealth and adventure. This, and poor economic prospects at home, enticed many to follow.

Interestingly, one key to Irish success was the link to Britain. Newly independent Argentina was decidedly Anglophile. The English were considered to be culturally advanced, and its people regarded as being from superior ethnic stock. To Argentines, any English-speaker from the British Isles was *Inglés*. And so, the Irish knowingly and strategically nurtured an Inglés identity. By doing this, they 'entered what was an elite social climate for "Ingleses" and one that facilitated social and economic mobility'. An Inglés identity was enormously significant. It affected how locals viewed the Irish and how the Irish presented themselves. It was in the interests of the Irish to be English.

Edmundo Murray has written extensively about the Irish in Argentina. In one online article, he says that, from the beginning:

dealing with...local people and cultures prompted the immigrants coming from a colonized island to regard themselves as colonizers. Confronted with, and sometimes feeling threatened by, the ways of living in Argentina...the Irish believed they came from the most modern culture in the world. They realised that they could be carriers of modernity and take advantage of what they perceived as...local backwardness and uncivilised ways...To the typical determination of most immigrants to adapt to their new milieu, the Irish added the attitude of behaving as modern conquistadores in what they perceived as an uncivilised territory.

25

The Irish settlers who arrived in Argentina in the 1830s would have found that some of their countrymen had preceded them. A sprinkling of Irish merchants had been in Buenos Aires for some time; others were ex-soldiers. The British invaded Buenos Aires in 1806, and again in 1807. Irish soldiers formed part of those invading forces; some stayed on in the country when the British left for home.

Plans for a British attack on Spanish South America had surfaced in 1804, when a Royal Navy captain, Sir Home Riggs Popham, submitted a memorandum to the First Lord of the Admiralty in London. In it, he proposed seizing four locations in Spanish America: Buenos Aires, Valparaíso, Venezuela and Panama. Popham's aims were to damage Britain's enemy, Spain, by urging its colonies towards independence, and to open up new markets for British trade. The plan was approved by the prime minister, William Pitt. At this time, France was at war with Britain. By the following year, Spain had joined with the French. Britain's ally, Russia, was keen to use diplomacy to break up this alliance. Not wishing to antagonise the Spanish, Popham's plan was put on hold.

In 1805, Major-General Sir David Baird captured Cape Town with an army of 6,500 troops. Popham was the naval commander of the expedition. Before he left Britain, Pitt had told him that the South American invasion could go ahead if Spain could not be won over to the anti-French side.

While in South Africa, news of Napoleonic victories on continental Europe convinced Popham that the Spain–France alliance was likely to remain intact. He persuaded Baird to give him 1,000 troops, under the command of Brigadier-General William Carr Beresford, and set sail for South America. More soldiers were picked up en route, at St Helena. Beresford was an Irishman, the illegitimate son of the 1st Marquess of Waterford, whose estates were at Curraghmore, in Portlaw. About half of Beresford's force was made up of the 71st Highland Regiment. In 1800, after eighteen years of duty in India, the depleted 71st had been transferred to Ballinasloe and Loughrea in County Galway. When it next left the country, for South Africa with Baird, the regiment was fully manned. Peter Pyne, in his research paper *The Invasions of Buenos Aires, 1806–1807: The Irish Dimension*, thinks it likely 'that a majority of the rank and file would have been Irish' at the time of their departure.

In putting together his force, Popham had neither informed London nor sought its permission. But he pressed on in the knowledge that 'the British Empire…[had]…been largely built up by similar examples of private enterprise'. It is possible that Popham had another motive. It is said that he owed money to William Pius White, an American smuggler and slave trader in Buenos Aires. White may have highlighted to Popham the large amount of bullion that was in the city, ready to be transported to Spain.

On June 25, 1806, Beresford and approximately 1,500 troops landed at Quilmes, seventeen kilometres south of Buenos Aires. The Spanish viceroy, thinking that a larger force had come ashore, hotfooted it inland to Córdoba. After a single clash, and the loss of one soldier, Beresford took Buenos Aires. The bullion never reached Spain. Instead, over $1m was shipped to England (Beresford and Popham retained enough to cover the expenses of army and navy; later, both received substantial prize money). There, its arrival was greeted with wild celebrations. The public believed they had found El Dorado.

Before he left for South America, Popham had been given to understand that the local population was ready to rise against Spanish rule. This information may have been provided by an Irishman, James Florence Burke. Burke was a British spy who arrived in Buenos Aires early in 1805. There, he fell in with Thomas O'Gorman, from Ennis in County Clare, a successful Irish merchant in the city. Burke was to gauge the level of local dissatisfaction with imperial rule. Before the year was out, he had returned to Britain to report on his findings.

The local support Popham had been expecting wasn't forthcoming. Pro-independence creoles were reluctant to make a move. Meanwhile, in Córdoba, the viceroy was attempting to put together an army. Spanish troops were already active on the outskirts of Buenos Aires, while in the city, natives were becoming ever-more hostile to the foreigners in their midst. Some pro-independence creoles were now co-operating with Spanish loyalists in planning to recapture the city. All the while, the British waited on official instructions from London.

On August 1, at Perdriel, just outside Buenos Aires, 2,000 Argentines confronted a 500-strong contingent of Beresford's soldiers. The locals were overcome in twenty minutes. Two days later, Santiago de Liniers, a Frenchman now leading local resistance, landed north of the city with 1,000 men. As at Perdriel, Beresford had hoped to meet the enemy in open country where his troops could put their military experience to best advantage. But heavy weather made the country roads inaccessible for his foot soldiers. Supplied with horses, Liniers' troops had less trouble advancing on Buenos Aires. On August 12, they launched their attack. The British fell back to the plaza in front of the city's fort. As they did, local snipers took up positions on the low, flat roofs of surrounding buildings and picked off the retreating foreigners at will. Beresford was trapped and he surrendered. After 47 days of British rule, local forces had brought about *La Reconquista* (Reconquest).

*

The Irish merchant Thomas O'Gorman, friend of the spy James Florence Burke, was one of the 'Wild Geese' who left Ireland to fight for European armies. He had fought with the Walsh regiment in the service of the king of France. When the regiment was disbanded after the French Revolution, he found his way to the French colony of Mauritius. There, he married Marie Anne Périchon de Vandeuil, the daughter of a colonial official. Involved in commerce with the Viceroyalty of the Río de la Plata, he moved his family to Buenos Aires. Although sources differ, it seems that O'Gorman was not in the city at the time of the invasion of 1806. His wife, *La Périchona*, was to have an affair with her compatriot, Santiago de Liniers, hero of *La Reconquista*, which scandalised the city. O'Gorman never returned to Buenos Aires. It is said that he died, penniless, in Spain.

26

It is Monday morning, and my clothes should have been in the wash two days ago. Sitting in a café across the road from the laundry, waiting for its doors to open, I eventually remember that today is a bank holiday. I drop the clothes back to Lulu. They very nearly made it there by themselves.

Today, I plan to visit Tigre, named for the *tigres* (jaguars) hunted there in colonial times. Some 28 kilometres north of Palermo, Tigre sits on an island in the Paraná Delta (the delta is approximately 65 kilometres wide at the mouth of the Paraná, where the river's various branches flow into the Río de la Plata). Jorge, the *fear a' tí* at Lulu, tells me that the town is a popular destination for a day trip. It is also where, in 1806, Santiago de Liniers landed his troops before advancing to retake Buenos Aires from the British.

The 118 bus from Avenida Santa Fe takes me to Estación Belgrano for the train north. There's a bitter breeze on Santa Fe; I fend it off with a zipped-up jacket and a green, woolly, beanie with a tapering tip that makes me look faintly gnome-ish.

At Belgrano, the train (2 pesos return) arrives almost immediately. On board, it is standing room only. This is not because the carriage is overcrowded. It's because it doesn't have any seats; it is bare. Many passengers sit on the floor, which seems a good idea. The top halves of the adjustable windows are broken and won't stay in place; standing rewards you only with a blast of the piercing wind. The window to my left is the exception; its top half clings to the window frame on a thin wire.

It is 40 minutes to Tigre; I don't notice where the city ends and Tigre begins. Outside the station there, monster Argentinian and provincial flags fly from tall poles. To the left, on a river, a single sculler carves his smooth way beneath a bridge. Along the bank, Avenida de las Naciones Unidas features a long line of flagpoles. At the foot of each, a small marble plaque names a country and its capital city.

From Uganda (capital, Kampala), I cross the bridge to the far bank and follow the river path. On the way, a plastic container partially filled with water sits on the roof of a Ford Taurus (it's like an old Ford Cortina). This alerts passers-by that the car is for sale. A notice in the window offers additional information. It claims that the car is '*Único. Joya total*' (Unique. A real jewel). Which it is, I guess, if you like your jewellery old and rusty. Rowing clubs have their headquarters on this side of the river. Sets of mini-tracks run up the sloping, concreted riverbank and cross the road to boat sheds on club premises. '*Precaución Cruce de Botes*' (Caution, Boats Crossing) is the warning.

The breeze here is as sharp as it was on Santa Fe, and my gnome-ish beanie provides welcome warmth. Veering left with the bend in the river, a stray dog keeps me company, past more clubhouses, before he slips away into the grounds of the Museo de Arte. Further on, the Museo de la Reconquista sits opposite the site on the river where Liniers landed in 1806. The small museum has a framed representation of the '*Banderas Inglesas tomadas en la Reconquista*' (English flags taken in the Reconquest), among them a *guion* (guidon) and *banderas* belonging to the 71st Highlanders.

A print shows General Beresford surrendering to Liniers '*frente a los arcos del Cabildo*' (in front of the arches of the Cabildo). Beresford bows his head, humbled before his victor. At the time, the Cabildo was in possession of all its arches.

After *La Reconquista*, Beresford and over 1,000 men were taken prisoner. The rank and file were removed to the interior of the country. Officers were to be returned to Britain. They had given their word not to fight again against Spain until they reached home. Eventually, however, they too were transferred inland. As 'gentleman' guests of well-to-do locals, theirs was not an overly unpleasant existence. The prisoners could carry side-arms, attend social gatherings and move about as they wished as long as they returned to their lodgings by nightfall.

Beresford's defeat didn't signal the end of Britain's engagement with South America. While officers were enjoying local Latin hospitality, events elsewhere were moving apace.

After he took Buenos Aires, Beresford had sent word to General Baird, the commander in South Africa, asking for reinforcements. Baird dispatched 2,180 men under a Lieutenant-Colonel Backhouse. They arrived at the Río de la Plata in October 1806. When he discovered that Beresford had already surrendered, Backhouse captured the town of Maldonado (in modern-day Uruguay) and waited for instructions from London.

There, in response to the arrival of Beresford's bullion, the government sent 4,000 men to Buenos Aires to consolidate the British position. Commanded by Sir Samuel Auchmuty, these included the largely Irish 1st battalion of the 87th Regiment of Foot (they later joined with another regiment to become the Royal Irish Fusiliers), under Sir Edward Butler. Auchmuty didn't fancy his chances of retaking Buenos Aires and instead laid siege to the Spanish stronghold of Montevideo. The city surrendered in February 1807.

Also, at this time, London was acting on a plan to invade Chile. They had sent 4,500 men under Brigadier-General Robert Craufurd to capture Valparaíso and Santiago (in 1798, during the United Irish uprising, Craufurd had been with the British Forces in Ireland, under the lord lieutenant, Lord Cornwallis, where he had led a flying column against rebels). When they heard about Beresford's surrender, London sent a ship after Craufurd, with instructions that he divert instead to the Río de la Plata. His force included 875 men of the almost wholly Irish 88th Regiment of Foot. (The 88th was formed in Galway in 1793 by Colonel John Thomas de Burgh; it later merged with another regiment to form the Connaught Rangers – 'the Devil's Own' – that disbanded in 1922 after the creation of the Irish Free State.) Craufurd arrived at the Río de la Plata in June 1807.

This combined force of over 10,000 men was commanded by Lieutenant-General John Whitelocke. On June 30, he landed his troops at Ensenada de Barragán (Barragán's Cove), 50 kilometres southeast of Buenos Aires. By the time they reached the city four days later, his soldiers were hungry and weary. The marshy land through which they had marched had sapped their strength and swallowed much of their provisions. On July 3, approximately 6,000 men assembled on the outskirts of the city. The remainder of the attacking force stayed a short distance to the rear.

Whitelocke spent a couple of days formalising a plan of attack. The delay gave Liniers time to prepare. It also gave an Irish bugler the opportunity to indulge in some light entertainment. Michael McCarthy, a deserter from the invasion force of the previous year, and now aligned with the city's defenders, crept towards Whitelocke's forces at night and amused himself by confusing the ranks with hoax bugle calls.

The attacking force, at the western edge of Buenos Aires, split into thirteen columns. Their targets were the city's main buildings, on the shores of the river, around a kilometre to the east. To hasten progress and to reduce possible civilian casualties, Whitelocke ordered that his men unload their weapons. En route, defenders sheltered behind the parapets of low-roofed houses. As the troops progressed through the streets, they were easily cut down.

Approximately 560 men of the mostly Irish 88th Regiment took part in the assault. They formed two of the thirteen columns, one of which was headed by a Colonel Duff. So concerned was he about the plan of attack that he ordered that the regimental flag be left behind, to prevent it falling into enemy hands. The two columns of the 88th attacked the vicinity of the city fort, one of the most heavily defended areas of the city. They suffered severe losses. Within a few hours, 240 men had been killed or injured. Both columns surrendered and were taken prisoner.

The second Irish regiment, the 87th – 'The Faughs', from their battle cry '*Faugh-a-ballagh*!' (Clear the way!) – also had a horrific time. Out of 642 soldiers, 87 were killed and 330 wounded. In total, in the morning's fighting, approximately 3,000 men were killed, injured or taken prisoner, 50% of the force that had started out just a short time before.

Whitelocke took the advice of senior officers and ordered the cessation of activities. On July 7, he signed a treaty of surrender. In London, the public was enraged at the humiliation of their army. On his return, Whitelocke was cashiered and declared unfit to serve in the military.

This resistance to the second British invasion was '*La Defensa*' (the Defence). Argentines were proud of their victories against the world's premier fighting force, and their efforts in 1806 and 1807 are considered to have given rise to a sense of nationalism among them. These events were the starting point of a process that, by the end of the following decade, would result in the country's independence from Spain.

27

Next morning, my unwashed clothes almost walk themselves out of Lulu's door. I accompany them to the laundry, on my way to visit Recoleta Cemetery.

Professional dog walkers do good business in Buenos Aires. *Paseaperros* (or *Paseadores de perros*; *el perro* – dog) stroll the streets with impossible numbers of dogs at the ends of leads. This morning in Palermo, at the junction of Paraguay and Borges, one *paseaperro* controls a posse of twelve. Another guy matches this total, further on, on Las Heras. But on Azcuénaga, the *paseaperro* of the day leads a bustling sixteen. It's an A-star for him, and a gold star for the first guy, who effortlessly led his dozen with one hand, while rolling a push bike with the other.

Covering around two hectares in the heart of Buenos Aires, Recoleta is, according to my guidebook, the city's 'most prestigious address', the resting place of Argentina's rich and famous. Twenty-one Argentinian presidents and two Nobel Prize winners are buried here. Inside the cemetery gates, I join a small group waiting for the start of the 11am tour. Our guide, Patricia, arrives and leads us along the main 'avenue' (for the most part, the cemetery is laid out in a grid pattern, with tombs lining avenues and cross-streets). En route, Patricia tells us in halting English that, on average, each of the approximately 4,800 vaults holds 25 to 30 of the deceased (this number includes cremated remains). Some of the older vaults, built with bricks and cement, are in poor repair; most are in durable marble or granite. Many of these memorials are magnificent. In what I suspect is a well-worn line,

Patricia tells us that the deceased had wanted a beautiful *palace* for living, and a beautiful *place* for eternal rest. Cats roam the cemetery. According to an old tale, we're told, they're here to ward off evil spirits. But it might be because a couple of old dears come and feed them every day.

Patricia stops at a 'crossroads', the cemetery's central point. Here, 'streets' branch off at diagonals from 'Cristo Central', a statue of Christ which stands mid-junction. Where two of these diagonals meet, lie the remains of Almirante (Admiral) Guillermo Brown.

Founder of the Argentine navy, William Brown was, according to Andrew Graham-Yooll (*The Forgotten Colony*), a 'national hero and star of the Irish community'. Born in Mayo in 1777, Brown arrived in Buenos Aires in 1810. His route to the Río de la Plata was a roundabout one. When he was nine, his family left Ireland for the United States. There, he joined the Merchant Navy as a cabin-boy. In 1796, he was press-ganged on to a British vessel. Imprisoned by the French during the Napoleonic Wars, he eventually escaped and reached England. In 1809, the newly married Brown sailed for Montevideo. The following year, he moved on to Buenos Aires where he earned a living trading up and down the coast. An extended spell of bad luck saw him lose his first ship to a Portuguese raider, before a second was wrecked in an attempt to get through a Spanish blockade of Buenos Aires. Later, yet another, the *Industria*, was captured by a Spanish frigate.

These setbacks prompted Brown into action. He recruited Irish, Scots and North American sailors from 'the seediest corners of the riverfront'. Posing as fishermen, they took to the Plata in a number of small vessels. They boarded and seized a Spanish cruiser (the Spanish were blockading the port in response to the ongoing Argentine wars of independence), forced its crew into boats and made their captives tow the cruiser back to Buenos Aires. Onshore, this poking-in-the-eye of their imperial masters thrilled the general public. It also impressed the governor, who offered Brown the post of commander of the Buenos Aires navy. The Irishman accepted, and in March 1814, on board his flagship, *Hercules*, Brown set out to confront the Spanish.

The island of Martín García sits in the middle of the Río de la Plata estuary, between Buenos Aires and the coast of the Banda Oriental (modern-day Uruguay). Its strategic location gave it the title of the 'Gibraltar of the River Plate'. After fierce fighting, Brown captured the island, and from there, sailed for the Spanish colonial base of Montevideo. There, he harassed enemy ships, luring them into combat. Victorious in a series of battles, Brown freed the estuary from Spanish control. In Buenos Aires, he was acclaimed a hero.

After a spell onshore, Brown acquired a privateer's licence and sailed for the Pacific. There, he was captured by the Spanish. Released in a prisoner exchange, he returned to Buenos Aires, found the port blockaded, and sailed onwards to Barbados. Arrested by the British for piracy, only the payment of a large fine secured his release. In 1818, back in Buenos Aires, he was accused by the government of 'leaving the country when he was most needed' (the war against Spain had been ongoing in his absence). The following year, he retired from the navy.

Brown ran a grocery shop in the centre of Buenos Aires for a time. Before long, however, he was coaxed out of retirement. In 1825, Buenos Aires was at war with Brazil over the contested territory of the Banda Oriental. As admiral of the fleet, he fought 29 battles in the two years of the war. Famously, at the Battle of Juncal, out of seventeen Brazilian vessels that took part, twelve were captured and three were burned. Brown lost none.

Graham-Yooll tells us that 'every battle that Brown fought in the Plata was watched by the population of Buenos Aires…[who]… flocked to the riverside, to await news…and to try to see Brown'. The conflict ended when Britain mediated between the two countries, the outcome of which was the creation of the state of Uruguay. When Brown returned to Buenos Aires, the people 'rushed to the streets and the riverside with bands of music and banners' to receive him; 'the…streets were thronged with enthusiastic crowds…[and]…he was taken to his dwelling in a carriage drawn by the people'.

In the civil wars that followed in the new state of Uruguay, the Argentine dictator Juan Manuel de Rosas supported the Blancos (Whites) against the Colorados (Reds). It was not long before Brown was again called into action – Rosas thought '*viejo Bruno*' (old Brown) was the man for the job. In a number of battles near Montevideo, he defeated an officer, John Coe, who had previously fought alongside him in the Argentine navy. In late 1842, he overcame a Uruguayan fleet on the Paraná river, led by the Italian Giuseppe Garibaldi (after a failed insurrection in Italy, Garibaldi had been condemned to death. He aligned himself with the Colorados after his move to South America).

Writing in *The Story of the Irish in Argentina*, Thomas Murray says that 'the story of Brown's naval career reads more like a romance of an enchanted knight…than of that of a man in real life.…He seemed to be able to win great victories under any and all circumstances and conditions'.

Stories about Brown are legion. Once, the dictator Rosas carried out an inspection of Brown's fleet. Afterwards, at a dinner arranged on his flagship, Brown took his customary seat at the head of the table. One of Rosas' men sought to redirect him to a position of less prominence, 'tactfully reminding him that the head of the feast was the place for the great Supremo...[He]...got the cool...reply, in... monosyllabic Spanish, that whatever Don Juan Manuel might be on land that on his ships, he, Brown was head man and would be in the head place'.

But even Brown's seemingly charmed life was not free from tragedy. His daughter Eliza was engaged to a Scotsman, Francis Drummond, who served in the Buenos Aires navy. In battle against the Brazilians in 1827, Drummond had his ear shot off. Then, with his ship incapacitated, he was shot again, in the hip, as he transferred to another vessel. He died shortly afterwards. Eliza was just sixteen and heartbroken. It is said that when she heard the news 'she dressed in her bridal gown, walked into the River Plate and drowned'.

In Recoleta Cemetery, Brown's memorial is a tall, green, mostly metal structure. A square base reaches above head-height; a column rises from there. Behind glass in the base, a casket holds the admiral's remains. The small, yellow, metal container is made from the cannon of one of his ships. The window is inscribed:

nacio el día 22 de Junio de 1777 en	born on 22 June 1777 in
Foxford condado de Mayo en Irlanda	Foxford, County Mayo, Ireland
Inglés de origen	English by origin
Argentino por sus servicios	Argentine for his services

After the tour of the cemetery, I ask Patricia if she knows the whereabouts of the Bradley (the Andes hot-air balloonist) and Murphy tombs (Murphy was a prominent *estanciero*, about whom I had been reading). I try to explain that Bradley was an aviator and spread out my arms and roll my upper body gently, like a child playing airplanes. I figured that this might help with my explanation; Patricia may have thought that I was mildly deranged. It was a long shot and she can't enlighten me. I make my own rambling search but have no success. Hungry now after almost three hours roaming a cemetery, I make to leave. Patricia is lingering at the gates; she has information for me. She thinks she knows where Bradley is. This is great news. She leads me to one side of the cemetery. 'Here!', she says, and waves her arm in a broad sweep that narrows the number of tombs down to the low thousands. I thank her and resume my search. I give it a further twenty minutes, but by now I'm starving, and with no sign of Bradley, I call it a day. Warily, I approach the cemetery exit. I keep an eye out for Patricia. She may be lurking with newly remembered, similarly pinpoint news of Murphy's whereabouts. But the coast is clear and I make my escape.

28

The Irish constituted the majority of English-speakers in nineteenth-century Argentina. The second most populous grouping was the English themselves; Scots and North Americans made up most of the remainder. According to Helen Kelly, in her book *Irish 'Ingleses'*, the main difference between the Irish and the English in the country was 'the rural nature of Irish settlement'. The English worked mainly as merchants and artisans and lived in the city of Buenos Aires. By contrast, prior to 1880, more than two-thirds of the Irish population ended up in *el campo* (the countryside, anglicised as 'the camp'). Early arrivals might have worked for a time with a city merchant, to save money or to repay a prepaid outward fare. Later, many left the city almost as soon as they arrived.

From the 1820s, when sheep-breeding became important, landowners needed people to tend their flocks. The Irish were the preferred choice (locals had little interest in herding sheep, and unlike the Irish, were obliged to undertake military service, often at very short notice). Under a system of *mediería* (halves), the shepherd would mind a flock of 1,500 to 2,000 sheep. Over the term of a contract (usually three to five years), with hard work and good fortune, animal numbers would increase considerably. When the contract ended, the shepherd would retain half the new stock, as well as a portion of the wool clip (later in the century, with more European migration and less access to land, contract terms swung more in favour of the flock owner; at this time, the shepherd's share might have been reduced to *tercería* or *cuartería*). The migrant now had a sizeable number of sheep of his own and he, in turn, might employ people to tend them. In this way, relatives and friends were brought out from Ireland, so that, Patrick McKenna (*Patterns of Migration*) says, 'a highly regionally specific chain migration began'.

Working life on the pampas was not easy (in Argentina, the pampas incorporate the province of Buenos Aires and adjoining parts of neighbouring provinces). In 1830, the only public roads were those that led west to Córdoba and Mendoza. Rivers had no bridges and heavy floods might alter sections of rivers that previously had been passable. Firstly, a shepherd would have to search for an area of land sufficient for his flock and with grass on which it could graze. At this time, much of the pampas had 'tall, coarse grass which the sheep could not eat and thistles which were taller than a man on horseback'. Thistles snarled in wool left a fleece unusable. Natural disasters were not uncommon. Flash storms could bring sudden flooding, ruining years of work in a single night. Extended periods of drought caused rivers to dry up and rich pasture to wither and die, leaving the shepherd to watch 'his flock...choke on the dust and blind themselves as they tried to eat the last of the surviving thistles'.

Some migrants did not survive. Alone on the pampas, an incapacitating injury might result in a protracted death. Loneliness sometimes took its mental toll. Distances between one dwelling and another could be vast; the shepherd could go weeks or months without human contact. His isolation also left him open to attack by the indigenous popuation. Thomas Murray mentions a shepherd, Cosgrove, living alone on the plains, who 'was stabbed in a score of places and thrown into his own well'.

The typical home for the Irish shepherd was a *rancho*, a one-roomed cabin. One writer described a visit: the door was a horsehide;

inside, on a dirt floor, the shepherd's table was an upturned chest, within which he stored his provisions. A shallow moat filled with water encircling the chest kept ants at bay and provisions intact. His seat was an ox's skull, its large horns a backrest. To one side, a horsehide stretched over a wooden frame formed a bed, with sheepskins for a mattress and a poncho for a blanket. A candle in the neck of a bottle provided light. Overhead, the roof was rushes and pampas grasses. A ladder on the outside wall of the *rancho* gave access to the roof. From here, the shepherd watched over his flock.

At some point, perhaps on an infrequent visit to Buenos Aires, the shepherd might acquire a wife, the result, often, of a match made by an Irish priest. This, or an increase in prosperity, might lead to home improvements: the addition of a wooden door (wood was not readily available on the open pampas), a framed window, or a second storey. The last might rest haphazardly on the original construction, the walls of the top floor sometimes leaning in a different direction from those rising from the ground (these particular Irish emigrants, it seems, hadn't quite mastered their construction skills).

In 1833, the dictator Rosas annexed land in the province of Buenos Aires that had belonged to the indigenous peoples. Soldiers cleared the way and the Irish followed in their wake. Land was rented from the government or from soldiers who had been granted *estancias* for their services.

Later, in the 1850s, after Rosas was overthrown, the country opened up more to international trade. Argentinian wool was in great demand. Also around this time, the government began to sell the land it seized, instead of renting it out as it previously had done. And many Irish, flush with cash after years of herding, made large purchases. While a sizeable number of Irish became landowners (one estimate is a figure of one in ten), most Irish laboured for their fellow countrymen. Edmundo Murray says that, on the Irish *estancias*, 'sheep farmers, shepherds, ranch hands, cooks, carpenters and other labourers lived and worked together, some of them with their families. They were primarily from a single Irish county or region, they spoke in English with their characteristic brogue, and they maintained frequent correspondence with their families and friends in Ireland'.

29

The Salado river (the Salado del Sur) cuts through the northern part of the province of Buenos Aires. Rising in the northwest, near the border with Santa Fe, it flows towards the Atlantic and reaches the ocean 170 kilometres southeast of the capital. For much of the nineteenth century, the Salado was the frontier. South of the river was hostile territory.

It was mostly north of the Salado that the Irish settled in the 1800s. With rent for land close to Buenos Aires too expensive to allow sheep-rearing in those areas to be profitable, the Irish moved out to a chain of *partidos* that encircles what is now Greater Buenos Aires. They started herding sheep in Chascomús, about 120 kilometres south of the city. As new districts opened up, they moved west and north. By 1840, Irish sheep farmers were in Monte, west of the capital. Next door in Lobos, in the early 1850s, there were far more Irish there than any other foreign nationality. By 1863, to the north, in Capilla del Señor, Irishmen owned more than 12,500 hectares of land. And in the following decade, according to Thomas Murray, Luján, one of the oldest settlements in the province, belonged 'almost exclusively to Irish sheep farmers'.

Where the Irish settled, they built their churches and their schools. In Chascomús, in 1864, work began on the first Irish chapel in the country. A Father Connolly had taken 100 children for First Communion the year before. And St Patrick's Day was still celebrated there, at Mahon's Chapel, up to the end of the century. Also in 1864, in Las Heras, the governor of the province instructed that the new church being built there be named St Patrick's, in honour of the area's industrious residents. Michael Allen built Kilallen on his land in Chacabuco in the late 1860s (*Cill*, anglicised as Kil: church, in Irish). In the same *partido*, Thomas Duggan built Duggan's Chapel on his *estancia*, near San Patricio railway station. Later, in the 1890s, in the cathedral at Luján, a Mrs Morgan donated five altars dedicated to saints Patrick, Brigid, Columcille, Malachy and Rose of Lima.

The official opening of Kilallen in Chacabuco was accompanied by a sports day, followed by dances in nearby houses. Unsurprisingly, the Irish were not averse to some play to complement their hard work. At Capilla, the race meeting in 1867 was the first of what became, in Murray's words, 'the most important and successful Irish race meeting in the country'. John Shanaghan's Fenian Boy was runner-up to Matthew Dillon's Chieftain in the main race that year. Shamrock trailed in third; Clear-the-Way and Volunteer were also-rans. In the same year, over 2,000 people gathered for the races held midway between the towns of Carmen de Areco and Salto. Carmen had been founded in colonial times as a fort in a bend of the Areco river, and used to be known as *Fortín* (*Fortín de Areco* – small garrison of the Areco). The Irish called it 'the Fourteen'. Some years after the 1867 meeting, the races were abandoned when quarrels developed after drink was taken. At a time when men in the camp went about armed, drink and guns were not a good mix. This brought an end to racing in 'the Fourteen'.

In Mercedes, the races were among 'some of the best and most largely attended in the country'. On one occasion, the crowd failed to disperse after the two-day meet and the carousing continued for a week. Locals were less than happy with the disorderly goings-on. The ultra-patriotic Murray is keen to tell us that 'the gathering was, of course, of all nationalities'.

In 1867, the races in Navarro (the equal of 'the best ever held in Mullingar') were accompanied by music and dancing and although the festivities at this two-day meeting also lasted a week, it seems that the revellers were well behaved.

These were wild and lawless times on the pampas. It was risky to venture outside government-controlled areas. In 1865, James Gaynor purchased cheap land in Nueve de Julio, south of the Salado. He employed two Irishmen to look after his sheep and seven Basques to build a mansion. A band of locals attacked the Basques, killed five of them and left with everything they could carry. The sheep were ignored, and the Irishmen escaped unharmed.

Often, the government-controlled northern *partidos* were not a great deal safer and, in the early days of settlement, 'murders of Irishmen…were frequent and terrible'. In Lobos, two Scally brothers were at home one evening, playing cards with their brother-in-law. One of the Scallys had had words with a local the day before. The latter arrived at the house and stabbed one of the brothers. The other was killed trying to defend him. Not far from Salto, a Martin Lyman was stabbed fifteen times and shot twice when he was attacked and killed by two gauchos. In Saladillo in 1875, Michael McCullough and John Cormack 'had their throats cut by bands of roving assassins'.

On occasion, it wasn't possible to depend even on official protection. Police were often ineffectual and sometimes colluded with thieves. In 1880, during an unsettled period, Patrick Cantlon from Kerry moved his wife and children from the camp to the safety of the town of Chivilcoy. Cantlon himself stayed on in the countryside to look after his flocks. On his way back to town some days later, a soldier from a nearby encampment ordered that he hand over his horses. The Kerryman refused, the soldier wielded his sword, Cantlon defended himself with his whip. The soldier reported back to his superiors and a road block was set up with orders to bring Cantlon in, dead or alive. The Irishman avoided the road block and found shelter at the house of a local Basque. Soldiers caught up with him there, shot him twice and beat him, before bringing him to their encampment. There, the commander wasn't entirely happy that the Irishman was still alive, and sent him to Chivilcoy as a prisoner. In town, where he was known, he was immediately released and with medical attention, he recovered (this particular incident was brought up by Irish representatives in the British parliament).

30

I've decided to visit San Antonio de Areco, over 100 kilometres northwest of Buenos Aires. The town is the capital of a *partido* of the same name, one of many that in the 1800s was home to the Irish. Evidence of their presence survives in local place names.

To the east of San Antonio de Areco is Diego Gaynor. James Gaynor from Westmeath arrived in Argentina with nothing and died owning over 80,000 hectares of land, more or less the size of County Louth. He is the same Gaynor whose Basque employees were murdered on his lands in Nueve de Julio.

West of town are the railway stations of Kenny, Doyle and Maguire. The last of these is named for Eduardo Pedro Maguire who, in 1907, donated the land on which the station is built. In the 1920s, Maguire was one of the 30 largest landholders in Argentina.

Also to the west, twenty kilometres from San Antonio de Areco, is the town of Duggan. In 1888, the three Duggan brothers, Michael, John and Thomas of Ballymahon, County Longford, owned approximately 300,000 hectares of land. An ardent Irish nationalist, Thomas Duggan once invited Roger Casement to his ranch here. Duggan's nationalism was such that he preferred not to do business with English-owned banks and cold-storage plants. In 1906, Duggan's son Alfredo was appointed honorary attaché at the Argentine embassy in London. Alfredo's son, Leo Alfred, grandson of the uber-nationalist Thomas Duggan, was educated at Eton and Balliol College, Oxford (where he ferried himself about in a Rolls-Royce). He later worked for London's Natural History Museum and, in World War II, fought with the London Irish Rifles. Leo Duggan wrote a great many historical novels, as well as works of non-fiction. His brother, Hubert, a Conservative MP for Acton, had also attended Oxford, where he was friends with Evelyn Waugh (he would later be godfather to Waugh's daughter, Margaret). Hubert Duggan lapsed from the Catholic faith during his youth, but with Waugh's intervention received absolution on his deathbed, a scene later transplanted by Waugh to his novel *Brideshead Revisited*.

I plan to return to Lulu after my time in the camp, and I leave some luggage there, behind the counter at reception. Nose-Ring Girl orders a taxi to take me to Retiro, Buenos Aires' enormous bus terminal, for my journey north. The taxi driver looks like Mr Burns, Homer Simpson's boss. And his driving is, to put it mildly, erratic. Not content with occupying a single lane, Burns straddles two. I reach for my seat belt, but there's no receiving piece into which to snap it. He crosses five lanes from right to left, darting between cars; in the search for advantage, no gap is too narrow. Almost immediately, he nips across lanes again, in the opposite direction. Clearly, indicators are for wusses; Burns certainly has no use for them (he may have looked in the side-mirror once). Near Retiro, he cuts directly in front of a bus. My backside lifts from the seat and my heels dig into the floor. Thankfully, the bus driver brakes and Burns nips clear. As the taxi pulls up at the drop-off point, I'm already half-way out the door.

Burns has frazzled my nerves; I decamp to the station restaurant and recover over coffee. At a nearby table, two women travellers sit, and write, silently. Both have new, almost-identical rucksacks; one has a smaller, matching daypack. They both write in purpose-bought travel diaries. Later, one reads a thick, pristine South American guidebook. She carefully underlines passages using markers and a ruler from a pencil case, and tags pages with small, colourful Post-its. Organised travellers. Germans, obviously.

From the bus station at San Antonio de Areco, on the blowy outskirts of town, a smiley cab driver drops me at a hotel and hands me his card: Marcelo of *Servicio de Remís Avenida* (Avenue Cabs) on Avenida Vieytes. At hotel reception, my haggling skills fail me and with no rate reduction forthcoming, I retreat to Tourist Information on nearby Patio (court) Guido O'Donnell. There, a lady hands me a local map and directs me to less pricey accommodation.

My stroll to the hotel leads through the centre of town. San Antonio de Areco seems quite a plain place, low-rise, with not much above a single storey. The only thing that stands out is local transport. Motorbikes and scooters are quite popular, while helmets seem surplus to requirements. Locks remain unused on push bikes piled in twos and threes against telephone poles. There are pick-up trucks and muddy cars, and beat-up cars with roaring engines and no exhausts. On the beat-up cars, vast islands of rust share space with bonnets and doors reclaimed from other vehicles.

I drop my bags and make my way to San Patricio's church, a neat building of grey, stone blocks perched at the edge of the Information Lady's truncated map of the town. Above the doorway, St Patrick raises a small Celtic cross in one hand; in the other is a bible and a crozier. A snake gasps, trapped beneath his feet. The small interior of the church is simple and tidy. Inside the entrance, two pillars support an organ loft. Holy water fonts sit on the wall, one on either side of the door. Above each, a Celtic cross and strings of shamrock are engraved on marble plaques. In the body of the church, a narrow bank of pews sits on either side of the short aisle. Fans stand outside the pews; heaters and long, thin speakers hang on the walls. Tall, narrow, stained-glass windows face inwards, oddly, at an angle. At the rear, on the right wall, the alumni of Clonmacnoise school ask you to remember in your prayers their '*directores ... hermanos, educadores y companeros*' (directors…brothers, teachers and friends).

On the wall opposite, a plaque says that this chapel was built by Margarita Mooney de Morgan. This is the same Mrs Morgan who, in the 1890s, donated the five altars in the cathedral at Luján. She was also a benefactor of the Clonmacnoise school for boys. Next door to St Patrick's, the school closed in 1940. And down the road is the María Clara Morgan Hospital, named in memory of Mrs Morgan's daughter, who died in Chicago in 1893. While in the US, María Clara Morgan had been cared for by the Sisters of the Little Company of Mary. In 1900, Mrs Morgan founded the hospital with the intention that it be run by the Sisters, but it wasn't until 1913 that four nuns arrived from the US to belatedly take up its management. In Ireland, the Sacred Heart Church in Roscommon has an altar donated by Mrs Morgan. She visited the area in the 1890s and some £2,000 in donations towards the building of the church came from Argentina.

At the head of the church, a Celtic cross sits on the front of a simple wooden lectern. Behind the altar, long strips of Argentine blue and white are stretched from ceiling to floor, to left and right. Behind them, Vatican yellow and white are draped in a similar manner, with, to the rear, Irish green, white and orange.

As I leave the church, I notice a marble slab on the floor, near the plaque to Mrs Morgan. It is in memory of the Right Reverend Monsignor Richard J Gearty, 'born on January 1st 1863 in Roscommon Ireland [and] ordained in Maynooth June 24th 1888'. Their 'soggarth aroon' (*sagart arún*, in Irish – dear priest) was Irish chaplain of San Antonio de Areco, Giles and Baradero for 35 years (1902–37). Father

Gearty was one successor of the first resident Irish chaplain in town, Father Thomas Curran, who had arrived in the country in 1862. Another was Pallottine priest Father Alfredo Kelly, murdered along with colleagues in Buenos Aires in 1976 during the *Guerra Sucia*. In 2001, the Pallottines asked the country's hierarchy that Kelly and those who died with him be considered martyrs. Now, the Argentine Church is working to have them declared saints (proof of two miracles is required for sainthood; martyrdom counts as one). In 2005, this course of action had been approved by Kelly's erstwhile confessor and friend, Archbishop Bergoglio of Buenos Aires. A Vatican tribunal will eventually make a ruling on the application for sainthood, but the final decision lies with the same man, Jorge Bergoglio, Pope Francis.

*

Later that evening, and after their weekend defeat, River Plate play the first leg of their relegation play-off, against Córdoba. It is not going well; they're losing 2–0 and play has been suspended. In the stands, River fans tear at chain-link fencing. Some have made it on to the field and are berating and pushing their players. The River manager strides on to the pitch and gathers his team together; a TV cameraman follows him to the huddle. River do better when play resumes, but not well enough and there's no further score. On TV the next morning, a banner headline reminds River fans of the unthinkable: '*River a un paso de la B*' (one step from the B division). There's a more cheery message for their opponents: '*Córdoba, Una Fiesta*'.

31

Next morning, on a ramble through a chilly San Antonio, I end up at Plaza Ruiz de Arellano, the town's main square. In the centre of the plaza, steps rise to a small, circular, paved area enclosed by a low wall. Opposite the steps, against the wall, is a statue of local patriot Juan Hipólito Vieytes, born in the town in 1762 (he fought during *La Reconquista*). On the plinth holding his statue, a plaque commemorates the 1995 visit to San Antonio de Areco of Ireland's President Mary Robinson, her stop-off here an acknowledgement of one of the more obscure outposts of the Irish diaspora.

Calle Arellano runs along the eastern side of the plaza. At No. 133, a plaque commemorates where the patriot Vieytes spent his early years. By the door of No. 137, four small, ceramic tiles form a square at above head-height. These declare the house to be a *'Lugar Significativo'* (a significant location), although it's unclear why. Further along, off the southeastern corner of the square, La Esquina de Merti restaurant is an *'Antigua Pulpería Parrilla'* (Old Tavern, Steak Restaurant), its *antigua* credentials emphasised by an old-fashioned messenger bike on a stand at the edge of the footpath. The corner opposite La Esquina is a magnet for stray dogs. The sun's rays reach them here and the dogs lounge about and launch themselves at passing cars and at each other. Their squeals and howls bring other strays running from canine outposts around the plaza. As I linger at the corner, Marcelo, the smiley cab driver, passes by, beeps and waves.

The parish church of San Antonio de Padua, dated 23.10.1730, is off the southern side of the square. Marble plaques, one on either side of an inner vestibule, name the priests who have served since that date. In 2006, the Rev. Santiago Whelan took over from Rev. Tomás O'Donnell. The church is bigger than St Patrick's and, inside, it is far more ornate. Near the doors, on the right wall, four large marble plaques list the names of long-dead parishioners. Most are Spanish, but the first plaque begins with Boyle, Davern, Kelly, O'Neill, Dunleavey, Leahy, Walsh, Carroll, Whelan, Leaden.

In the afternoon, I return to San Patricio's with my camera. On the way, oranges lie in a gutter. I suppose at first that they have fallen from a passing lorry, but overhead, orange trees at the edge of the footpath have shed their sweet load, as naturally here as trees in Ireland drop chestnuts.

Trees also line the footpath outside St Patrick's, and I cross the road in search of a better vantage point from which to take a photo. But it's difficult to get a clear shot. A passer-by who stops to explain this hooks a finger at the neck of his jumper to reveal a clerical collar. The padre continues on his way, but returns minutes later carrying a sickly, almost hairless dog. We fall into a stilted Spanish conversation. When I ask if, today, there is any Irish presence in San Antonio, the padre leads me and the dog into the parochial house beside the church. In an office there, an elderly lady sits behind a large desk. The desk has a protective glass top. On top of the glass is a shamrock keyring, beneath it a poster with a Celtic design and a postcard from Kilkenny. The lady stands to greet me. Isabel is white-haired, wears glasses, and has a face that can only belong to an Irish countrywoman.

But, of course, Isabel is Argentinian. 'My grandparents were from Ireland', she tells me, 'Westmeath/Cavan area, but they went back to Ireland a long time ago. My parents were born here, in Argentina; my father worked nearby, on an *estancia*.'

I compliment her on her English.

'English was the working language on the *estancia*', she says. 'We spoke English at home. And at boarding school, we spoke Spanish in the morning and English in the afternoon.'

Isabel is known to her friends as 'Lizzie' (it is common that, among themselves, the Irish give each other English familiar names). She worked in Buenos Aires after she left school, with Caterpillar, the British company, and Johnson's, a transport business.

'There was no problem finding a good job if you had English.'

She continued to live locally, though, while working in the city. There was a train service in those days and she commuted every day.

I wondered if people here retained any links with Ireland.

'No, there are no more priests coming out', she says. 'The priest here is an Argentine, but there's an Irish priest in the other parish.' She's talking about Santiago Whelan, at the parish church on the main plaza.

There were many Irish landowners around here, she goes on, 'but they have all died out now. Some Irish came with the railroads, saved and bought land and added to their land over time. The priests arranged marriages with other Irish families. We were kept separate from the locals. They were bad.'

The building we are in, she explains, had housed the Clonmacnoise school for boys. There had been an Irish girls' school nearby and the Morgan hospital down the block is for the elderly.

Had Isabel ever visited Ireland?

'I was in Ireland about five years ago', she says, 'on a Speedy Gonzales tour, twelve days. I wondered about all the flowers. It must be hard to keep them, but then, with all the rain…The rain is different in Ireland. It's softer. Here, it's stronger, you get wet very quickly. I hope to visit Ireland again.'

We chat for a while longer before I leave Isabel to get on with her work. I was delighted to have met her, and not a little taken aback that, despite a lifetime in Argentina, her near-perfect English was delivered in an Irish country accent.

*

Outside the parochial house, I pause to take my bearings. My map tells me that the cemetery is at this end of town, and I aim east, in its direction, along Avenida Vieytes. Soon I reach Plazoleta Eva Perón. Both Calle O'Higgins and Pasaje Irlandeses are here, their prominence on my map prompting me to imagine that the area might provide some reminder of an Irish past. But there's no evidence of this. Calle O'Higgins is a row of small bungalows on the southern side of the Plazoleta, parallel to Vieytes. Small, bare trees stand on the verge by the road. The footpath is uneven slabs; grass and weeds sprout through the joins where the cement has split. A small cairn in one front garden shelters a miniature Madonna.

On the western side of the Plazoleta, perpendicular to O'Higgins, Pasaje Irlandeses has bungalows with corrugated-iron roofs and unplastered block walls. A Renault 4, '*Se Vende*' (For Sale) on the side of the road, has an all-over coat of white house-paint that tries to camouflage vast patches of rust.

I continue on, past the edge of town, but with no sign of the cemetery I return towards St Patrick's. En route, a Juan A Bué has a corner shop. No mere butcher, Señor Bué is a decidedly more impressive '*Artesano en Carnes*'. Further along, in a yard off Vieytes, and opposite Hospital María Clara Morgan, smiley Marcelo buffs the paintwork of his cab. He can bring me to the cemetery, he says, and will call back in an hour.

The town's graveyard has a number of Recoleta-size mausoleums towards the rear of its large site, but mostly, the plots are discreet. Many headstones are weather-stained, grey with age and difficult to read. But there are Clancys and a de Clancy, a Loughlin de Clancy and a Sills de Clancy and Mary Imelda Cunningham de Clancy, who was known as 'Molly'. Edward Morgan from Glanworth in Cork died in 1860 and is remembered by his wife Catherine O'Farrell from Kinsale, who survived him by 22 years. Their son, another Edward, is nearby, with his wife, Margarita Mooney de Morgan, the benefactor of churches and schools, hospitals and altars. In a plot of three headstones, theirs is the middle one. To one side is their daughter 'Mary Clare Morgan', to whom her mother dedicated the hospital in town. The stone on the other side tells the sad story of their children over twenty years. George died not long after his tenth birthday. Neither Margaret nor Sonny lived to see their first. Catherine and Micheal (sic) Anthony were not yet three, John Joseph was only four.

The Little Company of Mary, who, in Chicago, had looked after María Clara Morgan in her illness, remembers Mother Columba Kealy and Sisters Fintan Kealy, Raphael MacCarthy and others. There are Farrells and Dunnes, Fitzsimons and Egans, Geartys and McDermotts, the infant Devereux children and the Mooneys from Milltown in Westmeath.

All about me is evidence of more than 150 years of an Irish presence in San Antonio de Areco. Celtic crosses are scattered throughout the yard. But there are too many plots to see. And it is time to leave. Marcelo is waiting at the gate.

32

Saturday morning is grey, overcast and very cold. I slip on my green, gnome-ish beanie and pull up the zip of my jacket so that it reaches almost to my lower lip. With the jacket's raised hood drooping over my forehead, I look like a polar explorer, my face only partially exposed to the raw wind. It is just after nine and the town is quiet as I cut along the northern end of Plaza Ruiz de Arellano at a brisk pace, on my way to catch the bus to Buenos Aires. The quiet is broken by a pack of dogs howling down the side of the square in my direction. I look around for a stick with which to fend them off, and am still searching when another morning stroller appears on the square. The galloping hounds divert their attentions to the misfortunate new arrival.

The bus station is near the highway, on the western side of town. En route, as I approach a junction, a rackety car turns from the right. What I had thought was a squeaky suspension is, in fact, a sickly, honking, car horn. In a different cab this morning, the ubiquitous and ever-smiley Marcelo beams and waves. The hardest-working cabbie in San Antonio, the man is everywhere.

The terminal is off the road, a low-rise building facing on to a broad, open area. As I wait outside its entrance, a glacial wind slices through my multiple layers of clothing. I withdraw indoors to the shelter of a small waiting area. Here, a display case shows the work of local artisans. *Mate* gourds come short and round like a ball, and tall and thin with a lip. A *mate termo* 'holder', covered in cowhide, is like a tall, furry binoculars case.

Leaving San Antonio, in a premises just off the Ruta, old cars are stacked one on top of the other in a hillock of rust. This may be the source of, or the graveyard for, all those beat-up cars in town.

Final reminders of the area's lingering Irish links come from a business with a large green shamrock painted on the roof of a shed inside its gate, and parked trucks belonging to *Transportes Egan* and *Casey Transportadora*. Soon, San Antonio is behind me. On the open plains, only clumps of evergreens and skeletal, leafless trees break the monotony of the view for as far as the eye can see.

*

In the city, almost two hours later, the wind is no less bitter. I escape it, and nip underground on to the Subte. On a train, a guy sells Parker pens for 10 pesos. He hands them out as he passes through the carriage, then revisits each passenger, and reclaims the pen or completes a sale. In the time it takes for a single stop, he has two buyers.

Before returning to Palermo and Lulu, I have decided to spend a few days in a different part of Buenos Aires. I take a spotless, comfortable double room in a hostel in the centre of town, off Avenida Nueve de Julio (July 9, 1816, the day on which Argentina declared its independence). A block in width, Nueve de Julio is one of the broadest avenues in the world. Up to nine lanes run in each direction, and just now they're all blocked with traffic. The noise is dreadful. Whistle-blowing policemen prevent cars from entering junctions as the way ahead becomes clogged; drivers slam their horns, unhappy with the slow progress.

Lunch comes from Gran Pizzeria La Rey, a lively restaurant just off the *avenida*. In my limited experience, pizzas in South America are somewhat hit-and-miss. It's the cheese, or more specifically, the right amount of it. Today, my Hawaiian is running with the stuff. I remove the first slice from the pan, and cheese from next-door slices seeps, lava-like, into the vacated space. This goo, now lodged in my stomach for the day, fortifies me for an afternoon trip to the suburbs.

33

The first English-language newspaper published daily in South America was *The Standard*, established in Buenos Aires in 1861 by Dublin-born brothers Edward and Michael Mulhall. Its readership was mainly urban, its tone was pro-British and, according to the first edition, it intended to be representative of 'the bond of fellowship between the various members of…[the]…Anglo-Celtic race'. The English-speaking community was depicted as one entity. For the Irish, according to Helen Kelly (*Irish 'Ingleses'*), 'maintenance of a separate Irish identity had, perhaps understandably, been subordinate to the more immediate and attractive proposal of integrating into an existing system of social and cultural superiority at an unusually advantageous level'. *The Standard*'s imperial bent did mean that there was no distinct Irish voice; all issues were reported from a pro-British standpoint.

The expansion of the Argentine economy in the second half of the nineteenth century saw large-scale European immigration, particularly from Italy, but also from Spain, Germany and France. However, like the Irish before them, these groups did little to integrate into local society. This did not impress their hosts. Argentine newspapers stoked native dissatisfaction, creating the image of a transient immigrant population earning what riches they could in Argentina before returning home (although there was an element of truth in this, most immigrants did stay in the country and invested their wealth there).

But newcomers did fail 'to cast off their Old World allegiance for a New World identity'. The census of 1914 showed that only 2.25%

of the foreign-born had been naturalised. Immigrant groups wanted to remain separate and were intent on retaining their language and culture. They established their own newspapers and formed their own cultural associations, hospitals and social clubs. This 'cultural detachment…complemented immigrant perceptions of Old World superiority', which, in turn, resulted in the rise of an Argentine national movement. Not unreasonably, their hosts wanted immigrant groups to give their allegiance to their new home.

European culture, once revered, was being rejected. Faced with this, the Irish began to emerge from a cover-all 'Inglés' identity that no longer served their interests. Also, political events in Ireland (Home Rule, Parnell, land reform…) began to reopen divides that the 'Inglés' label had masked. Key to the emergence of this separate Irishness was *The Southern Cross* newspaper.

The Southern Cross was founded in 1875 to cater to the Irish Catholic community. At its foundation, it too, like *The Standard*, stressed the common interests of all Argentine English-speakers. However, a new owner in 1896 signalled a change in editorial tone. William Bulfin, born in 1864 at Birr, County Offaly, was twenty when he arrived in Argentina. An ardent nationalist, he was a future member of Sinn Féin, and a friend of Arthur Griffith and Douglas Hyde. When Bulfin returned to live in Ireland, he sent his son Eamon to be educated at St Enda's, Pádraig Pearse's school in Dublin. Eamon Bulfin was with Pearse during the Easter Rising in 1916 and raised an Irish flag on the roof of the GPO (not the tricolour, but a green flag, on which were the words 'Irish Republic'). After the insurrection's failure, his Argentine citizenship saved him from a death sentence. He was deported and later, in Argentina, was appointed diplomatic envoy to Buenos Aires by Éamon de Valera. In 1922, he returned to live in

Ireland. (Eamon Bulfin's sister, Catalina, was married to Nobel Peace Prize winner Seán MacBride, co-founder of Amnesty International.)

William Bulfin tried to uncouple the Irish and English communities. Also, among the Irish themselves, he pointed up uncomfortable differences between those with nationalist and those with British sympathies. As the Argentine state was asserting itself, he pushed 'an Irish national position' but at the same time declared an allegiance to Argentina. This was a 'watershed in the evolution of the Irish community'. Irishness was separated from Englishness and 'a hybrid Irish-Argentine identity' was formed.

Irish nationalist feeling in Argentina was not strong. Bulfin's personal political commitment far exceeded that of his newspaper's audience. He founded a branch of the Gaelic League in 1899 but it struggled to get members. He had more success, however, with his support of hurling. Although played in the country from 1887/88, it was not until 1900 that attempts were made to organise the sport. And Bulfin's *Southern Cross* played a key role in its promotion. In the early 1900s, the newspaper published many articles explaining the rules and supporting the game. New clubs flourished, among them La Plata Gaels, Bearna Baoghail, Saint Patrick's Mercedes, Fahy Boys, Irish Argentines, New Lads. Today, one club remains.

Hurling Club (usually called Hurling) is a short distance from the centre of Buenos Aires, in the Hurlingham district of the city. After polishing off my cheese-laden pizza, I take a train to Estación William Morris, which Google Maps informs me is nearby. There, outside the station, vendors sell food at stalls by the side of the road. Hard-faced, staring guys lounge about, doing not very much. Grubby, low-rise buildings run along untidy streets perpendicular to the rail-line. I had expected to find Calle Río Colorado here, and for it to lead me towards Hurling. A grumpy, shifty-looking, corner shopkeeper has never heard of it, or he doesn't understand me. Either way, he hooshes me out the door towards a cab office across the street.

It is clear that I've chosen the wrong stop for Hurling. In the cab office, staff launch into a lengthy discussion before they finally agree on its location. A cab driver nods in my direction and heads for the door. The driver is hugely overweight. The material of his extra-large tracksuit bottoms is at full stretch to cover his monumental arse. I follow him as he waddles to his car. I struggle to open the door; the driver says something I don't understand, but I continue to have difficulty. He repeats himself, more loudly this time, and then he shouts. None of which helps. I notice a push-button on the handle, open the door and climb in.

The drive to Hurling is through side streets. Anyone unaware of the correct side of the road on which to drive in South America might not have been any wiser after this trip. We weave from right to left, avoiding huge pot-holes. I smile to myself as we arrive at speed bumps. Picking up speed while crater-dodging is near-impossible.

From the gates at Hurling's entrance, tall, thin trees line a driveway that curves right and leads to a sizeable clubhouse. Above the door, a green sign offers a '*Céad Míle Fáilte*', with, underneath, the Spanish translation, '*cien mil bienvenidas*'.

I follow a path around the far side of the building. Through lounge windows, men and women play cards at separate tables; a teenager spread out on a sofa wears an IRFU sweatshirt. Behind the clubhouse, four red-clay tennis courts are set in a square. To the left of the courts is a playground. On the other side are two swimming pools, one small, one large, both equally uninviting on a freezing afternoon.

I veer right and follow the path past the pools. Further along, a hockey pitch with an artificial surface runs lengthways on the left. Opposite is Cancha No. 1, the main rugby field. The scoreboard declares it's 'Hurling Club, since 1922', like a clothing brand.

*

In Buenos Aires, the first 'official' game of hurling took place in July 1900, between teams from the districts of Palermo and Almagro (south of Palermo). A shortage of hurleys made it a nine-a-side game. The following month, the Buenos Aires Hurling Club was founded as a branch of the Gaelic Athletic Association.

In the camp, hurling was played by *estancia* workers. In the city, it was the Irish middle classes who took part. They worked for banks, businesses, insurance companies and railroads. The Catholic Church was keen to promote the sport in the city. In a business environment dominated by Protestants, they saw it as a way of preserving identity and religious affiliation. Many priests and student priests, both Irish-born and of Irish extraction, were enthusiastic players.

At this time, hurling was without a dedicated home. In the city, facilities were rented in Boedo and Floresta and, in 1924, in the western district of Villa Devoto (at Floresta, the clubhouse was painted green, white and orange). In 1922, the Argentine Federation of Hurling was formed. Almost twenty years later, in 1941, members of the Federation formed Hurling Club and, later in the decade, finally purchased their own grounds, seven and a half hectares, here at Hurlingham.

While the present site was being developed, Hurling again used the grounds of other sporting bodies, among them the Porteño

Athletic Club. Originally named Club Atlético Capital, this was a football team formed in 1895 by a group of students of Irish descent. At the time, with little money to fund their activities, the students decided to try and improve their financial situation with a trip to the races. They pooled what funds they had and placed it all on an outsider, Porteño. The horse won, the bet paid out handsomely and the winnings covered the cost of the team's kit. As a tribute to its unknowing equine benefactor, the club became Club Atlético Porteño.

With a small number of teams in regular competition, and resultant, intense rivalries, hurling games in Argentina were often violent. The concern of Church and community leaders was such that they felt the sport should be abandoned. This, along with the absence of hurleys during World War II (it was impossible to import them), brought about the game's decline. From then on, hurling would be played annually, as an exhibition sport.

The club turned to rugby and hockey, and with some success. Five members of the men's hockey team were in the national squad that travelled to the London Olympics in 1948 (Tomás Quinn, Luis Scally, Tomás Scally, Tomás Wade and Guillermo Dolan). And excluding 1952, they were First Division champions from 1949 to 1956.

In the early days of hurling in Argentina, and with the rise of nationalism both there and in Ireland, the sport provided a way for the Irish to differentiate themselves from other groups, ie: the English, the Anglophile Irish and the rich Irish-Argentine landed families (they never played the game). This differentiation, although initially welcome, also led to insularity, and it was only when the club took up rugby and hockey that it found its place within the broader community.

Today, Hurling maintains an Irish identity, which can be difficult as non-Irish outnumber Irish-Argentines among new members. But regular visits from Irish sports teams and the activities of the club itself help to keep the link alive.

*

There's a viewing area by the side of the hockey pitch at Hurling and I join a sprinkling of spectators there at a ladies game. A team in white shirts with a green trim play a side in green and blue quadrants. It is unclear which is the home side. Eventually, I notice a shamrock crest on a white shirt. It's a competitive game. Hurling's opponents have the upper hand and dominate, but don't score. At full-time, the girls troop past each other on half-way and plant kisses on opposition cheeks.

While this match was in progress, other players were warming up on a practice pitch, sprinting between small, bright, green and red cones. They're about to take part in the upcoming game. Before it begins, each side forms a huddle; there are shouts of encouragement and brief team chants. It is even colder now, in the late afternoon, and most of the girls wear sleeveless shirts. It's an enjoyable contest, just as competitive as the first. The visitors score from a short corner. Hurling fight back. A ball is swept out right from centre-field. It travels down the wing to the end-line, across to the centre, bodies in a tumble and the hard ball smacks the wood at the base of the goal.

At half-time, it's 1–1. Hurling's players sit in a goal net, backs to the wooden base; their coach barks instructions. I'm keen to see the end of this match, but it's getting dark now, and Estación William

Morris was scary enough in daylight. Leaving Hurling, I spot a train station not far from the club's entrance. I hadn't noticed it on the journey here (it is possible the view had been blocked by the cab driver's arse). I quiz a girl on the platform but can't make out where the line leads, and continue on to the next junction where there's yet another station. There, I hop on a train bound for Federico Lacroze, in the city, pleased to have avoided a further brush with William Morris.

34

One of the many stops on the return to town from Hurling is the station at Santos Lugares (Holy Places). In the nineteenth century, another Santos Lugares in the city (since renamed San Andrés) was the improbably named location of the military headquarters of the governor of the province. And in 1848, it was the scene of the execution of twenty-year-old Camila O'Gorman.

Camila O'Gorman was the granddaughter of Thomas O'Gorman, the Irish merchant whose wife, *La Périchona*, had had the very public affair with Santiago de Liniers, the hero of *La Reconquista*. When Thomas O'Gorman left Buenos Aires, his family had remained in the city with his wife.

At the time of Camila O'Gorman's death, the governor of the province was the *caudillo* Juan Manuel de Rosas. In South America, the breakdown of law and order that accompanied the wars of independence helped to create conditions which saw the rise of the *caudillo*. In a culture where clientelism was the norm and where politics was carried out through a series of alliances between factions and clans, the *caudillo* was a political and military boss whose aim in acquiring power was to gain access to public funds with which to dispense favours, and thus build up networks of influence. *Caudillismo*, says Edwin Williamson in *The Penguin History of Latin America*, 'embodied the political culture of patronage and clientship in its primitive state'. The phenomenon was nothing new. In medieval Spain, a military leader would build up a power base to a point where he could extract lands and titles from the king. Originally, in essence, Spanish America was subdued in the same way. In time, *caudillismo* declined as patronage came to be carried out through the royal bureaucracy. After independence, with the monarchy rejected, new administrations were unable to generate the loyalty that had been accorded the Crown. They did not have the authority sufficient to intervene and modulate disputes between rival factions. *Caudillos* once again rose to prominence. In Argentina, chief among them was Juan Manuel de Rosas.

From a very wealthy family, Rosas was an *estanciero* with lands south of the Salado river. In 1820, he became head of the provincial militia and, by the end of the decade, as leader of the Federalists, he was elected governor. In 1833, when his term of office was up, he conducted a brutal military campaign against the indigenous peoples of Buenos Aires province. In the meantime, his wife remained in the city and started a movement, La Mazorca, to see him restored to the governorship. When Rosas was re-elected in 1835, he was accorded full dictatorial powers and went on to rule for another seventeen years. La Mazorca became his secret police force and served his interests in bloodthirsty fashion. Death squads terrorised the city. Kidnappings and murders were commonplace. Liberal opponents fled into exile.

Rosas was a great admirer of Britain, with the result that the Inglés community mostly survived the horror. At this time, many Irish flew the Union Jack from their roofs; the governor had ordered that any home bearing the flag was to be left untouched. The Irish did not escape wholly unscathed, however. Dr James William Eborall was the Irish father-in-law of Edward Mulhall, owner of *The Standard* newspaper. Eborall had once attended to Rosas and remained on a standby list of doctors to be called on by the dictator. At some point, he fell out of favour; he was likely suspected of having had contact with opponents of the regime. One morning, when he reached his front door, Eborall looked out to find his servants strewn about the lawn, their throats cut. The doctor had received his warning not to fraternise with the enemy.

Camila O'Gorman was a friend of Rosas' daughter, Manuelita. She grew up in a well-to-do family and had a traditional, religious upbringing. The family attended the Socorro church in Buenos Aires, where the curate, Father Uladislao Gutiérrez, had been a friend of Camila's brother in seminary.

Gutiérrez and Camila became lovers. On December 11, 1847, the priest told his superiors that he was travelling to Quilmes, south of the city. Instead, he met with Camila, and they both travelled north, to Goya, in the province of Corrientes. Under assumed names, they established themselves as teachers and founded the town's first school.

Meanwhile, in Buenos Aires, Rosas issued orders for their arrest. 'Wanted' posters went up around the city. Camila's father declared the affair a scandal. In Montevideo, Rosas' exiled enemies relished the chance to attack the governor. The affair, they said, highlighted the decadence into which Buenos Aires had descended under his rule. A future president, Domingo Sarmiento, blamed the moral corruption of Argentine women on the tyranny of the dictator.

Meanwhile, the couple continued their work in Goya. Their school became a success, and at a formal function to honour their achievements they were recognised and betrayed by Father Michael Gannon, a nephew of the wife of Admiral William Brown. It is likely that the Irish community were embarrassed by the couple and that the priest disclosed their whereabouts in an attempt to curry favour with Rosas and declare the community's public condemnation of their conduct.

The pair were transported to Santos Lugares and imprisoned. Rosas' daughter, Manuelita, eased Camila's discomfort by arranging for a piano and books to be placed in her cell. Camila asked Manuelita to intervene with her father on her behalf. Under interrogation, however, Camila declared that she had committed no crime. She insisted that she had been determined to elope (Gutiérrez had been accused of kidnapping her). This lack of repentance enraged Rosas. Manuelita's entreaties came to nothing.

By this time, Camila was eight months pregnant. On August 18, 1848, her unborn child was baptised by the prison chaplain. Camila was given holy water to drink and ashes were sprinkled on her head. The two lovers were tied to chairs in the prison yard and shot.

Even those scandalised by the pair's elopement were shocked by the punishment. Thomas Murray called it 'the most inhuman and unpardonable of the many atrocities of that reign of terror'. Over generations, the couple's story has captured the imagination. In 1910, *Camila O'Gorman* was one of the first films made in Argentina, and the 1984 movie *Camila* received the country's second-ever Oscar nomination, for Best Foreign Language Film.

35

Sunday morning's *Buenos Aires Herald* (the city's English-language daily) has a piece about the second leg of River Plate's relegation play-off against Córdoba. It's being played this afternoon and River need to overturn a 2–0 first-leg deficit. The omens aren't good. They haven't scored more than a single goal in a game since March. Fans have hung posters outside *El Monumental*. The message is blunt: 'Win or we will kill you'. The most hotly contested games of River's year, those against Boca Juniors, are normally patrolled by 1,200 police officers. Today, 2,200 will be on duty. The *Herald*'s reporter had intended to go to the match, but he has changed his mind. His friends have warned him that, win or lose, *El Monumental* will burn.

In the afternoon, I make my way to a busy street market in San Telmo (the oldest barrio in Buenos Aires, it is named for San Pedro González Telmo, the patron saint of seafarers). En route, locals are glued to River's match on TVs in cafés and restaurants. San Telmo's main thoroughfare is Calle Defensa (named for *La Defensa* against the British invasion of 1807). Today, both sides of this long, cobbled street are lined with stalls. Here, gumpf of every description is on offer. There are *mate* gourds and *bombillas*, knives, hats, leather bags, antique cameras, belts, necklaces…Chess sets have a South American twist: opposing, carved pieces are Incas vs Espanoles (sic). The supply of tat is endless. It is Tat Heaven; it is Tatville, capital of the Republic of Tat.

Outside a small shop, a crowd spills from the footpath on to the street. The shop isn't, in fact, open for business; instead, River's match is being projected through the open front door on to its rear wall. I join the milling spectators. It's 1–1, and just now on screen players are jostling each other. When the dust settles, a River player places the ball on the penalty spot. It's a poor kick, easily saved. The penalty-taker puts his head in his hands. He is distraught. Perhaps he has seen the posters outside *El Monumental*.

I detach myself from the football scrum and wander on between endless stalls. Match commentaries blare from portable radios. Soon, a stall-holder holds up a metal plate and hammers it, like a gong; River's death knell. The match is over and there has been no further score. River have been relegated for the first time in their 110-year history. I think of Paula, our football guide; I picture her in La Boca, smiling broadly between deep pulls on a celebratory cigarette.

36

Later in the week, and after a brief return to Lulu, I decide to visit Uruguay. I book a passage on an early-morning ferry to Colonia del Sacramento, across the Río de la Plata estuary from Buenos Aires (it is sometimes difficult to think of the Plata as a river; at its widest point, the estuary stretches for more than 200 kilometres). The ferry is a modern catamaran; on board, the upper deck is cordoned off, the seating on the main deck more than enough to cater for today's small number of passengers. I take a pew in an empty row by the left-hand window. Directly ahead, as the boat eases away from the dock, a brightening ball of a sun colours the horizon orange. Closer at hand, and at a certain angle, its reflection on the surface of the water is blindingly bright. Overhead, speakers spew out dreadful Latin, Eurovision-style ballads. After safety instructions in Spanish and English, it's 'nul points' for the Latin ballads and they're replaced by modern pop.

On the southeast coast of South America, Uruguay is the second-smallest country on the continent (the smallest is Suriname). It is bounded to the north and east by Brazil, and to the southeast by the Atlantic Ocean; the Río de la Plata is to the south, while west is the Uruguay river and Argentina.

In 1516, the Spaniard Juan Díaz de Solís was the first European to explore the country. He came to an unfortunate end when he and some of his men were killed and eaten by the indigenous population. In 1526, Sebastian Cabot avoided that fate, but nonetheless showed little interest in the *Banda Oriental del Río Uruguay* (East Bank of the Uruguay River). There was none of the mineral wealth that the *conquistadores* sought and very few Amerindians who could be put to work on their behalf. At this time, the aboriginal population totalled only between 5,000 and 10,000. By the following century, their already-small numbers had been reduced further, the *nativos* struck down by European diseases for which they had no defence.

Uruguay has always been associated with the raising of livestock. The basis for this may have been laid as far back as 1603, when, it is said, cattle shipped from Asunción by the governor of Paraguay were set loose on the shores of the Banda Oriental. The animals roamed wild on the pampas of the interior; in time, they numbered in their millions.

In 1680, Portuguese soldiers founded Colónia do Sacramento, and for years the town was an important smuggling centre, mainly for British goods, as traders worked around the monopoly of trade that Spain operated with its colonies (for simplicity, further references to the town will use the Spanish 'Colonia'). To counteract this, in 1726, the Spanish founded San Felipe y Santiago de Montevideo further east, and used it as a base to attack the Portuguese settlement. The original old town of Colonia, the *Barrio Histórico*, sits on a small peninsula that juts into the Río de la Plata. Its winding, cobblestone streets and old, Portuguese-style houses make it a popular draw for tourists.

'Calle Florida?' I ask the security guard at the exit door of the ferry terminal at Colonia. It should be directly opposite the front of the building, but with my shambolic navigational skills, it's best to check. The guard leads me in a different direction. This can't be right. I write the street name on a pad.

'Ah, Floreeeda!', he provides the correct pronunciation, and points me across the road.

I'm staying at a hostel nearby, on the south side of the peninsula that holds the *Barrio Histórico*. I drop my bags and follow Floreeeda along the shore. Ahead, facing me, is the remaining section of the old walls of the town. Set into them is the *Portón de Campo*, the restored city gate, its lowered, wooden drawbridge operated by heavy chains. From the *portón*, the tall, fortified walls run left, towards the river. They stop just short of the bank, cutting off a small patch of greenery that pokes into the Plata. Here, two benches looking out on the water encourage a moment's relaxation. To the right, a ferry approaches in the distance. Behind me, tourists linger behind railings at the top of a lighthouse. To the left, a long breakwater stretches parallel to the rocky shoreline. Soon, the ferry ploughs by, passes inside the breakwater and slows towards the dock.

Back along the old town walls, and through the *portón*, a short walk leads to a pleasant plaza with tall palm trees and screeching parakeets. Golf buggies carrying sightseers rumble over cobbles. This is Plaza Mayor 25 de Mayo. On a wall, a rectangle of ceramic tiles shows a map of the town in 1777. Some of the tiles are weathered and worn and the layout is partly unclear, but the tiny settlement can be seen, enclosed by fortifications that stretch the width of the headland.

Nearby is Plaza Manuel Lobo, the original Plaza de Armas '*de la antigua Colonia del Sacramento*'. Here, wooden walkways lead over low-lying foundations, the basement walls of a house intended for the governor but destroyed by the Spanish in 1777. Not far away, Avenida General Flores bisects the headland, running to its tip. I follow the *avenida* inland. Soon, street cobbles meet a sealed road, the edge of the *Barrio Histórico*, where old meets new.

I'm in need of local currency, and continue along Flores in search of a bank. On the way, and for no obvious reason, a guy plays a trumpet by the side of the road. Standing at an ATM, I realise I have no idea of the value of a Uruguayan peso. I withdraw 700 and retrace my steps towards the old town. By this time, the trumpeter has been joined by a sidekick. Both wear matching black trousers, white shirts and wine-coloured jumpers. The trumpet is set aside and they sing and shake rattles. The attention-seeking musical preamble concluded, the sidekick preaches with a bible in a raised hand, the erstwhile trumpeter pitching in with an occasional 'Aleluya'. Further on, a menu on a stand outside a restaurant has meals for 600-plus pesos; I return to the ATM for more cash (£1 = c. 33UYU).

Calle Ituzaingó runs from Flores to the opposite side of the headland from which I had arrived; the street peters out in a sandy patch. To the right, a beach is at the head of a small bay; sunshades on four legs, with roofs of palm fronds, are built into the sand. Directly across the bay are offices and residential buildings. From there, the land, wooded and less built up, stretches left, several tiny islands dropping off its tip in the distance. It is peaceful here. The river laps at my feet. The only sound is the washing water and the distant wails of the preacher.

Calle de España is parallel to Ituzaingó, further on towards the point of the headland. A small wooden pier extends from the foot of España; wooden benches sit back-to-back at intermittent points down its centre. Tall lampposts each hold five glass-ball lampshades. Upturned cones, in gun-metal grey, are put to use as flower beds. A line of these cones float in the bay, pointed side up, a metal ring at each tip. Boats bobble near the shore, tethered with rope passed through the rings.

37

Avenida Flores leads on, to the tip of the headland. There, a bust of San Martín faces west, towards the waters of the Plata and Buenos Aires. Although originally a Portuguese settlement, Colonia received regular attention from the Spanish because of its involvement in smuggling and, until the creation of the state of Uruguay in 1828, control of the town switched continually between the two countries. In 1763, a small squadron of ships arrived off the headland at Colonia. The squadron was commanded by an Irishman, and his aim was to bring about yet another change in the ownership of the colony.

This intervention came about in the context of wars in Europe. Early in 1762, France had been joined by Spain in its Seven Years' War against Britain. In May of that year, Spain invaded Portugal, Britain's economic ally. They also planned to attack the Portuguese in South America, at Colonia del Sacramento. In September, the governor of Buenos Aires, Pedro Antonio de Cevallos, sailed his forces across the Plata. Early the following month, Colonia was under siege, and by the end of October 1762, the town was in Spanish hands. Meanwhile, in London, merchants of the East India Company, working with the Portuguese, were developing plans to invade Spanish South America. British plans for an invasion of the continent were not new and had long predated the 1804 memorandum of Sir Home Riggs Popham (which eventually led to the Buenos Aires invasions of 1806–07). Throughout the eighteenth century, there were regular reports of impending invasion in the region of the Río de la Plata. But they came to nothing. Many sightings were said to be of merchants smuggling goods south from Brazil. In 1762, however, the governor of Buenos Aires was informed that Britain planned an attack.

In London, the East India Company merchants had bought two ships from the Admiralty, the HMS *Kingston* (renamed the *Lord Clive*) and the *Ambuscade*. These left for Lisbon under the command of Irishman Robert McNamara, an officer of the East India Company's marine. Sources differ on the detail of events that followed. It seems that in Lisbon, they were joined by two ships and 500 soldiers. From there, they crossed to Brazil. By the time they left Rio de Janeiro for Buenos Aires in late November, the fleet had been further enlarged to include a frigate, *Gloria*. En route to the Río de la Plata, they were passed by ships travelling in the opposite direction, transporting Portuguese prisoners to Rio de Janeiro, after the previous month's victory by the Spanish at Colonia.

At Buenos Aires, McNamara, aboard the *Lord Clive*, had no river pilot to negotiate the area's notorious sand banks and dangerously shallow waters. He turned his attention instead to Montevideo. When he was in front of the city, and about to attack, new orders arrived from Rio de Janeiro. McNamara was to retake Colonia del Sacramento.

On January 6, 1763, *Lord Clive*, *Ambuscade* and *Gloria* positioned themselves off the headland at Colonia and bombarded the town. Resistance was stronger than expected. After three hours, a fire on board the *Lord Clive* caused an explosion. The ship sank quickly, with 272 victims, including her captain. The other ships, also damaged, withdrew and slipped away to Rio de Janeiro with the remainder of the squadron.

In February 1763, the Treaty of Paris ended the Seven Years' War. Its terms dictated that, in many cases, territories captured during the conflict were restored to their former owners. As part of the deal, Portugal regained Colonia del Sacramento.

When *Lord Clive* sank in the waters of the Plata, the town's defenders had thrown heavy rocks on to the wreck to ensure that it couldn't be refloated. The ship remains there today, in her shallow, muddy grave.

38

Next morning, climbing on board a bus to Montevideo, I park myself at the front, second row on the left. As I settle myself, an old dear lowers herself into the seat ahead of me. Her daughter has delivered her to the bus and she is standing on the steps. All of three metres apart, the pair launch into a lengthy, shouted conversation. It concludes only when the driver closes the door of the bus, and not before the daughter passes on a phone number. By the time she has roared it for the fifth time, I've memorised the number myself. Predictably, not long after leaving Colonia, the shouted phone number has facilitated a shouted phone conversation.

My urge to strangle the old crone has subsided by the time we reach Montevideo, over two hours later. The city's main bus station is Tres Cruces (*el cruce* – intersection, crossing). Inside the busy terminal, the kiosk with the Tourist Information symbol in the centre of the concourse doesn't, in fact, provide tourist information, but I'm directed to an office that does. There, a helpful lady provides a city map on which she circles the main tourist sights. I tell her where I'm staying, she lets me know the bus I need and points me to the back door of the building, where number 187 is about to leave. Soon, we're on Avenida 18 de Julio, the main thoroughfare leading to *Ciudad Vieja*, the Old City. Unsure when to get off, I keep an eye on passing street names and follow progress on the Information Lady's map. Conveniently, passing through each junction, street signs are in the same position on the sides of corner buildings. Until we reach *Ciudad Vieja*, where there seems to be no standard. Soon, I realise I've gone too far. I hop off the bus and stop an old guy to ask directions. But it's difficult to concentrate on what he's telling me. He's got the most enormous, red, hooked nose. I try to look him in the eye, but my gaze continually slides to his massive honker. He ignores my rudeness, kindly leads me to the nearest junction and points his beak several streets back, to pedestrianised Pérez Castellano.

Ciudad Vieja, where Montevideo began, is at the head of a peninsula that lies between Bahía (Bay) de Montevideo and the Río de la Plata. Pérez Castellano runs almost the width of the peninsula, and my lodgings are here, at the Posada al Sur. Like its environs, the façade of the Posada is worn and crumbling in places. Inside, however, it is beautiful. Elegant doors lead to flights of marble steps. Rooms on the second and third floors have high ceilings, tall windows and handsome shutters. My double bed is low on an old, varnished and spotless wooden floor.

I drop my bags and search for a place to eat. In a small takeaway-cum-restaurant near the Posada, I labour over the menu with my pocket Spanish–English dictionary (restaurant menus are, of course, in Spanish; those in tourist areas might include an English translation). The owner sees me struggling and offers English words. I end up with slices of ham and slabs of chicken slathered in melted cheese, wrapped in a bun.

Afterwards, as I wash it down with coffee, a scruffy, unshaven guy approaches my table. He's wearing open-toed sandals and no socks on a freezing afternoon. He has a stethoscope in his hand, which he raises towards me. I'm not sure what service he's offering, but I shake my head and he shuffles off to the next table. His medical credentials seem to amount to possession of the stethoscope and a white medical coat, worn underneath a tatty lumber jacket.

A football match has just finished on a TV high in a corner by the door. The waitress tells me it's a play-off to decide who will join River Plate in the National B Division. At the mention of River, she gives me a thumbs-down. I'm not sure whether she's confirming their relegation, or if she doesn't like them. It seems that River's match on Sunday had ended in chaos, abandoned in the final minute when supporters invaded the pitch. Players had to be escorted to the dressing rooms. There were clashes between fans and police inside, and later outside, the stadium, as helicopters hovered overhead. That night, Molotov cocktails were thrown at the house of one of the club's board members. Firefighters arrived in time to prevent major damage.

Violence has always been part of football's subculture in South America (as, of course, it has been elsewhere). In the game's early years, rowdyism was rife and clashes between rival *barras de hinchas* (gangs of fans) were not uncommon. Bottles and missiles were the weapons of choice; firearms made an occasional appearance. Once, it is said, this resulted in *el gol de la casilla* (the goal scored in the dressing room). At half-time in a match, a gun was waved in the referee's presence; a goal, disallowed before the break, suddenly appeared on the scoreboard at the start of the second half.

Violence was also common *on* the pitch. In 1964, in Argentina, 82 players were sent off in First Division matches. In 1977, the number had risen to 186. In Brazil, in the mid-twentieth century, the British referee, Jack Barrick, sent off nineteen players in eight and a half months. In 23 years working in Britain, he had dismissed six (around this time, many South American countries 'imported' European, mostly British, referees in an attempt to raise local standards).

This violent play was exposed to a wider audience during the infamous 1967 World Club Championship (last contested in 2004, this was also called the Intercontinental Cup). Played annually between the champions of Europe and South America, the two-legged fixture that year involved Glasgow Celtic and Racing (*La Academia*, the Academy), of Buenos Aires. Celtic were at home in the first leg and won by the only goal of the game. Two weeks later, 80,000 people gathered in Buenos Aires for the return fixture. During the warm-up, the Celtic keeper was struck on the head with a stone, and had to be replaced. The Argentinians took a 2–1 lead shortly after half-time. They were determined not to let their advantage slip. Celtic players were spat at, thumped and kicked. The rough-house tactics had their intended effect; there was no further score. The Argentine president was at the match. He thought Racing's win was 'a triumph for Argentina'. One newspaper maintained that 'it wasn't football, but it was a beautiful victory'.

With one win apiece, neutral Montevideo hosted a play-off the following week. Twenty thousand Argentines crossed the Plata. On this occasion, in what was another brutal affair, Celtic fought back. Three of their players were sent off, two from Racing. The Argentines won 1–0. This didn't impress the locals; Uruguayans in the crowd pelted the winners with missiles as they left the field. Later, police baton charges were needed to disperse a local mob outside their dressing-room. 'Racing win the World War', reported a Uruguayan newspaper. For their part in the rowdy on-field proceedings, Celtic directors fined their players £250 each (at the time, their weekly wages were approximately £30). It is said that Racing's players each received a new car.

39

It is overcast and bitingly cold next morning, on a stroll through *Ciudad Vieja*. Out of the Posada, and to the right, Pérez Castellano leads towards the Bahía. En route, ball-shaped light shades droop, one on either side, from the top of lampposts. Towards the end of the street, a stall-holder puts woolly hats on body-less dummy heads. Here, the outside seating areas of restaurants are enclosed within clear, thick-plastic shelters. Just a few steps further on, Rambla 25 de Agosto de 1825 cuts through Pérez Castellano on the way to the tip of the headland.

To the left, down the Rambla, three hard-faced guys in a doorway drink early-morning beer from cans. Beyond them is Calle la Cumparsita. Not so much a street as a narrow, gated walkway with flagstones underfoot, the *calle* leads to an indoor market, El Mercado del Puerto. A plaque on a wall by the market entrance explains that local streets take the names of tangos created by Uruguayan composers and writers, 'a tribute to their contribution in depicting one of the most appealing aspects of [Uruguayan] identity'. 'La Cumparsita' (The Little Parade) is one of the most famous tango songs in the world. In 1997, it was enshrined in law as the country's cultural anthem. Uruguayans were none too pleased then, three years later, when the Argentina team marched to it at the Sydney Olympics.

The old wood-and-glass roof of the *mercado* is supported by tall, rusty, metal posts. Inside are open-air bars, cafés and *parrillas* (steak restaurants). It is early yet and behind the counters of the *parrillas*, workers are busy chopping, cutting and preparing. Behind them, at counter height, wood fires blaze in bricked corners. Stretching from the base of the fires, large metal grills are loaded with hunks of meat, chicken and sausages, cooked by hot embers raked underneath the grills from the flames.

I retrace my steps on Pérez Castellano, past the Posada, to Calle Washington. Inland, towards the town centre, cobbled Washington has beautifully maintained colonial buildings with tall, narrow, double doors, columned balconies and elegantly carved window arches. Parallel to Washington, pedestrianised Calle Sarandí is home to fashionable shops and boutiques. Here, elegant women wear stylish, oversized sunglasses, despite the sunless, cloud-covered sky. Strolling men sip *mate*. They crook an arm (usually the left) and clamp the *termo* with an elbow to the side of the chest. The left hand, raised as a result, holds the gourd. In this position, the *bombilla* reaches the mouth, and allows the *mate* to be sipped with a minimum of unnecessary movement.

Further on, Sarandí runs along one side of Plaza Constitución, the hub of the old colonial town. In the centre of the square, under maintenance at the moment, a *fuente* (fountain) is shrouded in green plastic sheeting. Paths leading from the *fuente* are lined with stalls that sell antique bits and pieces. Nearby, a guy hawks CDs from an open case. His music plays loudly from tall speakers, pan-pipes versions of 'I Will Survive' and 'Rivers of Babylon'. It's bland stuff, Andean elevator music. Nul points.

Later that morning, I switch accommodation from the beautiful but budget-threatening Posada al Sur to the standard and quite cheap El Viajero hostel. El Viajero is in the Centro district, next door to *Ciudad Vieja*, and not far from Montevideo's Calle Floreeeda (*florida*: florid, flowery). In the communal bathroom, the single urinal hides in a tiny gap between the shower wall and a wall by the sinks. A broader guy than me would be peeing from a distance.

Montevideo's Naval Museum is at the edge of the Information Lady's city map, on the eastern side of the peninsula. The number 145 bus drops me nearby, at Playa de los Pocitos, a lengthy beach lined with mid-sized apartment blocks. At the northern end of the beach, two permanent soccer goals, complete with nets, are planted in the clean, bright sand. Here, behind the beach, tiny Plazuela Winston Churchill has a bust of the British prime minister. To Winston's left, three guys are asleep on a patch of grass, stretched out on a mattress of cardboard beneath a squat, thick-trunked, palm tree. Only the tops of their heads are visible beneath a layer of blankets that protects them from the bitter cold.

Nearby, on a slight elevation, the Naval Museum looks out on the estuary. A narrow driveway is an arc that curves left to the museum door and carries on to meet up again with the public road. The segment of ground cut off by the driveway holds cannon, a part-buried anchor and an anti-aircraft gun that points to the Plata. To the left of the driveway as it exits the museum is a larger grassy area. Here, three flagpoles stand front-right. The centre pole hosts the Uruguayan flag, fully stretched just now in a stiff breeze. Its neighbours hold only flag-hoisting cords; on one, a clasp clinks continuously against the metal pole.

Buried in the ground to the left of the flags is the top section of a gunboat, *Comodore Coe* (named for John Coe, ex-colleague of William Brown in the Argentine navy, against whom Brown later fought in the wars that followed the creation of Uruguay). Directly behind the flags is a 150mm gun rescued from *Admiral Graf Spee*, sunk opposite Montevideo on December 17, 1939, after the Battle of the River Plate.

The first naval combat of World War II, the Battle of the River Plate was also the only action of the war to take place in South America. *Admiral Graf Spee* was the pride of the German navy, a pocket battleship, small but heavily armed. Commanded by Hans Langsdorff, *Graf Spee* had left Wilhelmshaven in northwest Germany in August 1939. By the time war broke out weeks later, she was already in the South Atlantic. The captain's orders were to destroy enemy merchant ships, and so deprive England and France of much-needed supplies from Africa and the Americas.

By mid-December, Langsdorff had sunk nine merchant vessels (this was done without loss of life; crew members were disembarked before the ships were sunk). In response, the British formed a battle group, made up of a heavy cruiser, *Exeter*, and two light cruisers, *Ajax* and *Achilles*. Based in the Falkland Islands, this was Force G, under the command of a Commodore Harwood.

On December 13, 1939, Langsdorff spotted ships on the horizon off the Río de la Plata estuary. In normal circumstances, *Graf Spee*'s float plane would have been dispatched on reconnaissance. But the plane was out of service. Langsdorff approached the ships and, too late, realised his mistake. He had run into Force G.

In the night-long battle that followed, all four vessels were badly damaged. Listing and taking on water, *Exeter* broke away and limped to the Falklands. *Graf Spee*'s fuel system had received a direct hit and she needed to make land. Langsdorff sought advice from Germany; he was told to head for Uruguay. On December 14, *Graf Spee* entered the harbour at Montevideo. As this was a neutral port, various articles of the Hague Convention now came into play. The upshot was that the ship could remain in port only until Sunday, December 17 – not enough time to make the necessary repairs. Over the following days, the British fed false information to the Germans, such that Langsdorff believed a large force was waiting at the mouth of the Plata. In fact, the 'force' comprised only *Ajax* and *Achilles*, both damaged, along with another cruiser, *Cumberland*, sent from the Falklands. Although other ships were on the way, they would not be there by the 17th.

Langsdorff had three options. He could try to fight his way to the more friendly port of Buenos Aires (Uruguay was officially neutral, but pro-Britain), he could accept internment in Montevideo, or he could scuttle the ship. Again, he got in touch with Germany. Under no circumstances, he was told, was he to accept internment. If *Graf Spee* was detained in Montevideo, and the British got on board, naval secrets could be compromised. With an ailing vessel, the captain considered that an attempted escape to Argentina would result only in failure and avoidable loss of life.

Langsdorff arranged for the majority of his men to be transferred by tug and barge to Buenos Aires.

On Sunday, December 17, thousands of onlookers lined the waterfront at Montevideo. Langsdorff boarded *Graf Spee* with a skeleton crew, sailed from the harbour and scuttled his ship in the shallow waters of the Río de la Plata estuary. A waiting steamer brought the captain and his remaining men to Argentina.

Some days later, in Buenos Aires, Captain Langsdorff was found dead in his quarters, a gun in his hand. An honourable man, he may have felt that he should have gone down with his ship.

In the Falklands, the stricken *Exeter* was repaired and sailed for home. The First Lord of the Admiralty, Winston Churchill, took the salute in February, 1940, when she slipped quietly into Plymouth harbour.

Approximately 1,000 Germans from *Graf Spee* were interned in Buenos Aires. After the war, some found their way to Villa General Belgrano, the 'central European town in Córdoba'. There, they may have made some things out of wood.

40

The door of the Naval Museum is locked. A sign in the window encourages visitors to ring the doorbell; I do this, and then knock loudly, but there's no reply. Soon, someone leaves; I nip inside and leave the requested 20-peso contribution with the aurally challenged attendant seated in a small office by the entrance.

Past the office, and to the right, a large room holds exhibits from the colonial, independence and militarism periods. Directly ahead as I enter this room is a portrait of the man I've come to see, *el Almirante Gaucho* (the gaucho admiral), founder of the Uruguayan navy, Pedro Campbell. Campbell has a lean, hard face, flowing hair and long sideburns. A full moustache stretches diagonally from the corners of his mouth and touches the raised collar of a military jacket. A large circular earring hangs from his left ear; a neckerchief is tied in a knot at his throat.

When the 71st Highland Regiment returned from India in 1800 and was stationed at Ballinasloe and Loughrea in County Galway, one of the Irishmen who filled out its depleted ranks was Peter Campbell. A sergeant by the time the 71st took part in the British invasion of Buenos Aires in 1806, Campbell deserted and made his way to the northern province of Corrientes. He stayed on there when the British withdrew.

In Corrientes, Campbell worked as a tanner. He kept the company of tough gauchos, adopted their dress and customs and learned to fight like them, long knife in one hand, poncho wrapped around the other arm as a shield.

After the establishment of the *Primera Junta* in Buenos Aires, Campbell took the patriot side in the wars against the Spanish. He joined with José Artigas, the *caudillo* of a region that included much of the Banda Oriental, as well as the provinces of Entre Ríos and Corrientes. Campbell made use of his military experience to form a very effective, mobile, guerilla force of indigenous Guaraní. Their success in numerous exploits made the Irishman the 'hero of a country larger than England'.

From 1814, Campbell built up a squadron of 23 vessels that patrolled the Paraná, and led daring actions against Artigas's enemies. It is in this role as *Primer Comandante General de Marina* (First Commander in Chief of the Navy), that *el Almirante Gaucho* is known as the founder of the Uruguayan navy.

When the wars were over, Campbell returned to Corrientes. There, in an area bristling with outlaws, he offered protection to wealthy landowners. The Scottish Robertson brothers hired him after a personal recommendation from the governor of the province: 'Next to the Protector [Artigas], there is no man can be of such service to you in this province as Don Pedro Campbell'.

Campbell himself thought that 'there is not an *estanciero* that has the liver to...peep out of his own window, unless he knows I am out in the camp to protect him'. The Robertsons' subsequent opinion of him shows that this was not an empty boast: 'His personal prowess was prodigious; his heart as bold as a lion's... he was dreaded by the Gauchos, admired by the estancieros, and respected by the inhabitants at large...[he was] one of the most feared and respected men, in a province overrun with daring bands of assassins'. Campbell went on to become deputy governor of Corrientes for a time in 1819.

After the independence wars, once royalists had been defeated, the la Plata region was riven by strife in an ongoing battle for control between those who favoured a loose federation of provinces and those who wanted the centralisation of power in Buenos Aires (at this point, the Banda Oriental was one of many provinces that made up the United Provinces of the Río de la Plata). Artigas' growing influence and his support for federalism meant that centralists in Buenos Aires did nothing to intervene when Brazil annexed the Banda Oriental in 1820. (Brazil had long considered what it called the Cisplatina – literally, 'this side of the Plata' – to be part of its territory.) Artigas was defeated and exiled. Campbell was removed to Paraguay in chains. There, he settled in the town of Pilar, on the border with Argentina, and resumed life as a tanner. He died in 1832.

In 1961, Campbell's remains were repatriated to Uruguay from his burial place in Pilar, in the *Urna de Madera* (wooden urn) that sits here, at the foot of his portrait in the Naval Museum.

*

After the annexation of the Banda Oriental, its residents soon became unhappy about the 'Brazilianisation' of their province. Also, across the Plata, Argentines began to feel threatened by their powerful neighbour. In 1825, Buenos Aires supported Juan Antonio Lavalleja, an exiled ex-officer of Artigas, and his fellow nationalists (the *treinta y tres orientales*, 33 easterners), when they crossed the Plata to remove the occupiers.

A war followed for control of the province. It was mostly played out on the Río de la Plata. Brazil, with experience at sea but not in the shallow waters of the estuary, had the larger fleet. Buenos Aires had William Brown. According to Andrew Graham-Yooll in his book *Imperial Skirmishes*:

> Admiral Brown became a folk hero. Crowds…rowed out into the river in small boats to catch a glimpse of his actions against the Brazilians. He used small ships to lure larger vessels into shallow water and there ran them aground; he often challenged much larger craft than his own to the bewilderment of the Brazilians. He taught his local crews to sing Irish songs, and his English officers to sing with them. Ashore he was feted constantly… People hung pictures of Brown in their homes and pinned up newspaper cuttings about his battles; his portrait appeared next to those of saints and statesmen in offices and shops as well as in private houses.

'An extraordinary fellow this!', the *Manchester Guardian* wrote of him.

Brazil blockaded the Plata, preventing imports and exports, taking ships as prizes. This disruption of commerce persuaded Britain to get involved (at one point, the Brazilians held up to ten British ships). An envoy, Lord Ponsonby, was sent to arrange peace terms. By 1827, a settlement had been negotiated. A peace treaty was ratified in October of the following year. Both rivals would renounce their claims to the province. A new country, Uruguay, was created.

The British envoy, Ponsonby, had been a member of the Irish House of Commons. After the Act of Union, and until 1802, he represented Galway Borough in the UK House of Commons. He was later to become Viscount Ponsonby, of Imokilly in the County of Cork.

*

Back in Centro after my afternoon in the suburbs, I drop into a corner café. A waiter approaches with a small tray. It holds a coffee, a glass of mineral water, a glass of orange juice, a tiny meringue and two small bowls, one with popcorn, one with cream. I had ordered only a coffee and assume there's been a misunderstanding; I ask the waiter to take away everything but the coffee and water. He shrugs and reloads the tray. But this, it seems, is a *merienda*, a light snack, usually taken in the late afternoon, to fill the lengthy gap between lunch and late Latin dinners. And all for the price of a coffee.

41

It is Sunday morning and, too late, I find out about a rugby match taking place at Carrasco, in the city's eastern suburbs. The mid-afternoon kick-off means I wouldn't make it there and back in time for my pre-booked five o'clock bus to Colonia. The fixture, between Old Christians and Treból (Shamrock) de Paysandú, is being played at *El Campo San Patricio* (St Patrick's Field).

In the early 1950s, the Irish Christian Brothers were invited to Montevideo. Parents in the exclusive neighbourhood of Carrasco were keen to provide their sons with a private, Catholic education and had been encouraged by the success of the prestigious Cardinal Newman College in Buenos Aires, founded by *los Hermanos Cristianos* the decade before. The Brothers arrived in 1955 and established Stella Maris. Ten years later, ex-pupils, eager to continue enjoying the rugby they had played at school, formed the Old Christians.

From the beginning, rugby was an integral part of life at Stella Maris. If, in the classroom, the Brothers' teaching methods sought to build character and promote discipline, then, on the playing field, rugby was the medium through which these same aims were pursued. At a time when the game was almost unknown in Uruguay, the boys were steered away from soccer (the Brothers thought it promoted 'selfishness and egotism') and towards a sport which demanded 'humility, tenacity…and devotion to others'. According to Old Christians team member Nando Parrado, in his book *Miracle in the Andes*, 'To the Christian Brothers, rugby was more than a game, it was…a moral discipline. At its heart was the…belief that no other sport taught so devoutly the importance of striving, suffering and sacrificing in the pursuit of a common goal'. The Brothers passed on their love of the game, and their ex-pupils played 'proudly wearing the bright green shamrock' on their jerseys.

In October 1972, a plane carrying the Old Christians crashed in the Andes. Parrado, who was on the aircraft, attributes their subsequent survival in small measure to their time at Stella Maris. The survivors responded to their situation 'in the way…[they had]… been taught by the Christian Brothers – as a team'.

The Old Christians, with a number of supporters, had been travelling to play an exhibition match in Santiago, Chile. Bad weather had forced them to stop overnight at Mendoza. They resumed their journey the following day, Friday the 13th. In poor conditions, the plane ploughed into a ridge and came to rest on a glacier on the east side of a mountain.

Including crew, there were 45 people on board Flight 571. Of the 32 who survived the crash, only a small number, surprisingly, suffered life-threatening injuries. Parrado's sister, Susy, was among them. She lived on for eight days and died in her brother's arms. She was buried in the snow, near the plane's fuselage, beside her mother who had been killed on impact. With no medical supplies, others who were badly injured had no hope. For those who lived on, their means of survival is well known. They were sustained only by eating the flesh of their dead fellow passengers. In his book, Parrado writes simply and movingly about the time they spent in the mountains.

From the beginning, the elements proved almost unbearable for the survivors. They wore only what they had travelled in: light, summer clothes. They had no coats or blankets. At night, sheltered in the fuselage, the extreme cold caused their teeth to chatter so much that it made conversation difficult. During the day, the sun blistered their lips and skin. And always, their lungs gasped for more oxygen than the thin mountain air could provide.

At first, they waited to be rescued. After ten days, despair set in when a news bulletin on their transistor radio announced that the search for their whereabouts had been abandoned. Soon, it was agreed that a group (they called them the expeditionaries) would attempt to climb out of the cordillera. It was now the end of October. Summer in the mountains arrived in mid-November; they would delay their departure until then. One night as they slept, an avalanche buried the fuselage. There were eight more deaths. Nineteen passengers remained.

On November 15, the expeditionaries travelled east, but made little progress and were back at the fuselage within six days. To the west lay a daunting 5,000-metre peak (the plane was at 3,600 metres). They were convinced that Chile lay on the other side. But the mountain had already beaten off two attempts by the survivors to scale it. With no other option, they would have to try again.

By this time, any food they did have had run out (Parrado describes how a single chocolate peanut lasted him for three days. Its chocolate coating provided the first day's nourishment. One half of the peanut was then consumed on each of the following days; he savoured the last half in his mouth for hours before finally eating it). For the author, although he understood the taboo they were breaking, there was no guilt or shame about eating human flesh (some survivors refused it for a time). He did, however, resent that he had been forced into a choice between that and a certain death.

On December 12, after two months in the mountains, Parrado and two others set off to climb the peak to the west. Overnight, on the slope, they slept in a hollow beneath a huge boulder. The floor of the hollow was so steep, they slept almost in a vertical position. After a heroic effort, they reached the summit. Expecting to see the green fields of Chile on the other side, they were distraught to find nothing but mountains stretching into the distance. They had no option, however, but to continue west. One of the trio returned to the fuselage, leaving his ration of meat with the other two. Parrado and his Old Christians team-mate, Roberto Canessa, would continue. 'Now let's go die together', said Canessa.

On the afternoon of December 18, they broke the snow-line; for the first time in months, they were walking on dry land. The next day, they saw trees in a valley, and a horseshoe, and cow dung. By now, their bodies were on the verge of collapse. Late on the afternoon of the 20th, they heard a faint human voice and signalled across a torrential, roaring river to a man on horseback. The rider acknowledged them, turned and disappeared into the looming darkness. Help arrived the following afternoon. In ten days, in a state of almost permanent exhaustion, Parrado and Canessa had trekked more than 110 kilometres across the Andes.

In all, sixteen passengers survived. During their time in the mountains, Parrado says that, for all of them, each moment was lived in fear. Some descended into apathy, others did their best to lift their colleagues' spirits. A rift could have developed between 'the workers and the lost boys', but any resentments were reined in as they 'struggled on as a team...Perhaps it was all the years together on the rugby field. Perhaps the Christian Brothers had taught us well'.

The rescue received worldwide attention. In Ireland, the principal of the Christian Brothers College in Cork city gathered his students together to pray and give thanks for the safe return of the surviving passengers. Some months earlier, Brother John (Dicey) O'Reilly had first asked for his students' prayers when Flight 571 was reported lost in the mountains. Most of the players on board had been his pupils when Brother O'Reilly had taught at Stella Maris in Montevideo some years before.

Unsurprisingly, the press presented the story as a triumph over adversity. They praised the power of the human spirit, the survivors' story was an inspiration, the survivors were heroes. Parrado thought that these people were missing the point. He was no hero, he thought. The urge that propelled him west was 'the same urge that drives a man to jump from the top of a burning building'. He says that thinking about the disaster, and the pointless waste of young lives, brought no feeling of triumph. Their experience was not something to be celebrated, but rather, to be outlived.

Despite the horror and the waste, and seemingly in common with many who suffer near-death, Parrado's subsequent life was somehow enriched. His experience 'had swept away everything trivial and unimportant' and had given him 'a profound understanding of what a wonder it is…to be truly alive and aware, to savour each moment of life with presence and gratitude'. This, he says, 'is the gift the Andes gave us'.

*

Later that Sunday afternoon, I catch a cab to Tres Cruces for my five o'clock bus to Colonia ('Tre Cruce', the cab driver pronounces the name of the station. The 's' is often dropped from the end of words here). The Copa América, South America's international football competition, has just begun in Argentina. '*Comienza la fiesta*' (the party begins), runs the Fox Sports banner headline on the TV in the station café. Just now, it is nil–nil between Brazil and Venezuela. But I'm not really paying attention. It's difficult to keep my eyes off the table to my right, where a guy sips *mate* from a gourd in the shape of a cow's hoof.

On board the bus, I'm in a window seat and feeling a tad confined. The passenger in front has reclined his seat to its full extent. Beside me, a guy holds his young son in his arms. The boy has his head on his father's left shoulder, facing me, and is coughing and spluttering in my direction. To the rear, a baby has started screaming. Across the aisle, a teenager texts furiously; there's a click with every letter pressed. I'm very much enjoying my spin around South America and, in truth, miss very little from home. Except, from time to time, the privacy of my car.

42

Next day in Colonia, in a café on Flores, my place mat is an LP. My meal sits on Side A of 'Fiesta', six songs by Raffaella Carrà, an Italian singer popular in South America (although it's possible that her popularity is on the wane, given that her albums now double as place mats). Uruguay are about to kick off their first match in the Copa América, against Peru. As I leave Raffaella to catch the ferry to Buenos Aires, cafés and restaurants the length of the *avenida* are thronged. In the terminal, a crowd has gathered in front of a large-screen TV. On board the catamaran, safety instructions are shelved; instead, the screen at the head of the cabin shows the football. Passengers pack the two centre columns of seats for a premium view. The game finishes 1–1.

Despite the efforts of the Christian Brothers, soccer is by far the most popular sport in Uruguay. On today's evidence, its citizens are relatively passive football-watchers. This seems in keeping with a certain calmness in the national character. Their drivers, for example, actually stop at pedestrian crossings (this, of course, takes all the life-threatening, South American fun out of crossing the road here). I'm familiar with only one Uruguay player, Diego Forlán, who once played for Manchester United. At the 2010 World Cup, he won the Golden Ball, awarded to the best player of the tournament (he was also its top scorer). On the pitch, he is the captain and go-to man. Off the pitch, shops that sell football shirts seem mostly to stock Forlán's number 10. And just now, his face is all over newspapers and the covers of magazines (although this seems to have more to do with a blip in his love life, than anything football-related). Uruguay came fourth in that 2010 World Cup at which Forlán was the star turn. This was the first time I had been aware of the team at an international tournament. But it seems that Uruguay have an impressive footballing heritage.

In 1929, a Uruguayan politician claimed that 'Other nations have their history but we have our football'. History and football came together in a timely manner the following year; on the 100th anniversary of their independence (the first constitution was approved in 1830), Uruguay hosted the first football World Cup.

The politician's lofty claim about the part football played in Uruguayan life came a year after the country had been crowned world champions at the Olympic Games for the second time in succession. Until the football World Cup came into being, the Olympic Games served as the sport's world championships. At the Paris Games in 1924, Uruguay were the only football team from South America to take part. They were so strapped for cash that reports suggest players slept on the floor on their sailing across the Atlantic, and then on benches on trains through France. This was possibly the only discomfort the team endured, however. Uruguay eased through the competition. In the final, a 3–0 win over Switzerland had newspapers gushing about the elegance and style of their play.

Miffed by their neighbour's success, rivals Argentina immediately challenged the new world champions. A fixture was set, to be played over two legs. When the second match was abandoned due to crowd trouble, another was arranged. Played in Buenos Aires, this third game also never reached a conclusion. The Uruguay team walked off the pitch when missiles were flung at them from the terraces. One of their players, Scarone, was arrested for kicking a policeman. At the docks the following day, the team was pelted with coal as they waited to return home. These unruly goings-on were but the latest episode in the serial drama that was the fiercest football rivalry in South America (Brazil would not become a force on the continent until later in the century). Competition between the countries was, and is, intense. Between 1901 and 1914, they played each other 41 times. The fixture soon left England vs Scotland behind as the most frequently played international.

In 1928, Argentina joined Uruguay at the Olympic Games in Amsterdam, where the two teams met in the final. There was keen interest in this, their 102nd meeting; 250,000 applications were made for the 40,000 available tickets. After a replay, the Uruguayans retained their title, the winning goal scored by Scarone, the policeman-kicker from a few years before.

The popularity of football at the Olympic Games persuaded Jules Rimet, the president of FIFA (Fédération Internationale de Football Association, the game's international governing body), to establish a competition specifically for the sport. It was decided that a Coupe du Monde would take place in 1930. The tournament would be open to all FIFA-affiliated countries (this included both amateur and professional leagues).

Uruguay put forward the most convincing case to host the competition. As well as the tournament coinciding with the centenary of the country's independence, the double-Olympic (ie: World) champions agreed to build a new 100,000-capacity stadium; and, perhaps the clincher, they would pay the expenses of all competing teams.

But it seems the latter was not the inducement they hoped it would be. Just eight weeks before the World Cup was due to begin, no European team had entered the competition (there were legitimate concerns among amateur players about holding on to their jobs after a two- to three-month absence). The English were indifferent. Austria and Hungary said they wouldn't attend. That Spain and Italy also refused to send teams was particularly galling. Most of Uruguay's population of two million traced their ancestry to one or other of the countries. The hosts felt betrayed.

Eventually, four teams from Europe were 'persuaded' to travel: France, Belgium, Romania and Yugoslavia. Also expected in Montevideo were Egypt, the US and Mexico, and, from South America, Argentina, Bolivia, Brazil, Chile, Paraguay and Peru. The Egyptians sailed from Alexandria to Marseille, and when they missed their onward connection by a matter of hours, the competition lost its only African participants.

Uruguay were hopeful of success in their home tournament. The team that had achieved their Olympic victories remained mostly intact. One of the side's newer members was Héctor Castro. He had played on the 1928 winning team and stood out for his talented forward play and his missing right forearm, lost to a chainsaw as a teenager. His team-mate, right-back José Leandro Andrade, is believed to have been the first black player to have played on mainland Europe (in Paris in 1924, he was known as '*La Marveille Noire*'). He formed part of Uruguay's imposing back line, the *costilla metallica* (iron curtain). It is said that his father was 98 years old when Andrade was born.

Ticket sales for the tournament were slow. Uruguayans were grateful for the arrival of the Europeans who did turn up, but it seems they weren't particularly interested in seeing them play. For much of the competition, crowd numbers were dismal. Uruguayan officials ignored this embarrassing fact and published outrageously exaggerated attendance figures. Later, FIFA provided revised, more realistic numbers.

The host's arch-rivals, Argentina, were confident of doing well. Their star and playmaker was Luisito Monti. Talented but ruthless (imagine a Latin Ron 'Chopper' Harris), he was loved by his countrymen and hated by opponents. Argentine fans called him '*Doble Ancho*' (Double Wide) because of his ability to cover all parts of the pitch. Opposition fans were not quite as admiring. When Argentina played France (official attendance – 23,407; FIFA estimate – 3,000), Monti nobbled Lucien Laurent, scorer of the first-ever World Cup goal (Laurent would be incapacitated for the remainder of the tournament). Although Argentina won the match, Uruguayan onlookers left the stands and carried some of the losing team shoulder-high from the pitch. This annoyed the Argentines, whose mood wasn't improved when they were pelted with stones as they boarded the team bus. Argentina threatened to pull out of the competition. They were persuaded to continue but there seems to have been little change in the level of their popularity. Soon, they needed round-the-clock security and a mounted police escort to and from training.

It is no surprise that football in its early years differed in some ways from the game as it is played today. In the Chile/Mexico fixture (official attendance – 9,249; FIFA estimate – 500), the Belgian referee wore short trousers, a smart jacket and a hat. A linesman, his compatriot, Jean Langenus, had on a shirt, tie and traditional cap to go with his plus-fours. Langenus was also a referee, one of the most highly regarded of those at the World Cup. But his future in this role had almost foundered before it had had a chance to begin. He failed the referee's exam at the first attempt. He had left a question unanswered. Thinking it a joke, he neglected to detail the correct procedure to follow when 'a ball strikes a low-flying plane'. This game, which Chile won 3–0, included the World Cup's first own-goal (*autogol* in Latin America).

In their match against Brazil (official attendance – 25,466; FIFA estimate – 1,200), four of the Bolivian team wore berets. This helped when heading a ball whose stitching was so prominent that players complained about bruising to their foreheads. Both sides started this match wearing white shirts. There was confusion for fifteen minutes before Bolivia changed into red.

By the time Uruguay played their first game, on July 18, two teams (Yugoslavia and the US) had already reached the semi-finals. Finally enthused by the home side's delayed entry into the competition, the Uruguayan public showed up in numbers sufficient to make the attendance figure-massager redundant. Against Peru, in the reduced-capacity Estadio Centenario (official attendance – 57,735; FIFA estimate – 57,735), the one-armed Castro scored the only goal of the game. It was a poor performance from the home side. But Uruguay would improve, and they, along with Argentina, went on to fill the remaining semi-final places. Both South American teams overcame their opponents. The first World Cup final would be contested by bitter rivals Argentina and Uruguay.

Early on the day of the game, FIFA had not yet decided on a referee. Before noon, they appointed Jean Langenus, the Belgian. Acknowledged as the best referee at the tournament, he was a good choice (as long, obviously, as low-flying aircraft kept clear of the stadium). But Langenus would agree to referee the game only on condition that he receive a police escort from the stadium immediately after the match. For the final itself, he would wear his usual shirt, tie, jacket and plus-fours.

Meanwhile, at Argentina's team hotel, their playmaker, Monti, revealed that he had received death threats, as had his mother. He was reluctant to play but was named in the starting eleven.

Uruguay began the final with a flourish and went a goal ahead, but were 2–1 down by half-time. Monti was doing well, despite not wanting to play. But at half-time, he claimed to have received further threats. Again, he had to be coaxed on to the field. Soon after the restart, Uruguay drew level. They then went ahead, before at the death, *el Manco* (the one-armed man) Castro, made it 4–2.

After two minutes of extra time, Langenus blew the final whistle. Without changing clothes, he made a dash for the port and a boat bound for neutral Rio de Janeiro.

Monti (and his mother) survived the day. After the World Cup, he was signed by Juventus of Turin, became an Italian citizen, and played in the 1934 World Cup. He won a winner's medal when Italy beat Czechoslovakia 2–1 in the final.

Uruguay didn't enter the 1934 World Cup in Italy or the 1938 competition in France. After that, the next one played was in Brazil in 1950. There, in the final, Uruguay beat the hosts in front of 200,000 fans in the Maracanã stadium, Rio de Janeiro, and again became world champions.

43

In Buenos Aires, I return to Palermo and resume battle with the sliding door at Lulu. But, with my Buenos Aires sightseeing itch already scratched, I'm soon keen to move on. Months before, in Quito, I had picked up a copy of Bruce Chatwin's famous book, *In Patagonia*; I'm now on my third reading. Some of Chatwin's time in the region was spent among the descendants of Welsh settlers there. I take my cue; before the week is out, I'm heading south. It seems my search for things Celtic has now expanded... and it gives me an excuse to visit Patagonia.

From the early 1700s in Wales, there had been talk of creating a standalone Welsh community abroad, in which Welshness could flourish, free from outside (ie: English) cultural influences. It was a hazy notion, something that might happen, some day. In the 1840s, emigration from the country was at an all-time high. In the United States, the destination of choice for most of those who left, the Welsh assimilated easily into their new environment. And as they did, so their identity became diluted. For Welsh observers, what they now regarded as a pressing need to safeguard a separate Welshness began to turn the dream of a colony into a reality.

In 1856, a society was formed in Camptonville, California with the aim of promoting the formation of a Welsh settlement. A letter was sent to Welsh newspapers asking for support; this resulted in a number of similar societies being set up there. The focal point of the movement became the Liverpool Emigration Society, later re-formed as a National Committee. Among its main movers were

Edwin Roberts, a Flintshire native recently returned from the US, the Rev. Michael D Jones, Lewis Jones and a Captain Love Jones-Parry from Madryn.

The committee applied to the Argentine government for land in Patagonia and were invited to visit the country (Argentina was encouraging immigration from Europe at the time). Lewis Jones and Jones-Parry sailed for Buenos Aires. There, they met with government officials before travelling on to Patagonia, where they surveyed land at the mouth of the Chubut river. Back in Buenos Aires, they entered into negotiations with the minister for home affairs, Guillermo Rawson. A deal was struck, land was secured and the two Welshmen sailed for home.

In Wales, the National Committee advertised for people willing to begin a new life in South America. There was little interest. Despite this, a departure date was set, for April 25, 1865. Edwin Roberts and Lewis Jones left for Argentina a month before, to make preparations for the prospective arrivals. In time, a sufficient number of willing travellers was rounded up, and on May 25, a month behind schedule, the emigrants were ready to leave. They would sail from Liverpool on board a converted tea clipper, the *Mimosa*. On the day of departure, hundreds of well-wishers gathered at the docks. The Welsh banner was raised and passengers sang an anthem written for the occasion. To great applause, the anchor was weighed. Enthusiasm was dampened somewhat, however, by the absence of any wind. The ship dawdled in the Mersey for three days. Eventually, on May 28, they were on their way. Two months later, the *Mimosa* arrived in Argentina, at Golfo Nuevo.

44

At the barren northern edge of Patagonia, Golfo Nuevo is formed by the almost all-enclosing pincer formations of Península Valdés to the north and Punta Ninfas to the south. At the head of the bay is the city of Puerto Madryn, named for Captain Love Jones-Parry's estate in Wales. It is a hefty 1,300 kilometres southwest of Buenos Aires, twenty or so hours overnight on a bus. My guidebook bigs the city up. 'Having spent hours travelling through the…Pampas', it tells me, 'you may wonder why you bothered'. Yes, well, I guess it does seem a bit…bleak. Land on the approach to the city is barren and scrubby. The outskirts have dusty, unsealed roads and unplastered houses. But trendy cafés and smart shops *do* lend its centre a prosperous feel. Although not blessed with much in the way of tourist attractions itself, Puerto Madryn is the stop-off point for a world-famous nature reserve on Península Valdés. The city is twinned with Nefyn in north Wales, and when the Welsh rugby team toured Argentina in 2006, they played one of their two tests here to honour the country's link with the area (the hosts won 27–25).

The morning after my marathon bus journey, I take a stroll to the city's beachfront. Locals lined up at the sea wall look out at a flock of pink flamingos stretched in a long line parallel to the shore, wading and feeding in the shallow water. Beside me, a guy removes his breakfast from a holdall: a *mate termo*, a bottle of water and a small baked loaf in a tin-foil container. I thank him, but shake my head at the offer of a sip from his *mate* gourd.

At the head of the beach, close to the sea wall, the sand is churned up and dry. Towards the water's edge, the departing tide has left puddles and broad, damp patches. A guy with a camera walks towards the flamingos. At his approach, the birds split up and fan outwards. Moments after the photographer leaves, they slowly drift back towards the shallow water, re-form the long single line, stand and dip their heads. His morning meal complete, my breakfasting neighbour re-packs his holdall and smiles goodbye.

Far to the right, on a leg of the bay, is the Museo del Desembarco. The museum marks the location where, in 1865, the Welsh immigrants landed. After their arduous journey, the new arrivals had found little onshore to welcome them.

Having travelled ahead of the settlers to prepare for their arrival, Edwin Roberts and Lewis Jones discovered that the help they had expected from the Argentine government was not forthcoming. The country was at war with Paraguay and priorities lay elsewhere. Help came instead from the British residents of Buenos Aires.

Two ships were hired, and Roberts and Jones sailed for Patagones (almost 500 kilometres north of Puerto Madryn) to stock up on provisions. From there, 500 cattle were to be herded overland to their new home. The pair then sailed onwards to Golfo Nuevo. They arrived in mid-June.

Already behind schedule, the Welshmen were to suffer further setbacks. Jones returned to Patagones for more supplies, only to discover that their cattle had been stolen. Back at Golfo Nuevo, Roberts had been abandoned by servants while digging a well; it was two days before he got out. When the immigrants arrived on July 27, preparations were not far advanced. There was no accommodation onshore. A wooden storehouse *had* been built, and overnight, some of the newly arrived sheltered there. Mothers and young children returned to the ship; many slept exposed to the elements.

Today, in Puerto Madryn, off the road near the Museo del Desembarco, a monument records the names of those who arrived on the *Mimosa*. A boardwalk leads the short distance from the monument to a rocky sea front. From the boardwalk's furthest point, to the left along the shore, shallow indents can be seen in the soft, chalk-like substance that forms the low cliff face. Quite open to the elements, these manmade caves were homes to the settlers for a time.

The Museo del Desembarco is steps away. As I enter, the strains of a soft, choral version of 'Abide with Me' drift from overhead speakers; 'Flower of Scotland' follows in its wake. At points around the small museum, A4-size cards, mounted alongside exhibits, tell the story of Welsh settlement in the area. The colony's flag hangs on a wall: horizontal stripes of Argentine blue, white and blue, a red Welsh dragon in the white centre. A Patagonian Welsh kitchen sits in one corner; a radio here kept residents of the town of Gaiman in touch with the progress of World War II in Europe. Beside the kitchen, a map shows Puerto Madryn and Nefyn, *ciudades hermanas* (sister cities). From the museum's speakers, 'Jerusalem' and 'Danny Boy' complete the short musical tour of the British Isles, and 'Abide with Me' plays once more. An A4 card provides more information about Edwin Roberts and his unfortunate experience at the bottom of the well. Having previously dug to a depth of eight metres, Roberts had climbed down a rope to begin another day's work. At this point, for an unknown reason, his labourers pulled up the rope and left. 'After 30 hours', the card goes on, 'Jerry, a half-breed Irish Hindu, helped him out of his predicament'. Jerry's good deed marks the end of the museum's displays. The circuit hasn't taken long to complete and I consider a second lap. But by now 'Flower of Scotland' is playing for a third time; time to move on.

Not long after the immigrants arrived at Golfo Nuevo, it was decided that the men should make their way overland to the Chubut valley, where they intended to settle, almost 65 kilometres away. Exhausted by their lengthy overseas journey, and short of food and water, they faced a difficult trek. Eventually they reached the site of an old fort, which they named *Caer Antur* (Fort Adventure).

Back at Golfo Nuevo, spirits were low. There were four deaths while the men were away. Lewis Jones, who had again sailed to Patagones for supplies, had not yet returned. When he did arrive in early September, his ship was accompanied by another, the *Río Negro*, carrying a regiment of soldiers. The women at Golfo Nuevo were then transported to the mouth of the Chubut river, from where they made their way to Caer Antur. The ongoing difficult conditions took their toll; some women became seriously ill, a number of infants died.

The soldiers on the *Río Negro* were there to perform the official handover of lands on behalf of the government. At a formal ceremony, Argentine and Welsh flags were raised, and the just-named settlement of Caer Antur was re-christened Pueblo de Rawson. This didn't overly please the immigrants, who, thereafter, gave the town's name a Welsh spin; they called it TreRawson (Tre – town, in Welsh).

Immediately, the settlers went to work. A wooden storehouse was built. A basic construction housed the school; simple mud cottages sheltered the families. In time, land was cleared, farms were assigned and the immigrants moved inland, spreading through the valley of the Chubut river.

45

The following afternoon, I decide to visit Trelew (pronounced Tre-leh-oo), one of the original Welsh towns in the region. Not far from Puerto Madryn, it was founded as a result of the construction of the Chubut Central Railway. Work started on the railway in 1886. One crew, made up entirely of married men, began inland and laid rails from the Chubut valley towards the sea. A second crew, all single men, worked from Puerto Madryn in the opposite direction. The end point of the line in the valley became Trelew, named for Lewis Jones (Tre, and Lew, from Lewis).

At the station in Puerto Madryn, I have trouble locating the Maryvale bus. It is easier to find once I realise that it's a *Mar y valle* (sea and valley) bus that I need. Soon, I'm travelling the dusty 60 kilometres south to Trelew. A short stroll from the station there, at the junction of 9 de Julio and Fontana, a monument celebrates the *'centenario de la colonización Galesa de la Patagonia'* in 1965. The structure is a marble mini-obelisk, a tribute from the *'sociedad San David de Trelew'*. Behind it is the Museo Regional Pueblo de Luís. Its exhibits, my guidebook informs me, cover the history of Welsh settlement.

I'm the museum's only visitor, and this gets me the personal attention of the museum's sole attendant. María, my good-looking hostess, is in her late thirties. She has on jeans and a shirt; her straight, black hair falls almost the length of her back; hair clips pin it back at the temples.

When I tell her where I'm from (no María, not Holanda, Irlanda; in almost all cases, the answer to the 'Where are you from?' question is interpreted as the former), she informs me that her ex-husband is also Irish (Irish-Argentine, she means).

'Lynch is his name, Patrick Lynch', she tells me in Spanish. 'And his father is Patrick. They're all Patrick. Is Patrick a common name in Ireland?'

'*Sí*', I tell her, '*San Patricio es el…*' – I struggle for the word.

'*Patrono*', she offers, filling in the not-too-dissimilar blank.

She's taken aback when I tell her my own surname.

Our conversation strays into English. María is holding a bible in her right hand. She's reading through it, she tells me. Although raised Catholic, she no longer goes to church. She doesn't believe in saints and the Virgin and crossing herself and going to Mass.

'I talk directly to God', she says.

The book's title is *Santa Biblia*. She wonders what *Santa* means in English. 'Holy', I tell her. As we chat, she plays with her hair with her left hand. She twirls it and flicks it behind her ear and combs down its full length with her fingers.

María retreats to her office and leaves me to look around. The museum is made up of seven rooms which track the early history of Welsh settlement in more or less chronological order. In one room, various cabinets show the personal effects of the first settlers: a diary from 1877, an appointment book from 1878. In another, there's a '*Pinza para enrular el cabello*'. Its accompanying, enjoyably quirky, translation tells me it's 'a tweezers to make hair curly', a curling tongs. There's a shawl, a sunshade, shoes and hats and large framed photographs of the immigrants.

From time to time, María returns to see how I'm getting on. At one point, I'm looking at a framed newspaper report from 1899 about a '*gran inundación*'. '*En Inglés?*', she asks, pointing at '*inundación*'. I make out that it means 'flood'. She laughs at the word and asks me to repeat it. She is interested in Northern Ireland. I explain about the 26 counties and the six counties and the religious affiliations. She wants me to name the counties in the north; she likes the sound of Antrim.

The final room in the museum holds the bandoneón (an accordion, used in tango music) played by Domingo Celano. Señor Celano was, apparently, '*El Soberano del Valle*', the King of the Valley. Sharing the display case with the bandoneón is a violin that belonged to a Tom Mulhall, with, beside it, a black-and-white photo of Tom Mulhall's Orchestra. It seems more like a dance band than an orchestra, the slicked-back hair dating it to the 1940s or thereabouts. The band leader himself doesn't appear in the photo, but Mauricio Miguel Mulhall ('Becho') is there. He plays guitar and contrabass; Olivia 'Niña' Mulhall is on piano, a Señor Harris sits at the drums. I'm keen to know more about this Irish-Patagonian outfit, but María can provide no further information. By now, I've reached the last of the exhibits. As María walks me to the door, the picture in my head is of the Tom Mulhall Big Band entertaining waltzing patrons in the ballrooms of southern Argentina.

46

Towards the turn of the twentieth century, the relationship between the Welsh settlers and their adopted country took a turn for the worse. At the time, military drills were compulsory for all citizens. But they had to take place on a Sunday, and this offended the immigrants' religious beliefs. The authorities in Buenos Aires ruled that the drills could take place on another day, but the governor of the province, José Eugenio Tello, would not allow it. Tello's successor, Carlos O'Donnell, was hostile to the Welsh ('Nero', they called him); he also refused to budge. President Roca visited and announced that they could drill when they wished. But by this time, two of the valley's residents had already travelled to London to voice their dissatisfaction to the government there. When the local authorities in Chubut discovered this, they imprisoned a number of immigrants on trumped-up charges. Eventually, Buenos Aires sent a delegation to report on the ongoing squabble. Nero was dismissed, but relations with the authorities had been soured.

The Welsh were also concerned about the education of their children. In 1878, the government had appointed a national teacher in the valley. Although a Welshman, the new teacher was Catholic, and the settlers worried about his influence. In addition, a growing Argentine nationalism meant that the authorities were keen that schoolgoers should learn about the history and culture of Argentina. Then, in 1896, new legislation ruled that classes in all national schools were to be conducted in Spanish. The settlers were angry at what they saw as official interference in how they educated their children. And they feared for the effects on their community of what they saw as the continual erosion of their identity. In the short term, the 1896 law was ignored. In any case, most of their teachers could speak only Welsh. To counteract the government measures, an intermediate school was founded. An important development, it provided a secondary education taught in the Welsh language, something unavailable even in Wales at the time.

Further disillusionment set in with the *gran inundación* of 1899. Constant rain over several weeks caused the Chubut to burst its banks. The settlers headed for higher ground and no lives were lost, but the flood caused widespread damage. Over 100 houses were ruined. Chapels, post offices and schoolhouses were destroyed. Help arrived from Buenos Aires, but the river flooded again on three further occasions.

The combination of natural disaster and what was perceived as official harassment caused many to question their long-term future in Patagonia. Soon after the floods, two settlers left for Canada. The Canadian government sent a representative to Patagonia to promote resettlement in their country. More immigrants departed at their own expense. Others were keen to leave but couldn't afford it. In Britain, funds were raised, with donations from, among others, the Prince of Wales and members of Parliament. In 1902, 230 settlers sailed for Liverpool from Puerto Madryn. From there, 208 continued on to Canada.

47

Gaiman, says one guidebook, 'is the largest Welsh settlement outside of Wales'. Founded in 1874, it is twelve kilometres inland from Tre-leh-oo. The town is famous for its five Welsh teahouses; Princess Diana had a cuppa here during a visit in 1995. Here, also, another guidebook says, Welsh is still spoken on the streets. It is a 'pure' Welsh, it says, that has changed little since the first settlers arrived (sometimes, I would soon discover, guidebooks really do come out with total bollocks).

From a large roundabout on the edge of Gaiman, a short walk leads to a narrow, wooden footbridge that spans the green water of the Río Chubut. Over the bridge, on the right, Plaza Julio A Roca lies parallel to the river; blue, green and yellow concrete benches sit on the paths that run through it. Along the side of the plaza, between it and the Chubut, an empty stream bed seems to make the '*Prohibido Bañarse*' (No Swimming) sign superfluous. A bust of San Martín sits in the centre of the square, erected by the townspeople in the '*Año del Libertador*', 1950. The bust is a *Monumento Histórico*; this fails to impress one local who has painted tears and a moustache in white on to the face of the bronze Libertador.

Also in the plaza, a plaque pays tribute to '*los pioneros inmigrantes*'. It's difficult to avoid evidence of *inmigrantes* in Gaiman. On the way into town a large wooden sign, complete with Welsh dragon and crown and plumes, advertises the Caerdydd Casa de té Gales (Cardiff Welsh Teahouse). A party in the upcoming elections has a Griffiths and a Goodman on the ticket. On Avenida Eugenio Tello, parallel to the river on the other side of the square, a sign in a shop window advertises the *2011 Eisteddfod de la Juventud* (Youth Eisteddfod) in mid-September. (An Eisteddfod is like a Welsh Fleadh Cheoil, with musical performances and arts and literature events.) Evidence of Welsh settlement is all around.

I escape Tello's roaring car engines and heavy fumes, turn right at the end of the plaza, and aim back towards the river. Here, on Calle M D Jones, the Plas-y-Coed tea shop is '*Ar agor*' (open). Inside this small, tidy rectangle of a room, all tables are set for four. Each has two tablecloths, one in red overlaid with another in yellow in such a way as to leave a triangle of underlying red at each corner. Each place-setting has a red napkin. The chairs have red cushions. Pictures have red frames. Welsh red is all around. The walls, though, are yellow. What you can see of the walls, that is, because they are mostly covered with hanging tea towels. Tea towels show the castles of north Wales, the castles of south Wales and Carreg Cennen Castle. Others have details of Welsh recipes, Welsh cakes, the Welsh language, Welsh music and so on. To the left, Welsh dolls and a Welsh harp sit on the mantelpiece over a red-brick fireplace. On the wall above them are love-spoons (carved wooden spoons traditionally exchanged between lovers) and a love-spoon tea towel. By the fireplace, a door leads to a small room filled with arts, crafts, photographs…and tea towels.

On a stand in the main room, the open pages of a visitor's book have messages in Welsh and Spanish. I take a seat at a table near the front door. Behind me, a bookcase is built into the wall. Its mostly hard-backed contents are in Welsh, Spanish and English. The bookcase has no tea towels.

The menu is short on choice. It's tea and cakes, or it's tea and cakes, just different portions and variations. But the cheapest option is a very expensive 65 pesos, nearly £10 sterling. Bloody hell! I check again. But no, there's nothing cheaper. I'm about to leave, but I'm the only person here and the waitress is now standing over me. I tell myself I'll probably never again be in a Patagonian Welsh tea shop (at these prices, it's a fucking certainty!). I choose something from the menu. I go for tea and cakes.

Soon, the waitress returns with a pot of tea. The pot is enormous. You might find one this size on an Irish farmer's table for Sunday dinner when the relations come round...all of them. A red-and-yellow knitted tea-cosy sits on the pot. On its days off, the tea-cosy might double as a sleeping bag. Soon, a large oval plate arrives, laden with slices of cakes and tarts and breads. I'm determined to get my money's worth and launch into them, but get less than half-way through. I swill as much tea as I can, then lift the pot to gauge its remaining contents; it's more than half full. I hand over the pesos, undo my belt a notch and go for air. There's an ocean of tea in my belly. I splosh out on to the street. Ten quid! I leave the tea shop feeling totally stuffed and slightly screwed at the same time.

The Museo Histórico Regional Galés (Welsh Regional History Museum) is a short waddle from the the pastry-peddling hustlers of Plas-y-Coed. The museum is housed in the town's old railway station building (the Chubut Central Railway closed in 1961). Its green, corrugated-iron roof has a handsome, white, painted wooden trim at the eaves. From below this, a shelter extends from the face of the building, supported at the edge of the footpath by four evenly spaced white wooden posts.

As I enter the *museo*, an attendant steps from a small office inside the door. In his late thirties, Fabio is dressed casually in jeans and a warm jacket; he has black, bushy hair and a beard, and wears round

John Lennon-style glasses. As we chat, he half-removes the glasses to consult a book in his office. They hang by a single arm from his left ear, the eye-pieces somehow dangling in place under his chin. Our conversation, which begins in a mish-mash of Spanish and English, soon reverts fully to English. When he learns where I'm from, Fabio informs me that the current mayor of Trelew is a Mac Karthy, with a 'K' (and a space). Yesterday, I'd seen the name daubed on a wall on my way through the town.

In one of the museum's small rooms, Fabio leads me to a hand-drawn map in a glass case. It's from 1886 and shows the division of land in the Chubut valley. The valley is a long finger stretching inland from Rawson to Trelew and Gaiman, and on to Dolovan (*Dôl Afon* – River Meadow) and 28 de Julio. Farms of one square kilometre were assigned to settlers along its length. Plots are marked on the map, the immigrants' names noted within the squares assigned to them: Rhys, Parry, Owen, Williams, Matthews. Fabio points to the name of Juan Doyle, an Irish *marinero* (sailor) who had arrived prior to the Welsh migration. Canny Juan had managed to wangle a plot. When the sons of these settlers were grown, no further land was available locally. Some moved west, and founded the towns of Esquel and Trevelin (*Tre Felin* – Mill Town), near the border with Chile.

The Welsh built canals, the first irrigation system in Argentina, watering land for a number of kilometres on either side of a stretch of the Chubut. One of these canals was the empty 'stream' I'd seen by the plaza. It is 'switched off' in May and 'opened' again in September.

I quiz Fabio about the 'pure' Welsh spoken on the streets of Gaiman. No-one speaks Welsh in public these days, he says, and they haven't for a long time. It would have been considered impolite, for example, for Welsh-speakers to have a conversation in a shop to the exclusion of their Spanish-speaking neighbours. The language is almost dead, knowledge of it confined to a very small number of older people here and in Trelew.

As well as their language, the settlers brought with them their religion. The first chapel was built in Rawson in 1873, and a second, nearby, in the following decade. As the immigrants spread through the valley, more chapels were built to service their needs. The museum gumpf says that, in total, more than 30 were built. This seems an extraordinary number, given the relatively small size of the community. It is explained perhaps by the dispersed nature of settlement and the difficulty of nineteenth-century travel. Sixteen chapels remain in use today.

No less striking than the number of chapels is the range of religious denominations. There are Anglicans, Baptists, Methodists and Methodist Calvinists, the Independent Congregation, the Congregation of Independent Protestants, the United Denominations and the Union of Free Churches.

Before I know it, it is 5.30 and the museum is about to close. Fabio apologises for having taken up my time. I assure him there is no need to apologise. I was delighted with the chat. It had taken my mind off the churning sea of tea in my stomach.

48

Bahía Blanca, on the coast, is ten hours north of Puerto Madryn. The city hasn't a great deal to encourage a visitor to linger, but it *is* a convenient stop-off point on my lengthy return to Buenos Aires. Besides being conveniently situated for the long-distance traveller, Bahía Blanca also has a place in Irish-Argentine history, the location of an unhappy episode that took place towards the end of the nineteenth century.

In mid-February 1889, the *City of Dresden* arrived at the docks in Buenos Aires. Its almost 2,000 passengers were participants in a migration scheme organised by agents of the Argentine government in Ireland, Buckley O'Meara and John S Dillon. Initially, the agents had had difficulty enticing people to travel to South America. But they overcame this minor obstacle, and in the process gained a handsome agent's commission, by lying prodigiously. Prospective migrants were promised not only houses, but also good land, and machinery and implements with which to work it.

When they stepped ashore in Buenos Aires, the new arrivals were left to fend for themselves. At first, they found shelter at the Hotel de Inmigrantes in the city. There, they slept on bare floors, and on flagstones in a courtyard. Appeals for help went out to the Irish-Argentine community. A lucky few picked up work on the estates of wealthy landowners. Some women found refuge in an Irish convent in the capital; others drifted into the city's red-light district.

Around this time, a colony had been set up in Bahía Blanca by David Gartland, a wealthy Irish-American businessman. At the end of

February, 800 *City of Dresden* migrants arrived at Napostá, north of the city. Overnight, they slept by the railway tracks, exposed to the elements. Next morning, they made their way 24 kilometres south, to the site of the colony. There, they found neither houses nor materials with which to build them; Gartland had run out of money. The immigrants made do with what shelter they could find. Over the next two years, they struggled to scrape an existence from inhospitable land. Eventually, overcome by the effort, they abandoned the site and returned to Buenos Aires. Over 100 settlers had died in their short time in Bahía Blanca; more deaths followed on the long trek to the capital.

Today, La Viticola railway station stands on the site of the abandoned colony. At a ceremony in 2010, a plaque was unveiled there to honour the immigrants of the *City of Dresden*; I thought I'd pay it a visit.

As the overnight bus comes to a halt in Bahía Blanca, my straggly-haired neighbour in the window seat reaches out his hand.

'Some day we meet in Ireland', he says.

Last night in Puerto Madryn, no sooner had I dropped into my seat, than he had offered me a sweet from a bag he was dipping into. Moments later, as I was foostering blindly in my daypack, he gave me the use of his flashlight. I figured he wanted to chat.

'My girlfriend's grandfather was from Ireland', he told me, once we had negotiated the initial Holanda/Irlanda hurdle. 'She is Irene MacCarthy.'

I mention Mac Karthy, the mayor of Tre-leh-oo, but his girlfriend's surname is spelt with a 'C'. It's the more usual spelling, I tell him.

My companion's name is Roberts. His Welsh great-grandfather had arrived in the area around 1880, some years after the original settlers. After a time, he moved west, to the town of Esquel.

'And your girlfriend's grandfather?'

'He had to run away', he said, 'after the revolution in 1914. He was a Protestant.'

'Yes, 1916', I say, assuming he is referring to the Easter Rising.

Keen to know more about Grandad MacCarthy's enforced flight from Ireland, I'm about to quiz my companion further when the on-board movie blares into life. Further chat is impossible, I nod off before the movie finishes and wake only as the bus rolls into the station at Bahía Blanca early the following morning. I shake the straggly-haired one's proffered hand, disappointed not to have satisfied my curiosity about the family history of the Patagonian MacCarthys.

The station terminal at Bahía Blanca is a wide, airy rectangle. Bus company ticket desks line one side of the building; on the other, tall glass doors open on to departure bays. Shops and desks run down the centre of the concourse. At Information, I enquire about a bus to La Vitícola and am pointed in the direction of a separate Tourist Information desk. There, the *hombre* gives me a tourist map of the city. Which is fine, if a little unexpected, as I'd asked him for bus times. I try again. He seems to be telling me that I can't get the bus I want from here. But I'm having trouble understanding him. I ask if he can speak a little more slowly (*'un poco más lento por favor'*). He gets exasperated, I get frustrated and we abandon our difficult conversation.

I turn to the queue of taxis by the side of the building. Here, an expensive quote sends me scuttling back to Information. By now, my body is drooping under the weight of my bags, and I enquire about a left-luggage office. The station doesn't have one, I'm told. I'm directed instead to a shop across the road from the terminal. There, a sour-faced woman sits on a high stool behind the counter. She informs me that it's 10 pesos to deposit my bags for the day. This is very reasonable. When I take in my surroundings, I realise that I'm in a small grocery shop that does a sideline in luggage storage. I glance over my hostess's shoulder. She follows my eyes to an open space where bags and suitcases are piled in a heap on the floor. I ask if she has a safe area for luggage. She points to the pile. Tempted by her pricing, but unconvinced by the security of her operation, I thank her and gather my bags to leave. I don't think she's pleased. As I make for the door, her face achieves the almost-impossible and appears even more sour and thin-lipped.

Outside the shop, I pause for a moment to take stock. I can't get information on buses, taxis are expensive and there's nowhere to securely store my luggage. I'm making very little progress in my attempt to reach La Vitícola. I retreat to the station café. Here, it seems that the owner has attended the same customer service classes as Sourpuss, the luggage lady. His mouth is an unwelcoming straight line – service with a grimace. I decide to enquire again about buses. Back at Tourist Information, the attendant's face drops when he sees me approach. Another struggle of a conversation yields nothing new about buses. But he does direct me to a train station, a twenty-minute walk away. The service is irregular, he warns me. But I'm in no rush.

Shifting bags between achey shoulders, the trudge through bare streets takes more than twice as long as expected. The railway terminal building, impressive from a distance, is, closer at hand, old and quite worn out. It *does* have a left-luggage office, although a glance through the padlocked door, half-hanging from its hinges, suggests that nothing new has been left there in a long time.

'*Un tren a La Vitícola?*', I ask the attendant in an office on the platform.

I split the place name in two, and pronounce it Viti-cola, like Coca-Cola. He asks me to repeat it.

'Ah, La Vi*t*icola…', he smiles, stressing the second syllable.

'…*Mañana*', he carries on.

I hadn't quite figured on the service being *that* irregular.

Frequent pauses to ease the burden on my shoulders mean that my weary return to the bus station takes even longer than the slog in the opposite direction had done. I'm worn out, and as I pass Sourpuss's shop, her lack of super-tight security suddenly seems to matter very little. Inside, she is seated in the same spot behind the counter. I make to offer her my bags.

'*No tengo lugar*' (I have no space), she hisses.

I glance over her shoulder. The luggage pile has not increased in size since my earlier visit. I turn back to Sourpuss; she's all thin lips and hard eyes. I smile, thank her and cross the road to the terminal.

I make a third attempt to get bus times, but the Tourist Information desk is now closed. I suspect the *hombre* has fled for the day rather than suffer another of my visits. Back at the taxi rank, a second quote is dearer than the first. It is now early afternoon and I'm all out of options: buses, taxis, trains. The plaque at La Vitícola will remain unseen.

I had planned to stay overnight in Bahía Blanca, but now I can't wait to leave. I buy a ticket for a bus to Buenos Aires, leaving at 10pm. This leaves me with a lot of time to kill. The Revenge of Sourpuss has ensured that I remain chained to my bags and I'm unable to stray far. The terminal is a Wi-Fi-free zone, so mindless internet browsing is not an option. I buy a *Buenos Aires Herald* from the terminal's small shop and join the café's grumpy owner for another coffee. Before long, I've read the paper from cover to cover; and still, there are hours to wait.

49

Finally, I escape Bahía Blanca and next morning reach Buenos Aires. It's a brief stop-off; I'm on my way to the Iguazú Falls (from a Guaraní term, meaning 'great water'). One of the world's great attractions, the falls are at the northern tip of the country, near where Argentina, Brazil and Paraguay meet, and eighteen hours overnight in a bus from the capital.

Today, a volcanic ash cloud has disrupted all flights from the city, an intervention neatly timed to coincide with the start of a two-week holiday period in Argentina. On Friday evening, Retiro is thronged. My bus, leaving at 9pm, is one of ten departures scheduled for the same time.

Tonight, Argentina play Uruguay in the quarter-finals of the Copa América. In the terminal, Argentine flags fly from the ceiling for the length of the concourse. Small pay-TV screens broadcast the game in packed waiting areas by the departure bays. One youngster watches on a mobile phone, through a magnifying glass. I snaffle a stray seat in the crowded station café and watch through to the end of the first half (1–1 as I leave; Uruguay go on to win on penalties).

On the bus, waiting to depart, my attention is drawn to the TV hanging from the ceiling. An oval DVD logo floats about on the idling screen. When it 'bounces' off the edge of the screen, the logo's colour changes to red, or orange, or greeny-blue. I try to anticipate the colour that will accompany the next bounce, but there appears to be no set pattern. After a few minutes of this, I decide that, once I reach Iguazú, I really do need to get out for a beer. As the bus moves off, the logo is replaced by a video with information about facilities on board. The detail of one of the video's messages is underlined further by a sign on the toilet door:

Pis: Si   *Caca: No*

It's a long and uneventful journey north. Excitement peaked with the DVD logo.

There's a torrential downpour in Puerto Iguazú as the bus pulls in, late on Saturday afternoon. Thankfully, the skies have emptied by the following morning, and it's a dry walk to the station for a bus to the Iguazú National Park. Covering 677 square kilometres of subtropical rainforest, the Park is a UNESCO World Heritage Site. From its entrance, the Rainforest Ecological Train travels eight kilometres to the Cataratas (Waterfalls) Station (the train runs on a narrow-gauge track and can carry up to 150 passengers). Nearby, the Iguazú river falls off the edge of the Paraná plateau. Numerous small 'islands' on the edge of the escarpment over which the water plunges mean that the falls are, in fact, 275 separate cataracts. Today, it's as if the crowds from Retiro have relocated northwards. Boardwalks are jammed and viewing platforms are like heaving terraces at a football match. Sharp elbows are required to get a decent view of the showpiece, the *Garganta del Diablo* (the Devil's Throat), where water thunders 82 metres over a U-shaped precipice. It is breathtaking.

Later, on a ramble through the town of Puerto Iguazú, the streets are bone-dry. Last night, rain had flowed along them in rushing rivulets, swamping the small supermarket at an intersection downhill from the hostel where I'm staying. This evening, a carpet of cardboard over much of the supermarket's floor soaks up any remaining moisture. There is not a great deal else to do in Puerto Iguazú except view the Falls. Tomorrow I'm moving on, southwest, to the Jesuit Mission at San Ignacio Miní.

50

It takes almost three hours to get to San Ignacio. On the platform of the bus station there, I ask an official for directions to where I'm staying. She's not sure, and asks a colleague. The colleague, in turn, calls on a passer-by. All three agree that they don't know where it is and point me to a taxi.

My pre-booked bed at the hostel has been taken; I'm directed instead to a house around the block, down a bumpy, unsealed road of dark, impacted, red earth. Here, the owner, Monica, leads me to my single room in a separate one-storey building to one side of her garden. This building has another couple of bedrooms, an outdoor communal kitchen and a tiled terrace. Two hanging chairs bolted to the roof of the terrace are like deckchairs without legs. I drop my bags and ask Monica how to get to the centre of town. She tells me I'm in it.

San Ignacio Miní is a short walk away. The mission, founded in 1610, had originally been sited in the state of Paraná, Brazil. After attacks by *bandeirantes* (slave traders), it was moved to an intermediate location before, in 1696, the Jesuits finally settled here, in the San Ignacio valley. Once, there were 30 mission settlements of Guaraní in the region, within the territories of modern-day Argentina, Brazil and Paraguay. Called *Reducciones* (settlements of Christianised indigenous Americans, anglicised as Reductions), in 1732 they held over 140,000 people. A grouping of seven of these missions has been declared a UNESCO World Heritage Site. San Ignacio Miní (minor, in Guaraní) is one of the best preserved.

The gable ends of long, single-storey dwelling blocks line the approach to the *reducción*. Through the entrance is the plaza, the main hub of the mission settlement. More dwelling blocks face the square, left and right. Directly ahead is the church: on one side is a courtyard and workshops, on the other, a cemetery, with separate burial sites for men, women, children and the stillborn. The Guaraní lived in the housing blocks, the priests in a residence to the rear of the church. Built from local sandstone, the roofs of the buildings have crumbled away. Rust-red standing walls are all that remain.

The missions were well-organised and successful production units. Some men worked as carpenters, smiths and craftsmen. More tended crops of corn, wheat, cotton and yerba mate. Women maintained the home, spun and wove. Both sexes produced art, religious and otherwise.

The indigenous people were converted to Christianity, but weren't fully westernised; some elements of local culture were retained (the official language of the mission was Guaraní). The Jesuits did, however, introduce the Christian concept of monogamy.

For some Guaraní, the *reducciones* represented progress, a guarantee of regular food, and protection from other tribes. For others, life here meant a loss of freedom, and subjection to a regulated way of life to which they were not accustomed. Many thrived, others returned to the forest.

Away from the mission, a casino sits on the main road that bypasses San Ignacio, its tall façade all twinkling lights. It seems out of place here, in this small, plain town of low houses, as if removed from a city location and dropped, randomly, in the countryside. The town itself is a collage of different shades of red: the deep red earth of unsealed roads, the bright and darker tones of the mission's standing walls, the red dust that covers pavement slabs. The underbelly of a passing white dog has an earthen, auburn tint.

Next morning, what I had thought was something falling on to the roof of the shower room is in fact a loud clap of thunder overhead. It is pouring with rain, sheeting down in that subtropical way, and has been for hours now. I had woken earlier to a full-throated, early morning chorus from the local cockerel. He seems to have recovered his voice today. Yesterday evening, attempted crowings were strangulated efforts, cut off half-way through.

I plan to return further south for a few days, to Rosario. Today, a bus from San Ignacio will take me 60 kilometres west to Posadas, from where I can pick up an onward connection. I ask Monica if she can order a taxi to take me to the station. '*Tranquilo*', she says gently, putting me at my ease when I get tangled up in Spanish words.

I make it in time for the 11.15am departure. When I reach Posadas, I have a five-hour wait at the station there, a trifling inconvenience after my recent, marathon endurance session in Bahía Blanca. It is still raining. The station is murky and dull. In the toilet, you must pay for loo paper and only one cubicle has a working lock. The cubicle is tiny and, with luggage, it becomes impossible. I end up sitting sideways, my knees part-way up the wall.

51

Rosario is the easiest place from which to visit the town of Venado Tuerto, a further 150 kilometres to the southwest. Venado Tuerto was founded in 1884 by Irish-Argentine Eduardo Casey. Casey was born in 1847 at Lobos, in the province of Buenos Aires, to Lawrence Casey of Westmeath and Mary O'Neill of County Wicklow. Lawrence Casey had arrived in Argentina around 1830 and was the first man in the country to pay one million pesos for a league of land (the Spanish used the league as a unit of area measurement; one league is almost 1,800 hectares. Some years later, in 1879, his son Eduardo bought 72 leagues of land from the government (c. 130,000 hectares), on which Venado Tuerto was built (the town's name, which translates as 'One-Eyed Deer', had been given by the Mapuche to a nearby lagoon). When Casey started selling plots from this huge purchase, many of the buyers were Irish and English, and place names in the region include Armstrong, Duffy, Hughes, Ham and Cavanagh. These original settlers were soon swamped by an influx of Spanish and especially Italian immigrants. But still, today, Venado Tuerto's airport is Aeródromo Tomás Kenny, Calle Republica de Irlanda forms the town's western border, and Calles Juan Cavanagh and Roberto Cavanagh intersect by the Polo Club, at its northern edge.

From Rosario, much of the journey to Venado Tuerto is through open country. Land, flat on either side of the road, stretches endlessly in the distance. The pampas are not fields, as we understand them. They seem to have no boundaries. Only intermittent clumps of trees break the monotony of the view for as far as the eye can see. I read that Argentines call it the pampa, rather than the pampas. And the singular form seems apt: one, single, broad expanse of land.

Towards the end of the three-hour journey, the bus rolls into the town of Murphy. In 1883, John James Murphy bought more than 18,000 hectares of land from Eduardo Casey. It was Murphy's third *estancia*. His circumstances had improved somewhat from when he had arrived in the country in 1844. Then, he had earned a living digging ditches in Chascomús, south of Buenos Aires. He went on to work as a shepherd on *mediería*. The following decade, he bought his first *estancia*, over 1,800 hectares, at *La Flor del Uncalito* in Salto, 200 kilometres northwest of the city (*uncalito* – eucalyptus; the English word, difficult for Spanish-speakers, ended up as *ucalito* or *uncalito*). Within a year, the steeply rising price of wool had allowed him to pay off his debt. In 1865, in the next-door *partido* of Rojas, he purchased a further 4,000 hectares. At the end of his life, Murphy owned over 28,000 hectares of land. He died in 1909 at his city property in Almagro, Buenos Aires, a successful and wealthy man.

Born at Haysland, in the parish of Kilrane (near Rosslare Harbour), County Wexford, Murphy was 22 when he left Ireland. His younger brothers, William and Pat, joined him in Argentina; remaining family members stayed at home. Edmundo Murray has collected a series of letters (*Becoming Irlandés*), exchanged between the distant branches of the family. As well as providing an insight into Murphy's own life, the author's hugely detailed footnotes provide fascinating information about the lives of Irish settlers at the time. In his letters, Murphy comes across as businesslike, responsible and, occasionally, a sensitive man. He could also be domineering, dismissive of his brothers, and not a little self-satisfied as he tried to impress the folks at home with his achievements.

From the time he bought his first *estancia*, Murphy 'promoted and financed a steady flow of selected emigration from southeast Wexford to Argentina'. His letters contain regular requests for working men to be sent out to him; on occasion, he names those he wants. His brother Martin, in Wexford, facilitated the departure of so many emigrants that he wangled a 5% commission from the shipping company for those passages he arranged. Martin hired the men and paid their fare; in return, the migrants worked for John James for twelve to fourteen months, after which time they were free to do as they pleased.

Murphy would not employ local labour. He felt he could not rely on them. This was indicative of the generally lofty opinion the Irish had of themselves, and the low opinion they had of Argentines. When faced with gauchos and locals, 'the Irish united in a self-perception of British superiority'. As a result, the settlers kept to themselves. Middle-class Irish wanted their children to mix only with fellow Irish (some would remain single rather than marry an Argentine). And until relatively recent times, the wealthy Irish socialised only with each other, the wealthy English and the local bourgeoisie.

The Irish also kept their distance when it came to religion. They resisted integrating with local Catholic society until at least the start of the twentieth century. They insisted on being attended by Irish priests (in the parish church in San Antonio de Areco, a confession box marked 'P. Irlandés' is set aside for those who feel comfortable baring their souls only to an Irish padre). By building and maintaining their own churches, Irish chaplains kept their community intact, but apart from larger society. Among Argentines, this separate institution was known as *la iglesia de los ingleses* (the church of the English).

If the Irish thought that they were socially superior to the locals, it seems that, among themselves, there was also a perceived pecking order. In Buenos Aires province, feuds existed between settlers from Wexford and Westmeath. 'Wexford people thought very highly of themselves', says Edmundo Murray, 'in relation to the Ballinacarryas'. (By Ballinacarryas he means Westmeath people – Ballynacarrigy is a town in Westmeath near the border with Longford.) In *The Forgotten Colony*, Andrew Graham-Yooll reports that in 'the town of Salto Argentino, the parish priest held separate masses each Sunday to avoid a fight. Throughout the century, the church services a family attended were not referred to by their times but by the county of origin of the worshippers attending. However, they did mix at the "native" mass and ushers made sure that seating arrangements were such that rival families were kept apart'. In a letter home, William Murphy mentions that, on a visit to Ireland, a friend from Argentina had received a great reception in Wexford. Edmundo Murray notes that Murphy is delighted to report that the friend had thought the county 'fifty years in advance of Westmeath'.

In the 1860s, as more Irish emigrants flowed into the country, John James Murphy considered the newly arrived to be socially inferior to the migrants of his vintage. This was an opinion shared by the wealthier Irish landowners who, by the end of the nineteenth century, were, unsurprisingly, more socially at ease with the local Argentine bourgeoisie than with new immigrants from Ireland. Successful Irish settlers often perceived themselves to be of a higher social class. Some believed, as do their descendants, that their families had belonged to the upper echelons of society in Ireland.

The language of Murphy's *estancias* was English, although words of Spanish did seep into common use. He writes of *senaling* the sheep (*señalar* – to stamp, mark out, ie: to brand), the weather is a constant concern, particularly times of *seca* (drought), and he speaks proudly of the handsome mount planted on his land (*monte* – woodland, a grove of trees). The ongoing use of English by settlers was far from unusual. For most Irish, Spanish did not become their first language until the early decades of the twentieth century. Some remained more proficient in English even into the 1950s.

When they arrived in Argentina, most immigrants were taken aback by the native way of life. Unable to settle, many returned to Ireland or re-emigrated to the United States (between 1869 and 1895, it is estimated that, among the Irish, one person re-emigrated for every migrant that arrived). Murphy reconciled himself to his new situation, realising that he had landed in the right place at the right time. Still though, twenty years and more after his departure from Ireland, his letters are full of pining for the companionship of those he left behind. He continually expresses a wish to spend the rest of his life with friends and family, either in Argentina or in Ireland. For Murphy, home was not so much related to geography; it was more the company of neighbours from Kilrane. Like many immigrants, his mind is in two places. His working life is on his *estancias* in Argentina, his social links remain in southeast Wexford.

John James Murphy never quite got over his homesickness. He returned to Ireland on two occasions, planning to live there from the proceeds of his land in Argentina. He stayed between 1861 and 1863, and returned again with his wife and four children in 1878. Tragically, in 1879, his daughter Catalina (Kitty), 'a lovely fair-haired happy child of ten', contracted scarlatina (scarlet fever) and died. Later, Kitty's brother wrote: 'In those days scarlatina was fatal. No-one dared go near them for fear of contagion. The other children had been sent down to Haysland, my father's old home, where his sister and invalid brother lived. She [J J Murphy's sister] and the children went to see the funeral passing towards Kilrane Churchyard. My mother [in the funeral procession] said it nearly broke her heart to see the three small ones on the side of the road watching the funeral pass, not realising it was their little sister'. Later, in 1881, a son, Martin Herbert, also died. Murphy was distraught: 'I am leaving and not coming back; the Argentine has never treated me like this'. The following year, he returned to Argentina and never again visited Ireland. Murphy named his residence in Mar del Plata (a beach resort, c. 400 kilometres south of Buenos Aires) *La Angelita* (The Little Angel). His son says that they all knew 'it was in memory of little Kitty in heaven whom he adored, but [he] never mentioned her...until two days before he died'.

Today, says Edmundo Murray, most residents of Murphy know nothing about the man for whom their small, dusty town is named.

52

An old lady sitting on a wall outside the bus station in Venado Tuerto tells me it's *ocho cuadras* to the centre of town. On the way, every lamppost is hung with election posters. In a slight variation on a theme, one local candidate states that '*el cambio continúa*' (the change continues). The president, Cristina Fernández de Kirchner (CFK, according to newspapers), appears, smiling, with her local team.

In the town's central plaza, San Martín sits on a rearing horse, facing west (someone told me that all mounted statues of San Martín face the Andes). Nearby, a slim, bronze deer is the *venado tuerto* of the town's name. By the road, on the opposite side of the square from which I had arrived, a statue is set on a plinth, a tribute from '*El Pueblo de Venado Tuerto*' to Don Eduardo Casey, on the 75th anniversary of the establishment of the town (1883–1958). Casey has a beard and swept-back hair, and wears a knee-length frock coat buttoned at the chest. He takes up a statesmanlike pose, left foot forward, right arm slightly outstretched, palm outwards; in his left hand is a scroll. Plaques on the base of the plinth are tributes from various societies, including the town's Jockey Club. Casey was an accomplished horseman. As a boy, he and his brother would ride for hours on the open pampas. In later years, he would establish a stud farm to improve the quality of horses on his *estancia* (he once provided Buffalo Bill with ten gaucho horse-breakers for his travelling show). A co-founder, among many, of the prestigious Jockey Club in Buenos Aires, Casey also founded its equivalent here in Venado Tuerto.

The Jockey Club is several *cuadras* away. The building is plain, like an office block, all concrete and glass. Small Argentine flags fly at intervals along its front. Inside, official types lounge in the lobby. On the right is a plush dining room, out back, clay tennis courts and a swimming pool. I was hoping I might find some memorial to the club's founder here, but a brief wander reveals nothing. More members arrive in the lobby, I get some sideways glances, take my cue and make for the door.

Nearby, on Calle Alvear, I drop into Molly Malone's for a late lunch. The L-shaped bar has dark wood panelling on the walls, dark wood tables, and a tiled and wooden floor. Among the usual posters ('Best of Dublin's Pubs', 'My Goodness, My Guinness'), one announces that '*Une bonne Guinness ça fait du bien*'. Small, framed movie posters (*The Commitments*, *Michael Collins*) hang near a *Rolling Stone* cover that shows U2, their people of the year at one point. The themed-pub-tat *pièce de résistance*, however, is high in a corner by the door: a pipe-smoking leprechaun standing on a swing. A girl in a green T-shirt takes my food order. Soon, she delivers medallions of pork, with chips cut like crisps. A clear, thin plastic sheet wrapped around the cutlery is secured with a small green, white and orange sticker.

There's a museum in Venado Tuerto that I'd like to visit, in the town's Polo Club, which Google Maps tells me is at this end of town. After lunch, I aim in its direction, down Alvear, past the faded sign for Kenny the optician, towards Avenida Santa Fe. There, at the edge of Parque Municipal General Belgrano, an old guy gets on his knees and sketches directions in the dusty earth. The Polo Club is over a kilometre away he tells me, further than I had thought. At a nearby junction, I spend fifteen unsuccessful minutes trying to flag down a taxi. It is mid-afternoon now and time is running short. My bus to

Rosario leaves at 5.30 and I'm also keen to squeeze in a visit to the town's cemetery. Reluctantly, I abandon plans for the polo museum and return towards the centre of town.

Irish-Argentines have a long association with polo in Argentina, not least here, in Venado Tuerto. In 1887, they figured among the mostly English founders of the town's Polo & Athletic Club. A recent club president was Guillermo Cavanagh, great-grandson of Edward Cavanagh from Mullingar, who arrived in Argentina in 1851. Another was Tomás Kenny, a distinguished surgeon, for whom the town's airport is named (Kenny was married to a daughter of John James Murphy). The club has been a nursery for some of the sport's most distinguished players.

Polo was introduced into Argentina by British *estancieros* in the 1870s. In the first recorded match in 1875, Ciudad played Campo (City vs Country), in a kind of Jackeens vs Culchie showdown (in Ireland, Dubliners are jackeens and the rest of the country are culchies). Campo were easy winners. This was not a great surprise. The *Standard* reported that 'some of Ciudad's players had never seen a match before'.

The sport became popular throughout the country, but especially in Buenos Aires province and here, in southern Santa Fe. In 1893, the Argentine Open Polo Championship was held for the first time. Now one of the most prestigious events in the world game, it takes place at the Hurlingham Club in Buenos Aires. A six-time winner and Argentine legend was Luis Lacey, born in Canada of Irish extraction. A man whom the Prince of Wales (the future King Edward VIII) always wanted on his team, the main field at Hurlingham is named for him.

In 1924, polo provided Argentina with its first gold medal at an Olympic Games. Irish-Argentines Juan Nelson and Arthur Kenny made up two of the four-man team. The gold medal-winning team of 1936 included Luis Duggan and Roberto Cavanagh. In the 1940s, Argentine polo was dominated by clashes between Venado Tuerto, which included brothers Juan and Roberto Cavanagh, and El Trébol (The Shamrock), with Luis Duggan and his brother Heriberto. Venado Tuerto won the Argentine Open in 1944, and from 1946 through to 1950.

Today, Irish names persist. In 2006, the Argentine Polo Association's Juniors Cup was won by the 'Glascorn' team, three of whose members were Guillermo Cavanagh Jr and Guillermo and Francisco McLoughlin. Glascorn was the name of the old McLoughlin homestead in County Westmeath.

53

My trials with the Spanish language show no sign of easing up. Back in the centre of town, I linger by the car at the head of a taxi rank on Avenida Casey. Its driver detaches himself from a group of men chatting on a nearby wall.

'*El cementerio*', I say.

He looks at me blankly.

Again, '*El cementerio*'.

He shakes his head. I repeat it once more. He has no idea what I'm saying.

Deflated, I begin to walk away, but dig out a pen and paper and write the word down.

'Ah,' he exclaims, '*el cementerio*!'

Sweet Jesus!

From the main gate, an avenue of mausoleums leads to the rear of the town's sizeable municipal cemetery. There are Spanish names of course, and many Italian ones, but there are also Heffernans and Nolans and Dunnes, and the Long mausoleum sits across from a vault holding O'Brien family remains. Time, or an errant stonemason, has morphed O'Dwyer into O'Duyer. Off the main avenue, tombs on the 'side streets' resemble rows of tiny, flat-roofed, terraced houses. Each has its own full-size door. One is open just now; inside, two coffins lie one above the other, the length of a side wall, like a bunk bed.

At the end of the main avenue, a tasteful memorial holds the remains of Don Eduardo Casey. At the top of a set of steps, a red-brick wall rises to head-height. Here, a plaque records the date Casey's remains were transferred to this location, on April 26, 1973. To one side, a narrow, white construction, rising like a tall, thin chimney, holds a plain cross.

Eduardo Casey was a pioneer and serial entrepreneur. Born into money, he went on to accumulate enormous wealth of his own. At the age of 30, he owned a farming agent company. The first Argentine to export live cattle to Britain, he co-founded a cold-storage plant and served on the boards of a railway company and the Buenos Aires Provincial Bank. He was also a property developer, a newspaper proprietor and, of course, a landowner. Some years after he had acquired the 72 leagues of land here in Santa Fe, he bought a further 100 leagues in Cura Malal, in the *partido* of Coronel Suárez, in Buenos Aires province. According to Venado Tuerto historian Roberto Landaburu, 'Casey was one of the stars of the 1880s'.

Married to María – a daughter of John Gahan, from Westmeath, and his wife Mary Devitt – Casey had five children. He was a horse-racing fan, a good dancer and singer, a sociable figure. When visiting his lands in southern Santa Fe for the first time, he travelled in the company of friends. One of their supply wagons, liberally attended to on the trip, was set aside solely for wine and champagne. Generous with his wealth, at a request from the Irish ladies of Venado Tuerto, he financed the building of the original church in the town (along with the Virgin, St Patrick is the patron saint of Venado Tuerto).

In the 1880s, along with Thomas Duggan (one of the Duggan brothers from San Antonio de Areco), Casey invested heavily in Uruguay. He was overexposed and after a financial crisis there in 1890, he lost everything. His belongings, down even to his furniture, had to be sold (his brother bought some assets anonymously and returned them to him). He retreated to London in an attempt to get back on his feet. There, he secured loans worth £100,000. In Argentina, he repaid in full the small shareholders who had invested with him. For years, Casey tried to recover his former position. Though still energetic, and with plans and grand schemes, previous acquaintances no longer wanted to listen. In 1906, by this time abandoned by his wife, he threw himself in front of a train in Barracas, in the city of Buenos Aires.

For decades, Casey was a forgotten figure. But the combined efforts of the government, the people of Venado Tuerto, and his grandson Julián Duggan, ensured that his remains, along with those of his wife and two of his children, were finally removed to the town he had founded.

Returning to the bus station from *el cementerio*, I'm in plenty of time for the 5.30 to Rosario. Before long, we're rolling over disused railway tracks on the outskirts of Murphy. Darkness is falling quickly now. Along the edge of the endless pampa, the burnt horizon is sandstone red, like the walls of San Ignacio Miní.

54

After my spin to Venado Tuerto, I spend a lazy weekend in Rosario, catching up on sleep, and strolling by the broad Río Paraná. In a café, on Sunday afternoon, I catch the final of the Copa América. In River Plate's *El Monumental* stadium in Buenos Aires, Diego Forlán scores twice in Uruguay's 3–0 win over Paraguay. Uruguay now have fifteen Copa América titles, one more than rivals Argentina, and are the most successful team in the history of the competition. With these two goals, Forlán has scored 31 times for Uruguay to become his country's joint top-scorer, equalling the record held by Héctor Scarone, the cop-kicking forward from the 1920s.

Almost on a whim, perhaps swayed by their footballing victory, I've decided to return to Uruguay, to visit Punta del Este, a couple of hours east of Montevideo. (I've arranged to meet someone in Salta, northwest Argentina, in two weeks' time. Before then, I plan to spend a week or so in Paraguay; till then, I'm passing time.) For the 850-kilometre journey on Monday night, I've booked a seat on EGA, *Empresa General Artigas*, a bus company named for Uruguay's hero of independence, which, I guess, would be like travelling on Mick Collins' Coaches, or the Eamon Dev Express.

Punta del Este is the playground of South America's rich and famous. Twinned with Marbella, its permanent population of 10,000 jumps to 150,000 in the summer months. The town, which sits on a small peninsula that nudges into the Atlantic Ocean, is well known for its golden beaches and upmarket resorts (it also hosts a high-profile rugby tournament, the Punta del Este Sevens).

Just off the bus after my overnight spin, I'm given instant evidence of the town's swish credentials. In a café near the station, a waiter who has delivered a coffee remains hovering by my table. I have just handed him a 100-peso note (more than £3). Not enough, it seems. I pass him another. The tab for morning caffeine comes to 120 pesos, over £3.80.

My accommodation is inland, a hostel in a pleasant, residential neighbourhood. The owner, Rodrigo, tells me I'm his last customer of the season. Rodrigo is a surfer-dude, with a scraggly beard and long frizzy hair tied in a knot at the back of his head. His hands are permanently shoved deep in his pockets, which may be why the crotch of his jeans is almost at his knees. In a few days, he is closing up for two months to go surfing in Máncora, northern Peru. I mention Montañita, in southern Ecuador, as another popular surfing hangout. Rodrigo launches into a long spiel about rips and tides and swells that explains why Máncora outdoes Montañita as a surfing destination. I've tuned out five minutes before he finishes speaking. Rodrigo is also the only South American I have heard cursing (in English, at least), although his 'fugging' pronunciation removes the harshness from the word.

In the afternoon, I aim for the coast and follow a boardwalk that runs parallel to the shore, behind the town's beach. It's a bright day, but the sun, at mid-height, provides little warmth. A chill wind blows in off the choppy sea. A brisk walk leads to a breakwater that curves into the bay. Its huge boulders protect yachts moored alongside. In calm, open water, within the breakwater's embracing arm, sailing boats are tethered to upturned cones; they're the same as those gun-metal grey ones in Colonia del Sacramento.

Not far from the yachts, a lady estate agent advertises on a poster attached to a telephone pole. She wears a white trouser-suit, and is leggy and blonde and pretty. She welcomes you to '*un estilo de vida*' (a style of living). Clearly, she is saying, live here and you too can meet classy women like me.

It's a brief stay in Punta del Este. My path hasn't crossed that of any blonde, leggy lady estate agent and tonight I'm travelling north, into Brazil. An overnight bus will deposit me in Porto Alegre, capital of the southern state of Rio Grande do Sul, before I pick up an onward connection to Florianópolis, a further 500 kilometres along the coast.

On board, sidekick-girl asks for my passport. We'll be crossing into Brazil in the wee hours and she will deal with the formalities at the border. I'm uneasy letting the passport out of my sight, but it seems to be standard procedure. In the morning, she gently shakes me awake and returns it to me. Last night, at the ticket desk in Punta del Este, the attendant had put a small, numbered sticker on the passport's back cover, my seat number, enabling the organised redistribution of travel documents this morning.

Soon, breakfast is served: a very sweet coffee (nothing is ever sweet enough in South America) with a snack of water biscuits and an *alfajor*. An *alfajor* is a relatively recent discovery. It's a biscuit sandwich. There are many variations, but typically it's two shortbread-type biscuits with a *dulce de leche* (gooey caramel) filling, the whole often smothered in a chocolate coating. Exquisite.

As the day brightens, I take in the surrounding countryside. Southern Brazil in midwinter is not the Brazil of the imagination. This is a cold, early morning in farming country. In the mid-distance, mist lingers at the base of low hills. Close at hand, soggy green fields lie beyond red, earthen banks. At one point, we pass the cab of a lorry, half-sunk in boggy ground off the road, its backside sticking out into the left-hand lane. Soon, shacks and poorly built houses signal our approach to Porto Alegre. Sidekick-girl marks the end of the journey with the offer of boiled sweets from a bowl.

In Portuguese-speaking territory now, it is not long before I thud into the language barrier. At the ticket desk in the bus terminal, I resort to sign-language. A forefinger stubbed on the counter is correctly interpreted as meaning that I want to travel today. From the on-screen options, I point to the first departure time, 9am. A couple of hand gestures are needed to indicate my choice of seat number 30 from the seating plan. As the attendant passes over the completed ticket, we share a chuckle at our successful, non-verbal communication. I'm unable even to thank him, and offer a thumbs-up.

55

Over 1,000 kilometres south of Rio de Janeiro, Florianópolis is spread between the mainland and the island of Santa Catarina, the two parts of the city linked by suspension bridges. A thriving centre for services and information technology, it is one of the most prosperous areas of a rapidly developing country.

Directions to my hostel, on Santa Catarina, are convoluted and involve a number of local buses. But at this point, I've pretty much had my fill of buses. Instead, I flag a taxi that brings me to the east side of the island and across a bridge that spans the narrow point of a lagoon. Directly over the bridge, in the centre of the small town of Lagoa da Conceição, the taxi turns right and follows the water's edge for half a kilometre. My accommodation is 50 metres from the shore.

The hostel's young *bean a' tí* greets me at reception. Paula is in her twenties, trim, with long black hair, dressed casually in jeans, shirt and a denim jacket. She is strikingly good-looking. If she was at a Brazil football match during the World Cup, she'd be one of those girls that TV cameras zoom in on during breaks in play. I'm early, and as Paula leaves to prepare my room, her brother, tinkering with a motorbike at the front gate as I arrived, drops over to say hello.

My recent numerous and lengthy bus journeys have left me worn out. My stomach is cramped and there's an unwelcome irritation in my throat. In the afternoon, and again, later that evening, a stroll to the centre of town results in a drenching, providing the flu that had threatened with the further ammunition it needed.

After drenching number two, I retreat to the hostel's lounge. There, a bearded French guy is stretched on the sofa. Now watching his third movie in a row, he moves from the sofa only to switch DVDs. His only movement *on* the sofa is to adjust the volume on the remote control. He's been here for two weeks now and looks very much at home. I take a seat for the movie, but am unable to see it through. I take to my bed before 9pm and sleep through until morning.

I'm unwell for the remainder of my short stay in Brazil. That, and the almost-constant rain, means that most of my time is spent indoors. One afternoon, during a brief, dry interlude, our hosts throw a BBQ. The French guy raises himself from the sofa to attend. Which is good of him, as the BBQ is in his honour. It's a going-away treat. The previous day, following a momentary relaxation of his death-grip on the remote control, he had visited his room long enough to discover that his flight to Europe leaves a day earlier than expected.

Towards the end of the week, still feeling unwell, but by now bored witless, I decide to move on. In a travel agency in town, I book an overnight trip to Foz do Iguaçu, on the Brazilian side of the border at the Iguazú Falls. It's a stop-off on my way to Asunción, in Paraguay. The over-friendly travel agent, a local, speaks English with an American twang. In between regularly hoovering voluminous amounts of snot up his nostrils, he tells me that Paraguay is 'durdy', and warns me to be careful there. I assure him that I will and we conclude our business. 'See you, buddy', he says, my best pal, after five minutes.

That evening, at the bus station, the attendant at the ticket desk asks my country of origin and is already writing HOLANDA in his ledger before I have time to correct him. On board a short time later, the Battle of the Centre Armrest is a fractious affair. In a clear breach of seat-sharing protocol, the elbow of the half-snoozing lady in the window seat pokes me in the ribs. A gentle nudge persuades her to readjust. Soon, the pillow behind her head slips and is rubbing in my face. I move it aside. She pulls the pillow away and turns to face the window. Before long, she changes position again and places both feet on my footrest. I tap against the squatting shoes. She harrumphs, tosses and turns, flips the armrest up and down, and keeps shuffling about in her seat. Eventually, a passenger to the rear leaves the bus and my neighbour relocates; I exhale, at length.

56

It's a boiling hot early morning in Foz do Iguaçu, Brazil, as a bus arrives to take me the short distance across the border to Ciudad del Este in Paraguay. Climbing on board, it's a tight squeeze. Ahead, a low barrier sits at the top of the steps, at the driver's right hand. To the left, at the head of the aisle, is an unlikely turnstile. I heave my heavy bag over the barrier and drop it on to a grey plastic shelf. A glare from the driver persuades me to return the bag to my feet. It seems that the cash register is built into the shelf; cracks on its lid suggest I'm not the first to mistake it for a temporary luggage rack.

I push through the turnstile and flop into the first empty seat. After several stops, more passengers pile on board and I move closer to the exit door at the rear. Soon, even the aisle is packed. The traffic slows. 'Customs?', I ask the guy beside me in the window seat; I mime the stamping of a passport with my right fist on to my left palm. He thinks it is; I shift my bags again, stand by the rear door and press the bell on the nearest metal upright. There's no sound from this, so I try another, and then another. Nothing.

This is slightly worrying. My guidebook cautions that local buses don't automatically stop at Customs, and often carry on through the border. I need to reach the driver to let him know that I want to get off. I shuffle towards the front, bags hanging from both shoulders. But the aisle is crowded, and unhappy passengers urge me back. My stock among my fellow travellers plummets further when, turning around, I catch an old dear across the head with a notebook-enforced, swinging daypack. At the rear exit again and with Customs at hand, I'm in a mild panic. I really, really don't want to end up in Paraguay without exit and entry stamps. I try to catch the attention of passengers standing at the front. I'm hopping anxiously from foot to foot now, pointing from them to the driver; they avert their eyes from the bobbing lunatic at the rear. I try another bell. Not a peep. Without a word of Portuguese, and with bells that don't work, how are you supposed to let the driver know that you want to get off? My neighbours at the back of the bus provide the answer. They had noted my demented hopping and pointing, and they shout and whistle at the driver on my behalf.

My passport exit-stamped, I follow the steady movement of people across the Friendship Bridge to Paraguay. There, at the head of the queue in *Migraciones*, a grumpy-looking attendant (Fernando, says the name tag) greets me with a dismissive swipe of his hand. Which I take to mean that I should join the next queue along. It's a short wait for an entry stamp, and a great relief to be able to use again even my miserably few words of Spanish.

It is hectic on the Paraguayan side of the bridge. The road is stuffed with vehicles and street traders and hawkers. Pedestrians mill about on the paths and spill on to the road. One guy selling trainers somehow clutches six in a single hand and raises them to my face. Others hand out flyers for Ciudad del Este's electrical retailers (the city is well known for its black market in electrical goods).

I need to convert my remaining Brazilian reals to Paraguayan guaranís, and find myself wandering back in the direction of *Migraciones*. There, el Grump Fernando has left his desk and is leaning against a pillar outside the building, lighting a cigarette. '*Cambio?*' (bureau de change), I ask. He points behind me, to a guy sitting on a wall wearing a money belt. I had something a tad more official in mind. I thank the wordless Fernando and after a quick search, find a *Cambio* inside a nearby, dumpy mall. I queue at a window in a murky corridor. Behind me, steps lead down to a tiny landing. There, in semi-darkness, a woman shrinks into a corner among bags and clothes and three small, half-dressed children. It doesn't look like a temporary refuge.

Guaranís in hand, I flag down a bus from the side of the bustling road for the short journey to the city's central station. There, young guys in official blue jackets hover around arrival bays, standing between the shafts of small carts. The carts are like miniature versions of the ones farmers used to bring milk to creameries in 1950s' rural Ireland. The youngsters earn money lugging baggage to and from the holds of buses. Inside the terminal, I book the last seat on the 11.40am to Asunción, and in a small *tienda* (shop), stock up on water and crackers for the trip (crackers are the default stomach-filler for the unprepared traveller on lengthy South American bus journeys).

I'm on the lower deck of the bus, in the aisle seat, last row on the left. It's not the best position from which to view the movie showing on the small screen near the driver's cab; the tall guy in front of me keeps shifting in his seat, which means that I must continually adjust *my* position, in order to see something other than the back of his head. The movie is in Spanish, *Pirates of the Caribbean* number something-or-other, and in truth, I understand little of it. Eventually, I tire of trying to peer around the shifting black mop ahead of me, and my attention drifts from el Capitán Jack Sparrow to fleeting glimpses of red-earthed, rural Paraguay.

57

In south-central South America, landlocked Paraguay, almost five times the size of the island of Ireland, is surrounded by Bolivia to the north, Brazil to the east and Argentina to the south and west. Most of the country's borders are defined by the Paraná and Paraguay rivers and their tributaries. The Río Paraná, the second-longest on the continent, has its source in Brazil. As the Alto (Upper) Paraná, it enters Paraguay in the east, and for 800 kilometres forms the border with Brazil, and then Argentina.

The Río Paraguay also rises in Brazil, in the western state of Mato Grosso. It forms part of Paraguay's northeastern border before it cuts through the country north to south. From the capital, Asunción, it marks the frontier with Argentina for 240 kilometres before it joins the Alto Paraná. This merged river then flows onwards through Argentina as the Lower Paraná, and later meets with the Río Uruguay at the head of the Río de la Plata estuary.

The north–south route of the Río Paraguay divides the country into two distinct areas: the *Región Occidental* (Western Region), known as the Chaco Boreal, and the *Región Oriental* (Eastern Region), the Paraneña, an extension of the Brazilian Mato Grosso ('Thick Forest' in Portuguese). Most people live in the Oriental, in its western and southern parts. By contrast, the Chaco Boreal, roughly two-thirds of the country, and mostly covered with cacti and thorny shrub, holds less than 5% of the country's population.

Paraguay has one of the most homogeneous populations of any country in South America; and almost all are mestizo (part European, part Amerindian). It is also unusual in that the indigenous language (Guaraní) is spoken by most of its people.

Prior to the arrival of the Spanish, tribes of Guaraní lived in the Oriental. They were semi-nomadic; the men hunted, the women cultivated crops, and they inhabited temporary villages of thatched dwellings. In 1537, Captain Juan de Ayolas sailed up the Paraná from Buenos Aires, looking for *El Dorado*, the legendary Man of Gold (a mythical tribal leader who, it was believed, covered his body with gold dust). The Guaraní provided but a brief resistance. In local culture, it was customary for women to be exchanged between factions as a means of cementing alliances. The tribal elders presented Captain Juan with no fewer than six women to keep him company. His soldiers each had two to look after their needs. Apparently, the women were never less than enthusiastic in their roles. 'Polygamy was the basic law of Paraguay in those early days', noted one historian. He added that there was an 'extraordinary campaign of mutual acceptance through free and untrammelled love' and that these beautiful women were 'not frugal of their persons to anyone who [asked]'. The Spanish abandoned their search for gold.

Unsurprisingly, the result of this frenetic sexual activity was the mestizo. There was cross-breeding everywhere in Latin America of course, although possibly nowhere conducted with the same level of enthusiasm as in Paraguay. But whereas elsewhere the mestizo was socially marginalised, in Paraguay he was on almost equal terms with the traditionally 'pure' Hispanic ruling class.

Despite almost shagging themselves senseless, the Spanish did manage to summon the energy to found a settlement on the east bank of the Río Paraguay, dedicated, ironically, to the Virgin: the Fort of Our Lady, St Mary of the Assumption – Asunción.

It is after 6pm when we reach the city, rush hour on a warm, close evening. From the *terminal de ómnibus*, I grab a taxi to my hotel. En route, it becomes clear that the driver is only vaguely acquainted with the nuances of polite commuting. When it comes to high-thrills driving, this guy is right up there with Burns of Buenos Aires. He darts suddenly from behind cars, zooms ahead, then nips back in front, squeezing into seemingly non-existent spaces. Naturally, the indicator remains redundant during these manoeuvres. When the driver ahead slows to allow a car to exit a petrol station, his politeness is rewarded only with a lengthy blast of a horn. I keep an eye on the taxi-meter. We're in guaraní country; the meter starts at 5,000, and gallops along in bursts of 300 (£0.69 = 5,000PYG).

I've managed to mess up my hotel reservation. Online, I've mistakenly booked for tomorrow night, Saturday, instead of tonight, and the English-speaking *hombre* at reception plans to charge me the full room rate (the internet tariff is a lot less). Eventually, I persuade him to change his mind. He will switch tomorrow night's booking to tonight. And, he says, if I want to stay tomorrow night, I'll have to book online for Sunday. Or something.

The hotel is on Avenida España, near the Río Paraguay, in the centre of the old city. The building is bright and fresh and clean. My en-suite room on the first floor has cable TV and a balcony that looks out on a small courtyard. Downstairs, there's a small outdoor pool. I'm pretty chuffed. I haven't had this much comfort in ages.

After settling in, I ramble to the Britannia pub, which my map tells me is close by. It's a sizeable spot, with three separate downstairs rooms and further space upstairs. In the main bar, a poster shows a map of the London tube system. Another advertises Beefeater gin. Small, framed reproductions of English rural scenes hang on the walls. The Britannia is lively just now, with locals mostly. The music is good (Nick Lowe, Roy Orbison, George Harrison…) and not too loud. A couple of girls stand around looking pretty, offering Lucky Strikes to customers. On each table, a laminated A4 sheet lists food and drink options: 'Drink's [sic] – Good Food – and Rock 'n' Roll' runs the footnote. I decide against a Green Beer (*tradición Irlandesa*) and instead choose a Heineken Grande for 17,000 guaraní (about £2.50 for 650 cubic centimetres, not much over a pint). The bottle arrives clipped into a blue flask-like container marked *Fría* (cold), its neck poking through the top. There doesn't seem to be any way in which the 'flask' keeps the beer *fría*, except that it stops your hands from warming the bottle. As I sip my beer, the already-busy Britannia packs up some more, and I leave in search of a quieter spot. Across the road, I park myself at a tall table in an empty bar and pass a contented hour over a couple more Heineken Grandes.

Next day, I wake at noon. Lengthy bus journeys, the remnants of the flu and last night's beer have combined to take their tiring toll. My lazy day continues when I discover rugby on cable TV (*amistosos internacionals*, friendly internationals). Later, I stir myself in search of food. On España, I find a *supermercado* with a café/restaurant attached; a couple of slabs of cooked meat with rice is good-value fare.

Out for a stroll later that evening, I aim, in a vague way, for the Britannia. En route, I pass two young girls at a street corner. Minutes later, I realise I'm going in the wrong direction, and return on the other side of the road. The young whores mistake my reappearance for interest and call me over. I nod and continue on my way. The girls are heavily made-up but they can be no older than fourteen or fifteen.

This part of Asunción has a run-down feel. Some of the colonial buildings are well maintained, others are shabby and crumbling.

Footpaths are broken, the roads are littered and dim street lighting adds to an already shady vibe. The area's dodgy status seems confirmed by the presence of armed police, standing in pairs at street corners. When I find it, The Britannia is empty and I return to the hotel to see out my lazy day as it had begun, with cable TV.

58

Paraguay was one of the first countries in South America to declare its independence from Spain. When the Viceroyalty of the Río de la Plata crumbled in the wake of the Peninsular War in Europe, Paraguay refused to recognise the *Primera Junta* in Buenos Aires. The junta sent a military expedition under General Belgrano to enforce its authority. Belgrano was sent packing by the Paraguayan militia. But when the Spanish governor in Asunción appealed to Brazil for help in dealing with further potential attacks from the south, he was deposed, and the independence of Paraguay declared, on May 14, 1811.

The country was formally declared a republic in October 1813. The Paraguayan Congress appointed Dr José Gaspar Rodríguez de Francia as dictator for five years, and later for life. Paraguay had always been an isolated backwater. It had been only sparsely settled by Spaniards, it was far from the centres of power and its economy was not much above the level of subsistence. Francia wanted to maintain the country's simple structure. He wanted to isolate Paraguay from the region's main powers and protect it from the upheavals that occurred elsewhere in South America as a result of independence struggles. He more or less sealed the borders, banned most foreign visitors (some unlucky, uninvited guests were held under arrest for years) and conducted only minimal external trade.

Although personally scholarly and immune to corruption, Francia wasn't a democrat. He prohibited political activity. He reduced the power of the Catholic Church, closed their monasteries, seized their lands and nominated his own clergy. He also confiscated the estates of his elite, liberal, Hispanic opponents. To further dilute their influence, he instituted marriage laws whereby no European could marry anyone of Spanish origin. This guaranteed what one historian called the 'social downfall and destruction of the Spanish bourgeoisie in Paraguay'. It also had the knock-on effect of creating a more integrated population. In addition, a ruling was put in place, although not strictly enforced, whereby any marriage had to be approved by the dictator himself. The result was that common-law marriage became the norm and levels of illegitimacy soared. By the time of his death in 1840, Francia's absolutist rule left a Paraguay that was almost self-sufficient, relatively prosperous and probably the most stable country on the continent.

Like his predecessor, the new dictator, Carlos Antonio López, wasn't a big fan of personal liberty. But unlike his predecessor, he wasn't quite as incorruptible. He made every effort to increase his own wealth and that of his family, at the expense of the state. López was keen to modernise the country. He improved its infrastructure and military strength; he expanded industry and foreign trade. The Hispanic elite were again allowed to intermarry and the Catholic Church permitted to operate more freely.

The dictator's wife was Doña Juana Carrillo. Her Catholic sensibilities were offended by the 'free and untrammelled love' practised by the general populace in her midst. She had laws and decrees passed in an attempt to impose more traditional values. But her crusading efforts came to nothing. It seems the people were happy with their sexually freewheeling ways. There continued to be a high rate of illegitimate births. By mid-century, 50% of families were headed by single women (in Asunción, the figure was 70%). One historian has stated that 'cohabitation or "visiting rights" without commitment were very common'. This seems a studiously polite way of saying that everybody was at it hammer and tongs.

59

Next morning, on my visit to the *supermercado* for breakfast, there are two police officers standing behind a barrier at a crossroads on España. I'm expecting to see a march or a demonstration, but instead, marathon runners approach, and veer left at the junction. It is warm now, even at this relatively early hour, but the race is timed, I assume, to avoid the sun at its later, blistering height. There's a watering station further along España, beyond the police officers. Runners grab plastic cups, and get a dousing and roars of encouragement as they pass.

After two nights of hotel living, my wallet is in revolt. I leave my luxurious en-suite room and revert to budget accommodation, a hostel a couple of blocks further back from the river, on Estigarribia. It's a beautiful, restored colonial building with thick walls and high ceilings that provide a cool refuge from Asunción's searing heat. The hostel seems to be owned by a group of youngish guys, one of whom may be an ever-present big bloke whose role I haven't yet figured out, but who, hours after I arrive, has yet to stir from his horizontal position on a sofa in front of a large-screen TV.

Recoleta (*recoleta* – quiet, retiring; belonging to a convent) is a short bus ride from the old centre of the city. The cemetery's entrance leads on to Avenida A, its paving slabs rust-red, coated with ubiquitous Paraguayan dust. The *avenida* is lined with imposing mausoleums, many with small, metal plaques affixed to their walls. Blue with a green trim, these have been awarded by the *Municipalidad de Asunción* to those of the deceased it considers to have been of service to the country ('*sirvio a la patria*').

On its own in the middle of Avenida A, a tomb holds the remains of 'Corinna [sic] Adelaide Lynch', born August 6, 1856, died February 14, 1857. The infant is remembered with a (slightly misquoted) verse from Samuel Taylor Coleridge.

> Ere sin could blithe [blight] or sorrow fade
> Death came with friendly care
> The lovely [opening] bud to Heaven conveyed
> And bade it beossom [blossom] there

BM

Corinne Lynch was the daughter of *La Irlandesa*, Eliza Lynch, mistress of the president of Paraguay. Eliza Lynch was born in Charleville, County Cork, in 1833, and arrived in Paraguay over twenty years later. By the time she left the country in 1870, she was the most famous woman on the continent, the equivalent of a modern tabloid editor's dream, her image associated with sex, glamour and power.

Eliza Lynch was the only daughter of Dr John Lynch, a Catholic, and Jane Elizabeth Lloyd, a Protestant. At the age of sixteen, she married a French army officer in an Anglican church in Folkestone, Kent. The marriage did not last, and before long Eliza had returned to be with her mother, who was now living in France. In 1854, most likely at a ball at the Tuileries in Paris, she met Francisco Solano López, eldest son of the Paraguayan dictator Carlos Antonio López (although it is sometimes said that Francisco Solano López's biological father was his mother's step-father!).

The year before, the elder López had dispatched his son to Europe. Solano López's brief was to develop relations with European states

(Britain and France had recognised the independence of Paraguay only that year), buy weapons and railroad stock, and hire professionals to help in the modernisation of the country. López had an audience with Queen Victoria and Prince Albert, and with Emperor Napoleon III. After they met in France, Eliza Lynch joined López on his subsequent travels around Europe, before, late in 1854, the pair left, separately, for South America.

By the time Eliza reached Asunción, she had given birth to a son, Francisco. Prior to her arrival in the city, rumours circulating there hinted that she had lived as a courtesan in Paris. There is no evidence for this. The stories most likely came from López's brother Benigno, always resentful that Francisco was his father's heir apparent. However, this is the image of Eliza that would endure. And from the very beginning, her reputation tarnished, she was ignored and despised by the city elite.

She must have cut a cosmopolitan figure, though, in dreary, provincial Asunción (the city's population at this time was around 20,000). She was glamorous (reports of a great beauty seem exaggerated), sophisticated and well read at a time when most women, including those in higher society, had little education. She entertained foreign guests on behalf of government with a degree of ceremony not previously witnessed. She introduced fashions (parasols, hats, belts) and influenced cuisine and music (it is said that she brought the polka to Paraguay).

Eliza lived in her own townhouse in Asunción and later, had a country palace built 50 kilometres outside the city. She and López never lived together, although clearly he was a frequent visitor; over the next ten years, Eliza gave birth to six children. Throughout this time, López continued to see other mistresses.

*

In 1862, when Carlos Antonio López died, Congress voted unanimously to install his eldest son as president of the republic for ten years. Since independence, Paraguay's leaders had taken pains to avoid conflict with the country's neighbouring superpowers, Argentina and Brazil. Since his return from Europe, however, López had increased the size of the army from 10,000 to 100,000, by far the largest and most up-to-date force in the region. Before long, the new president's military urges would lead Paraguay into war – the most ruinous in the history of the American continent, North or South – the War of the Triple Alliance (known in Paraguay as *La Guerra Grande*, the Great War).

When Francisco Solano López came to power, a civil war in Uruguay had been ongoing for 30 years, the pro-Brazilian Colorados (Reds) in opposition to the Blancos (Whites). In October 1864, Brazilian troops occupied the Uruguayan town of Villa de Melo. Expecting Paraguay to be the next target of Brazilian aggression, López got his retaliation in first. He halted the progress of a Brazilian naval vessel travelling up the Río Paraguay, had it escorted to Asunción and informed the Brazilian envoy that Paraguay was now at war with his country.

In Brazil's Mato Grosso, north of Paraguay, López scored early military successes against unprepared locals. Next, he set his sights on liberating Uruguay. To reach its border, he asked for permission to cross the Argentine province of Misiones, to the southeast. This was refused; by this time, Argentina had allied itself with the Colorados, who were now in power in Uruguay. At a session of a supine Paraguayan Congress, war was declared on Argentina. On May 1, 1865, Brazil,

Argentina and Uruguay signed the treaty of the Triple Alliance, and came together to oppose López.

Almost from the beginning, the game was up for Paraguay. In June, its navy was almost wiped out. In September, an enormous Paraguayan force occupying the town of Uruguayana on the Argentina/Brazil border, surrendered after a six-week siege. At this point, remaining troops outside the country were recalled to defend the national territory. In April 1866, the Allies crossed into Paraguay for the first time. From this point, López, accompanied by Eliza, criss-crossed the country, trying to stay ahead of the enemy.

As the war progressed, López began to descend into paranoia. He saw spies everywhere and was inclined to kill any bearer of bad news. He spent hours in church and drank for days on end. He received evidence of conspiracies against him and set up what became known as the Tribunals of Blood to try those accused. By the end of 1868, 400 people had been executed, including his brother Benigno. López used torture to extract information from captives and his conduct was, at times, barbaric (after the war, his behaviour was condemned, with Eliza implicated by association).

The final scenes of the war took place at Cerro Corá, northeast of Asunción, near the Brazilian border. Cerro Corá is surrounded by the Amambay mountains and can be accessed via a pass in the southeast and through the Aquidabán river valley in the northwest. In February 1870, López arrived there with his remaining officers and approximately 200 soldiers. With them were wounded personnel, families and a number of prisoners. The last included his mother and two sisters, Inocencia and Rafaela, who had previously been found guilty of conspiracy. Eliza was there too, transported in a carriage with her children.

At a Council of War convened with his senior officers, López decided against fleeing to the mountains. He and his tiny force would stand and fight. Eliza knew that this was the end. She expected that López would be killed and she may not have held out much hope for herself and her sons; over the past year, the enemy had shown little mercy towards prisoners.

The Brazilians approached Cerro Corá from both the southeast and the northwest, cutting off any escape route. On March 1, 1870, 2,600 troops led by a General Câmara launched an attack. In the battle that followed, López was lanced in the stomach and in the side. Helped by his soldiers, he made it to the banks of the nearby Aquidabán river. Discovered there by Câmara and ordered to surrender, he replied, famously, 'I will not yield up my sword. I die with my sword and with my country'. When soldiers were unable to relieve him of his weapon, he was shot and killed.

The Brazilians cut off López's ear and some fingers; they battered his teeth and took clumps of hair and skin. Anyone found in the Paraguayan encampment area was burned alive. Women were raped, some Paraguayans escaped, others were taken prisoner. Among those spared, López's sister Inocencia took up with General Câmara (she gave birth to his daughter nine months later). His other sister Rafaela had a liaison with a Brazilian colonel, his niece with a captain. Eliza claimed British citizenship. Her children did the same, with the exception of her eldest son. Although only fifteen, Francisco was a colonel in his father's army. He struck out at a Brazilian officer with his sword and was shot dead.

Câmara ordered that López and his son be buried in a shallow grave. Eliza insisted on a proper burial and helped to dig their final resting places. Always gutsy, and particularly so now in the face of the rape and destruction around her, Eliza demanded that she be transported to safety. By the time she reached Asunción, the provisional government put in place by the Brazilians had embargoed her property (for the duration of the war, under instruction from López, she had made enormous land purchases in an effort to secure her family's future. By 1870, she owned land greater in size than the island of Ireland). Eliza moved on, made it safely to Buenos Aires and eventually to London.

Eliza Lynch settled in France on her return to Europe, and died in Paris on July 25, 1886. In the twentieth century, the Paraguayan dictator General Alfredo Stroessner set about restoring López's reputation. He also declared Eliza Lynch a heroine, and in 1961 her remains were transferred to Asunción. The Catholic Church would not allow her to be interred with López in the National Pantheon.

There's a small garden in Recoleta cemetery, not far from the tomb of the infant Corinne Adelaide Lynch. At its head, a short set of steps leads to a tall crucifix. To one side is an impressive mausoleum, its front a large, ironwork grille gate. Behind the gate, on top of marble steps, a casket holds the remains of Eliza Lynch.

On the front wall, the *Municipalidad de Asunción* has awarded her one of its plaques. Another has been dedicated to Elisa (sic) Alicia Lynch, by the people and the government. There's a statue on the mausoleum's flat roof; a woman in a tattered ball gown. Her feet are bare. She has a small shovel in her hands and stands proud and erect between two freshly dug graves, each marked with a small makeshift cross.

60

After a late lunch at the hostel, a stroll along Estigarribia leads towards the centre of the old town. There, four small plazas sit in a square off a busy shopping street, Calle Palma. At the edge of one, Plaza de la Libertad, a line of permanent stalls sells better-than-average tat. Between stalls, I join a circle of spectators at a game of draughts. The game is played with bottle-tops on a makeshift board. To 'crown' a piece, a bottle-top is upturned. A crumpled 5,000 guaraní note awaits the winner.

Unusually, the centre feature of this plaza is not a national figure. Instead, steps rise to a green metal sculpture that depicts what looks like a man grappling with an angel. Locals sit on the steps, taking their ease, sipping *mate*. It is late afternoon now and shoeshine stalls on the paths through the plaza are no longer manned. At the roadside, under-employed vendors sell Paraguayan football shirts from lines strung between telephone poles. Trade might be more brisk had the national team not returned as runners-up from the recent final of the Copa América.

In the square of four small plazas, Plaza Juan E O'Leary sits diagonally across from Plaza de la Libertad. A bust of the man for whom this quiet, green space is named sits at its centre. Juan Emiliano O'Leary was born in Asunción in June 1879, grandson of John O'Leary, an Irish immigrant to Buenos Aires, and son of Juan, a travelling salesman, who had arrived in Paraguay during the War of the Triple Alliance.

Active in politics, Juan E O'Leary was a supporter of Bernardino Caballero, who was president of the country from 1881–86 and who, in 1887, founded the Colorado Party, which would dominate politics in Paraguay for much of the twentieth century (politics didn't consume all of Caballero's energy – one source says that he was twice married, and fathered 90 children out of wedlock). Caballero had been one of López's generals in the War of the Triple Alliance. In 1874, he was part of a diplomatic mission to London, and visited Eliza Lynch in Paris in November of that year. She told him that she would reveal the whereabouts of monies belonging to the state in return for help in recovering her properties in Paraguay. This information was passed to President Gill who encouraged Eliza to return to Asunción. (President Gill was descended from an Irish immigrant, John Thomas [*el Inglés*] McGill. In Paraguay, McGill became Gill when the dictator Francia decreed that the prefixes of foreign names could no longer be used.) Although Eliza did travel to Paraguay, a proposed meeting with Gill never took place and her properties remained beyond reach.

O'Leary was minister for foreign affairs, briefly, in the government of General Stroessner (leader of a military coup in 1954, Stroessner led the country until 1989). But it is as a revisionist historian that he is most widely remembered. Initially critical of López and his role in the War of the Triple Alliance, in time he rebranded him a patriot and a national hero. O'Leary was also a poet, concerned mainly with national identity and with the preservation and development of the Guaraní language. He died in Asunción on October 31, 1969.

Not far from his plaza, a street named for Juan E O'Leary runs along the side of Palacio de los López, the seat of government. A guard sits on the footpath, by a barrier that blocks vehicular access to O'Leary. I point down the street, planning to walk in that direction; the guard dismisses me with a tetchy flick of the hand which vaguely directs me around the front of the Palacio.

Palacio de los López was intended to be the home of Francisco Solano López. Building work started in 1857, but the War of the Triple Alliance intervened and López never saw its belated completion, in 1892.

The white, two-storey structure is the shape of a 'U' lying on its side, with a long base and short legs, its façade a series of columns and arches. The columns are wrapped in the national colours, and long strips of red, white and blue stretch from the roof to the ground for the length of the building. This patriotic display is in recognition of the bicentennial of the country's independence. Just now, all public buildings in Asunción have similar, if less extravagant arrangements. A square tower encased in scaffolding rises from the roof of the palace, at its centre point; a large Paraguayan flag flaps loudly in the fresh breeze.

Parallel to Calle O'Leary, Calle Ayolas runs down the other side of the building, towards the broad Río Paraguay. At the rear, the Palacio has a fine location, overlooking Asunción Bay. A gunship is docked at a small pier on this side of the river; the national colours are visible on buildings on the distant, far bank. Looping around the back of the Palacio, I begin to walk up O'Leary on the other side; a guard running along the lengthy balcony at the rear of the building toots me away with urgent blasts of a whistle. My alternative route, past miserable slum dwellings, leads towards the Congreso Nacional and on to the Plaza de Armas of old Asunción.

On my meandering return to the hostel, personnel of the *Fuerzas Armadas de la Nación* (national naval forces) pass by, impressively decked out in very smart, blue uniforms. Less impressive is their method of transport, in the back of an open truck. Along the waterfront, a number of imposing colonial buildings stand out from their more dilapidated neighbours. Some are in use as government ministries, although 'El Ministerio Dance' is unlikely to be one.

61

Next morning, a heavy, oppressive heat lands on me when I step from the cool confines of the hostel. It's another hot, hot, cloudless day. This area of the city, quiet over the weekend, is alive now with traffic and pedestrians. It's not difficult to spot the gringo; I may be the only person in Asunción wearing a long-sleeved shirt. The remainder of my clothes head for the laundry. The *señora* tells me they'll be ready tomorrow; at the hostel, I book *una noche más* (another night).

On the way to the *supermercado* for lunch, I drop into a small café on España. Inside, I can barely hear myself think. The café's double doors are open to allow a flow of air; buses and lorries roar past, while inside, the radio is up to eleven so it can be heard over the thundering traffic. A street kid with a thick mop of black hair gets bread crusts and a drink in a plastic cup from the café girls. His bare, dirt-blackened feet stick out from oversized tracksuit bottoms rolled up to his calves.

I pass the afternoon rambling around the centre of the old city. At a guess, they don't get too many tourists here (I have yet to come across one); outside a police station, a high-ranking officer stops to help as I turn a street map every which way and try to get my bearings. I make a judgement of his exalted rank solely from the impressive colours on his peaked cap, absent from the headgear of his colleagues.

Nearby are the open doors of Iglesia Universal de Reino de Dios. The façade of the church is almost indistinguishable from that of neighbouring shops and houses. Inside, five people at the front of a short set of pews stand, facing a preacher, and raise their hands in the air.

Placards have been hung from telephone poles in this part of town by the *Municipalidad de Asunción*, in recognition of the country's bicentennial. These show images of notable figures from Paraguayan history, each '*una luz del bicentenario*' (a guiding light/inspiration of the bicentenary).

Later in the afternoon, returning from town, I pass through untidy Plaza Uruguaya. Ropes are tied between the trunks of trees in one quarter of the square. Thin plastic sheeting, like that of a refuse sack, is drawn over the ropes and pegged to the ground on either side. These makeshift tents are the permanent homes of the plaza's residents. The residents themselves, along with most of their belongings, sit outside the tents. The grass is mostly worn away, the exposed red earth thinly carpeted with a layer of pink blossoms deposited by the trees. Children play in the dust. On a footpath by one side of the plaza, water gushes from a broken hand-pump, and campsite inhabitants take advantage of the running water to wash themselves and their clothes. Jeans on the ground are half-scrubbed with a bar of soap; a woman is topless while she squeezes water from her blouse. There are a couple of bookshops on the plaza (the only ones I've seen in the city). According to posters, there's a bicentennial push for '*el libro en su casa...leer y creer*' (a book in your house...read and believe). I suspect the promotion is unlikely to impinge too much on the lives of the tent dwellers.

Nearby, the life of Juan E O'Leary (by now, in my head, his name is a hibernicised Johnny Leary) is celebrated on one of those bicentennial placards. He was, it says, a '*poeta, ensayista, historiador, periodista y político*' (poet, essayist, historian, journalist and politician). O'Leary is '*una luz del bicentenario*'.

At teatime, I pay yet another visit to the café/restaurant at the *supermercado* on España. En route, splintered plastic cups are strewn on the road beside the location of the watering station for yesterday's marathon. Further along, a bustling junction seems particularly popular with street urchins; a small posse of them clean windscreens and beg at car windows. Here, yesterday, a disabled man had ventured into the stopped traffic. He had levered himself from the footpath using his backside and his one good arm, shuffled between cars until the lights turned green, then scuttled back to the path. Today, a policeman regulates traffic at this very busy rush-hour intersection. As I cross the road, he chooses the very moment I pass him to toot ferociously on his whistle. My ears are ringing as I sit to eat.

Returning to the hostel a short time later, ears still faintly humming, I see that small tables have been set up on the footpath at various points. They hold notepads and books of tickets. This is *La Nueva Quiniela* (the new lottery), the big bloke at the hostel tells me from his supine position in front of the large-screen TV. Three games are played every day, he says, *Matutino, Vespertino* and *Nocturno;* punters bet on the occurrence of numbers that are subsequently announced on the radio. It is not unlike the numbers game, played illegally in the United States, an income generator for city gangsters.

62

It is Tuesday morning, and somewhere in Asunción a mosquito is kicking back. I imagine him as a cartoon mosquito, his oversized face the shape of an M&M, a broad grin exposing a set of even, super-white teeth. He is relaxing on a sun lounger, wings folded back, arms behind his head (my cartoon mosquito has arms), spindly legs crossed at the ankle. He wears sunglasses and there's a cigarette hanging from his lower lip. Floozies buzz around him, refilling his drink, lighting his cigarettes. He's fat and bloated and can barely move. And that's because he's spent the night gorging on my fucking ankle. A hard, red, scratchy lump is a reminder of his visit. Bastard.

It is time to move on from Asunción. I need to be in Salta, northwest Argentina, in a week. To get there, I can loop up into Bolivia and then dip south, or I can drop into Argentina and make my way cross-country. But I've been thinking about the options for so long now that I can't make up my mind. Either way, to be sure of a seat, I need to buy a ticket in advance; I make my way to the bus station, still undecided.

The busy terminal is decked out in bicentennial red, white and blue. Inside, opposite the departure bays, the far wall of the building is lined with small shops. Much of what is for sale seems to be *outside* the windows. Soft drinks and snacks are stacked low. Football shirts, T-shirts and racks of sunglasses hang above them. Young girls sit on stools out front; if you glance in their direction, they launch into a spiel.

I climb to the first floor, where a line of ticket booths runs the length of the building. As I parade past them checking out my options, guys inside the booths stick their heads to window openings and shout out their destinations. After a ridiculous amount of stalling, I book a ticket to Santa Cruz, Bolivia. The fare for the overnight journey is 250,000 guaraní (c. £37). When I ask if my seat is *semi-cama*, the attendant points to the image of a bus on a poster. Only later do I realise that I hadn't gotten an answer to my question.

An ancient and rackety bus returns me to the old town. Underfoot, worn-out floorboards have a broad, protective, metal strip tacked over them, down the aisle. Up front, a wavy, blue strip of material, like the fringe of a curtain, runs across the top of the windscreen; small red and white bobbles hang from it. The bus has no air conditioning. When it's on the move, open windows provide a cooling breeze; when it's stationary, you boil. It's 29 degrees, according to the digitised screen at a junction near Recoleta. On board, it feels like a lot more. On the short journey, a quick double-take confirms a passing street name: Calle MacMahón.

Martin McMahon, son of Irish parents and hero of the American Civil War, was US minister resident in Paraguay (US ambassador) for a time during the War of the Triple Alliance. McMahon was born in La Prairie, Canada in 1838 (La Prairie is on the St Lawrence river, opposite the island of Montreal). His family had emigrated from Ireland a short time before – his two older brothers, John Eugene (b. 1834) and James Power (b. 1836), were born in County Waterford. Around the time of his birth, McMahon's father and uncle were involved in rebellions that took place in Lower Canada (mostly modern-day Quebec), and the family left abruptly for the United States.

The rebellions in Lower Canada in 1837–38 were the culmination of decades of political activity that sought accountability from government. At the time, the latter was made up of three strands:

the governor, appointed from London; the Legislative Council, an all-powerful upper house appointed by the governor and dominated mainly by wealthy British businessmen; and the Legislative Assembly, an elected lower house with little influence. Repeated pleas for reform were ignored and this led to the formation, in August 1837, of the Société des Fils de la Liberté.

The Société had both a civil and a military wing. One of the leaders of the former was Edmund Bailey O'Callaghan, a doctor and journalist, born in Mallow, County Cork in 1797. He emigrated to Canada in 1823 and became editor of the *Vindicator and Canadian Advertiser*, a newspaper dedicated to the cause of democratic rights and reform. In its columns he urged citizens to revolt. (The newspaper had been founded in 1828 as *The Irish Vindicator and Canada General Advertiser*, by Daniel Tracey, another doctor and journalist. From Roscrea, County Tipperary, Tracey moved to Canada in 1825. Imprisoned for a month in 1832 for demanding the abolition of the Legislative Council, he was released after public disquiet about his arrest. He died of cholera in the same year).

There were a number of clashes between rebels and British forces in late 1837, before martial law was declared in Montreal in December of that year. Arrest orders were issued for 26 rebel leaders, O'Callaghan among them. He escaped across the border to the US where he settled in Albany. In 1848, he gave up medicine and became secretary-archivist of the state of New York. Later he moved to New York City, where he died, in 1880.

Canadian rebels based in the US attempted two invasions of Lower Canada in 1838, both put down by the British. The aftermath of the uprisings saw the merging of Lower Canada and Upper Canada to form the Province of Canada. The rebellions of 1837–38 have since become a symbol for those in favour of the independence of Quebec.

Fleeing south, the McMahon family settled in New York; there, Martin McMahon attended St John's College, Fordham. (Founded in 1841 by the Tyrone-born coadjutor bishop – later archbishop – of the Diocese of New York, John Hughes, in 1907 St John's College became Fordham University.) He went on to study law at Buffalo and headed to California to work as special agent for the post office. At the outbreak of the American Civil War, McMahon was elected captain of a company of cavalry. When he learned that the company would not be sent to the front line, he resigned his command and returned east. There, he was appointed captain and aide-de-camp to Major-General George B McClellan. He stayed with the Army of the Potomac (the Union Army of the East) for the remainder of the war, achieving the rank of brevet major general. He received the Medal of Honor, the highest military decoration awarded by the US government, for his bravery at the Battle of White Oak Swamp in June 1862. McMahon had volunteered to burn a train abandoned between opposing army lines. In doing so, he managed to save the train's valuable instrument-wagon (no, I don't know what that is either).

McMahon's two brothers died in the war. John Eugene McMahon was the first colonel of the 164th New York Volunteers (one of four regiments that made up a brigade of Irish soldiers, the Corcoran Legion). On his death, his brother, James, succeeded him; he was killed in 1864, at the Battle of Cold Harbor.

After the war, McMahon served as corporation counsel (chief legal officer) for the City of New York, before being appointed US minister resident in Paraguay by President Andrew Johnson. On December 14, 1868, McMahon presented his credentials to López at Piribebuy, east of Asunción. A week later, he witnessed the Battle of Lomas Valentinas (55 kilometres south of Asunción, on the border with Argentina), where 7,000 Paraguayans faced a Brazilian force almost four times their number. Fearing the end, López made a will and left it with the American. He also entrusted him with custody of his children, and McMahon withdrew with them to Piribebuy. In his will, López had left everything to Eliza.

McMahon was hostile to slave-holding Brazil and was critical of the Triple Alliance for continuing to pursue the war well after a time when it was clear that Paraguay was defeated. In mid-1869, after a brief tenure, he was withdrawn from the country. When he returned to the US, he wrote movingly of the sacrifices and difficulties suffered by ordinary Paraguayans as war raged around them.

In New York, McMahon became involved in local politics. He served in the State Assembly (the lower house of the State legislature) and the State Senate; in 1896, he was elected to the bench. He died of pneumonia at his home in Manhattan in 1906, and is buried in Arlington National Cemetery, outside Washington, DC.

63

Having bought my ticket for the journey to Santa Cruz tonight, I pass the remainder of the day doing not very much. On the way to the *supermercado* for lunch, the plastic cups at the roadside are now more splintered, and lay up against the footpath, urged there by passing traffic.

At the hostel, the big bloke is slumped on the sofa. It is unclear whether he has moved since morning. On the big-screen TV, Brazil play Germany in football. '*Amistoso?*', I ask, trying out my most recently acquired Spanish word. '*Sí, Amistoso*'.

At teatime, I gather my bags to leave. I thank my hosts, the big bloke hoists himself from his reclining position to shake my hand, and I catch a rush-hour bus to the station. On board, the guy beside me in the window seat sips *mate* non-stop. He continually tops up his gourd from a fat *termo*. The *termo* is too big to hold in one hand. Two leather grips attached to its sides, when grabbed together, function as a handle and allow him to pour. The bus isn't due to enter the station but will pass close by, and from time to time I half-stand in my seat looking out for it in the darkness. My neighbour unclamps his lips from the *bombilla* long enough to tell me he'll let me know when to get off.

In the terminal, a TV screen at the head of a bank of seats shows Paraguay vs Mexico, another *amistoso internacional*. With time to spare before my 9pm departure, I take a pew towards the rear. In the row ahead of me, a very pretty Paraguayan girl turns in her seat, and for a brief moment, we catch each other's eye. This is enough to set my mind on a wander. I think about Paraguayan women, about the six of them who 'tended' to Ayolas. I think about López and his many mistresses and Caballero and his 90-plus children. I think about all that 'untrammelled love' in the colonial years, and the women who gave themselves freely to anyone who asked. And I think, bloody hell, Paraguayan women don't half put it about! Slowly, I return my gaze to the beautiful girl in the seat in front of me. But I'm shaken out of my mildly lustful reverie by the sight of her index finger excavating almost to the knuckle in her left nostril. I turn back to the *amistoso*.

Later, at the departure bay, a policeman strolls through the waiting crowd. He stops people at random, looks at IDs and makes notes on a clipboard. He wears a gun at his side, the way a gunslinger would in a Western, the holster kept in place with drawstrings tied around his lower thigh. The departure bay is spilling over with luggage. Some passengers seem to be relocating, rather than merely travelling, and carry with them the largest of suitcases and taped-up canvas and plastic sacks. When the bus arrives, the hold quickly fills up, and I end up taking my bags on board.

My *boleta* (ticket) states that the bus is '*convencional*', and it's not wrong – it is an ordinary bus. Which would be fine, if this was an ordinary bus journey. But this will be my longest in South America, 27 hours, through a semi-desert. The discomfort of long-distance South American bus travel is often eased by luxurious, *semi-cama* seats, air conditioning and rolling movies. Tonight on board, the standard seats recline only very slightly (mine flips into the upright position whenever I lean forward), there's no air conditioning, and a movie that plays as the bus moves off soon breaks down. The TV screen stares blankly from the ceiling for the next 26 hours.

At 4am, we stop in a dusty parking area and gather outside a *Migraciones* building. A sickly dog with a droopy head mopes about, and coughs and wheezes as if something is lodged in its throat. A Paraguayan official appears, collects our passports and returns to her office. Everyone shuffles closer to the doorway. Each passenger is called in turn (at first, I don't answer to *Mee*-tchel), and documents are exit-stamped.

From here, and for what seems like an eternity, we travel bumpy, dirt roads through a dusty landscape of low, scrubby trees. We're in the Chaco Boreal, that area of thirsty lowlands (c. 260,000 square kilometres), west of the Paraguay river. The Chaco (it rhymes with Jacko) Boreal also incorporates southeast Bolivia and northern Argentina, and is itself part of the Gran Chaco, an even vaster area of aridity (c. 725,000 square kilometres) bounded by the Andes in the west. It is truly desolate, and when the day awakens fully the heat is stunning. Mosquitoes use me as a buffet cart and snack on my ankles. Happy with the fare on offer there, they find further nourishment later, beneath my chin and on the back of my neck.

At 8.30, an insubstantial breakfast barely troubles the walls of my stomach: a small, tetrapack chocolate drink and a four-pack of custard cream-type biscuits. Soon, at a military checkpoint, a soldier comes on board, checks passports and ticks names on a passenger list. A little further on, Bolivian *Migraciones* is a ramshackle place in the deserted middle of nowhere. Stepping from the bus, I half-expect tumbleweed to blow across my path. We complete forms (never been arrested, not carrying drugs, not bringing too much money into the country…) and under shade in a blowy yard, wait to enter a small shack. Here, in return for completed forms, a stern Bolivian official stamps our documents. Outside, two old women sheltering beneath large umbrellas clutch fistfuls of notes, and I exchange my remaining guaraní for bolivianos (£1 = c. 11BOB).

Back on board, and within minutes, the bus comes to a halt. At another military checkpoint, we again line up with our passports and again are ticked off on a passenger list. Once more, we take to the endless dirt road. A relentless sun beats through the windows. There's no escape from the heat and the sweat and the stickiness, and unending hours in an upright seat in a cramped space. I don't think I've ever been more uncomfortable.

It's hard to believe that a war was fought over this godforsaken place, the Chaco. But, in the 1930s, Bolivia and Paraguay did just that. Its genesis goes back further, to the 1880s, when Bolivia lost its coastline to Chile in the War of the Pacific. Bolivia saw the Chaco Boreal as a possible route to the sea, through the Paraná river system. Historically, there had always been a question mark over the rightful ownership of the land and, initially, Bolivia advanced its claim through peaceful means. Things hotted up, however, in 1928, when oil was discovered at the western edge of the Gran Chaco, in the foothills of the Andes. It seemed like an oil rush was in the offing. From then, there were intermittent clashes and by 1932, larger-scale fighting was under way. In May of the following year, Paraguay formally declared war.

Bolivia seemed to have every advantage in the conflict: a larger population, a bigger army, a better air force and an enemy that was very short of cash. Most of the war's battles, however, were won by Paraguay. Better leadership and familiarity with the terrain proved crucial and, by 1935, the Bolivians were almost pushed out of the Chaco. But by this time both countries were worn out. Some 100,000 were dead. In June 1935, there was a ceasefire, arbitrators were convened from other South American countries and in 1938 a treaty was signed in Buenos Aires. Three-quarters of the Chaco Boreal was awarded to Paraguay; they, in turn, conceded port privileges to Bolivia. No further oil was discovered.

Eventually we escape the monotonous, scrubby Chaco and stop at the outskirts of a town. I wait, standing stooped beneath the overhead rack, as a line of guys troop up the aisle and off the bus. 'Santa Cruz?' I ask hopefully. '*Quince minutos*' is the part of the response I pick up. Fifteen minutes to Santa Cruz? Fantastic. It's selective hearing on my part, however. It is soon clear that we're *stopping* for fifteen minutes. Santa Cruz is another seven hours away. Sweet Jesus!

After the *quince minutos* leg-stretch, a meal on board is fried chicken, rice and chips…with a spoon. But it's tasty, and it comes with a very welcome ice-cold drink. Dessert is a large bag of what look like overblown sugar puffs that I had bought at the last stop (later, I see them advertised in a supermarket as *maíz inflado*, inflated corn).

By now, a number of passengers have left the bus and the guy beside me moves to an empty seat. This is bliss. I stretch myself out. A group of Spanish-speakers gather round seats in front of me and chat and pass the time. They're friendly, and try to include me. I use my simple Spanish and they practise their words of English. When speaking among themselves, however, their rapid speech loses me, and I soon tune out. On my notebook, I listen to a random series of documentaries I had downloaded from the BBC website. I listen until the battery is almost dead. There is still no sign of Santa Cruz.

At last, at long, long last, and approaching midnight, the journey comes to an end. My mouth is dust-dry as I jump from the bus and grab a taxi to my hostel. There, I swallow half a litre of chilled mineral water and grab a shower before bed. It has probably been the most drawn-out day of my life.

64

The roads around Santa Cruz are blockaded. There's a general strike in Bolivia and the owner of the hostel says it could go on for days. After a brief stay in the city, I had planned to take a bus southwest, to the small village of La Higuera, before travelling on to Sucre in the south-central part of the country, en route to Argentina. Instead, with no end to the blockade in sight, I book a flight to Sucre, for tomorrow, Sunday.

Before that, I pass time around Santa Cruz's very pleasant main plaza. In the centre of the square, high on a plinth, Colonel Ignacio Warnes is a '*Héroe de la Independencia 1816*'. An Argentine soldier, Warnes fought with Belgrano when he tried to bring Paraguay under the control of the *Primera Junta* in Buenos Aires. In 1813, Warnes successfully liberated Santa Cruz from Spanish forces. He was killed three years later, in battle with royalists.

Off one side of the plaza, a plaque on the wall of a bistro states that Santa Cruz de la Sierra was founded on '*26 de Febriero de 1561…* [by]…*El Capitán Don Ñuflo de Chaves*' in the presence of '*nativos y 90 hispanos*'.

Opposite the bistro, and of a more recent vintage, the Irish Bar is upstairs in a mall (pub logo: a cartoon leprechaun, one hand holding a foaming beer mug, the other giving a thumbs-up). The main area of the bar leads on to a balcony that overlooks the plaza.

From here, Colonel Warnes is shielded from view by trees. In the centre of the square, the tops of these trees sway gently. Nearer at hand, somehow, the wind seems stronger. Across the street, palm fronds bend sharply; on the outside wall of the pub, two flags are fully extended, right to left. Away from its blowy, blustery edge, I take a seat beside the dark-glass partition that separates the balcony from the dim pub interior.

At either end of the balcony, walls are rust in colour above waist-high, dark-wood panelling. Pub tat comes with a Bolivian twist: a display case contains knives, rifles and a conquistador's shield. Beside them is an old-looking, yellowed map of Bolivia. I do think that this might be a genuine, antique map until, a short time later, a street vendor tries to sell me a similar one, from a sheaf of them draped over his arm. Trinkets and Guinness bottles make up some of the more standard Irish-themed-pub gumpf, along with prints of Irish scenes: a country kitchen, the Cliffs of Moher and Molly Malone and her barrow.

A girl in jeans and a green top provides a menu. I decide against the *Estofado Irlandés* (Irish Stew) and order the Irish Club, a standard club sandwich that's impossible to handle without spilling half its contents. I wash it down with a soft drink, avoiding the more potent 'Nutty Irishman' (Baileys, Frangelico, *leche* [milk]).

It's very pleasant here on the balcony, warm and sunny. Across the road, beneath the palm fronds, old men on concrete stools play chess at concrete tables. Beyond them, locals stroll the plaza's paths. It is just after midday now and the Irish Bar is doing a good trade. Like many Irish-themed bars in countries with no pub-drinking culture, or without hoards of travellers or expats, it seems more of a pub-cum-restaurant than a 'drinking' establishment. An Irish pub is the in-thing. It's the trendy place to be, even if not utilised for the original Irish purpose of swilling copious amounts of beer.

65

The following afternoon I take a cab to the airport for my flight to Sucre. Inside the terminal, slow-moving queues snake through the concourse. A glance at the Departures board tells me that my flight has been cancelled. Passengers line up looking for information; no reason for the cancellation is given. After several conversations with different attendants, I discover that the flight has been rescheduled for 8am the following morning, information offered almost as an afterthought.

That night, I set the alarm for 4.45am. When I wake, I half-doze for a few moments and then jolt upright. My fuzzy memory recalls setting the alarm to 'Snooze', before then, for some reason, switching it off. My small travel clock is hiding among the bedclothes; instead I check the time on my notebook. It is 6.30, and as I hadn't reset the notebook to Bolivia time, it is, in fact, 7.30. Too late! I consider getting a taxi to the airport to book another flight. But I don't even know if there *is* another flight. I rapidly sift through options in my head; eventually, I lean back, resigned to the fact that I can do nothing about it now. Last night, the road blockades around Santa Cruz had ended. Later that morning, I book an overnight bus to Sucre.

In the afternoon, I download radio podcasts to keep me company on my trip. The internet connection is weak and it's a slow business. Later, having ordered a taxi to the bus station, and bored after the day, I pace the hostel's inner courtyard. The kitchen faces the courtyard, and one of the girls from reception is at an open window there.

'Where you going?' she asks.

I move indoors. 'Sucre.'

She gives an appreciative sigh. 'Nice place', she says. '…About eighteen hours.'

'Well, leaving at five and due to arrive around nine in the morning, so hopefully a bit less.'

I tell her about the cancelled flight, and missing the rescheduled one. She quizzes me about costs.

'Did you get a refund?'

'No', I say, 'it was my fault that I missed the flight.'

'…and the bus was eighty (bolivianos)?'

'Ninety.'

These figures are relatively small by European standards. But the average Bolivian wage is equivalent to less than $100 a week. The missed flight and its frittered-away cost must seem wasteful.

'Not a good road', she goes on, talking about the journey to Sucre.

Ah, I thought, another dirt road, like the one from Asunción.

'…Don't know how to say in English', she says, '…precipice'.

'Oh!'

She baby-steps across the kitchen, heel-to-toe, one careful foot in front of the other. Then she holds her hand palm-down in front of her chest and makes a slicing, angled, movement to waist-height.

No English required: narrow road, sharp drop. Marvellous!

'…For about five hours.' She's still talking about the bad road.

'Right.'

'You should be OK…not many accidents recently…'

If she's trying to make me feel better, she could probably try harder.

'…Depends if the driver is drinking', she says. '…They're always drunk.'

Oh, for fuck's sake!

Later, at the bus station, I present my ticket to an attendant standing by a narrow turnstile that leads to the departure bays. '*Informaciones*', he says, and turns me away. At Information, I'm directed to another desk where 3 bolivianos buys a yellow ticket marked '*Uso de Andén General*' (Use of the General Platform). Back at the turnstile, I show this ticket; the attendant ushers me through and points me to Platform 21.

After my chat with the girl at the hostel, I am now paranoid about my journey. At the departure bay, I keep an eye on the driver as he jumps from the steps of the bus and makes his way into the terminal. Well, at least he doesn't fall over! I check the bus for roadworthiness. But I'm not sure what attributes would make it less likely to tumble down a steep precipice. All I *can* tell is that it is old.

A guy checking travel tickets at the bus door is, moments later, selling drinks on board. He jumps off at the terminal gates, where another official boards and checks passengers for those yellow '*Uso de Andén General*' tickets (this seems to be a departure tax). Up front, the driver's compartment is curtained off. A man is entitled to some privacy I guess, when he takes a drink.

My neighbour in the window seat wears a white Liverpool football shirt, 'Maximo S', number 6. He slides back the window and sticks his face to the open air. The bus is basic, *convencional*, like the one that brought me to Santa Cruz. I reach for the seat belt. If I'm going to be hurtling down a steep slope, I want to be strapped in. But there is no belt. There are wires and an empty space where the TV screen used to be, the overhead light doesn't work, there's no toilet, and air conditioning is my neighbour's slid-back window. This is my second time on a bus in Bolivia. Soon, I would come to the conclusion that the country is the nursing home for South American buses. When they've seen service on the remainder of the continent, they are sent here to see out their weary days.

At dusk, we come to a halt at a road toll; women and children surround the bus and reach to the open windows, selling small baskets of food. From here, the road climbs steadily, and gets rougher and bumpier. It's a dirt road, and mostly it clings to the side of mountains. I strain from my aisle seat to get a view of the precipice that, depending on driver sobriety, we might soon tumble down. Luckily, it's dark, and I can see very little. At one point we pass through a tunnel. Its walls and roof are roughly hewn, not smoothed or concreted, and there's jagged rock all around. The seeming haphazardness of its construction leaves an uneasy feeling; I'm half-expecting it to collapse in at any moment.

At 10pm, the bus stops at a hamlet in the hills, outside a Hotel Mairana. The hotel's toilet facilities are spare, but welcome. Some passengers sit for a meal. Even at this late hour, there are vendors on the footpath. Parched, I buy a small tub of ice cream. Its spoon is almost fully buried, and I excavate around the top of it with the tub's plastic lid. Using the partly revealed spoon as a stick, I remove the frozen ice cream from the tub and eat it like a short, fat ice pop. It is a welcome treat.

On the road again, and not long after first light, we pull into a makeshift lay-by on the side of a mountain for a toilet break. Women disappear behind dunes, guys relieve themselves into a small ravine that falls away just off the road. On the bus again, and after five minutes on the open hillside, the air on board is foul.

At one point, as the road weaves around the side of a hill, roadworks block the way ahead. There has been no warning and there is no diversion. The driver speaks to the workmen, reverses and crosses a flat, empty valley. We splash through shallow streams and join a track on the other side. Soon, the driver turns back and moves off in a different direction. I've lost my bearings now, but eventually we make it to a sealed road and continue on our way.

Seemingly in the middle of nowhere, a young guy steps on board. He's hawking something. He stands at the top of the aisle and launches into a lengthy spiel. His patter seems to hit the mark; passengers respond to his questions and laugh at his jokes.

Slowly climbing yet another mountain, there are shouts from the seats ahead. '*Que pasa?*' I ask an old guy near me, as we roll to a standstill. '*La aqua*', he says. And as we troop off, steam is pumping from the open hood at the front of the bus. Water poured into the engine spills through to the ground. Passengers move from the shade of the mountain to the sunny side of the road, and sit on a metal crash barrier. The old guy is beside me. 'Sucre?', I ask. He points over my shoulder. Across bare hills, the stretched-out city is a short distance away. A car going in that direction is flagged down, and passengers crowd round looking for a lift, but there's only room for one. A couple of lorries going in the opposite direction are also stopped, and quizzed, I guess, for whatever is needed to fix the stricken bus. It is still spewing steam.

Eventually, we're on our way. I hadn't noticed earlier, but the floor of the bus is coated with dust, from windows left open for the duration of the journey. The young hawker carries on with his patter. First he hands a bauble to each passenger, a clear stone with a small, metal hoop attached. He then distributes necklaces, thin strips of leather, on which the bauble can be attached. He has everyone laughing and does some business.

The bus isn't fully recovered and gives up the ghost at the foot of a hill leading into Sucre. I ask the driver for directions to the bus station and he points after passengers already traipsing up the incline ahead. As I drag my bags after them, a taxi blows its horn on the other side of the road. I flag it down, climb in with two other bus refugees and make the short trip to the centre of town.

66

Tomorrow, I plan to move on to Potosí, to the southwest, from where I can catch a bus to Villazón on the Bolivian border on my lengthy way to Salta. So my stay in Sucre is a short one, which is a pity – it seems a fine city. It has been a UNESCO World Heritage Site since 1991, and my guidebook assures me it is 'the most sophisticated and beautiful city in Bolivia, with some of the finest colonial architecture in South America'. But by now, I've overdosed on colonial architecture. And a fissure-like gash where my heel has split means I've been hobbling for days. Sightseeing is curtailed.

Next morning, a passer-by gives me an earful as I almost remove her head, flinging open the door of a taxi outside the bus station. Inside, attendants at ticket desks shout out their destinations and pester me to use their service. I choose a company at random and book a seat on a 1.30pm service to Potosí. At a restaurant-cum-takeaway in the terminal, the *papas fritas* (chips) look tasty, heated under glass behind the counter. But the owner won't sell them unless I also buy some *pollo* (chicken). Beside the *papas fritas*, the odd, angular shapes of the hunks of *pollo* are off-putting. I retreat instead to stalls by the roadside and stock up on crackers.

'*Panorámico o bajo?*', the lady had asked when I booked my bus ticket. Upstairs, my *panorámico* seat doesn't quite deliver the quality of view its description seemed to promise. I'm sitting at the very front, and the lip of the bus roof overhanging the windscreen limits my range of vision to about ten metres. Two horizontal bars in front of my knees make it difficult to get comfortable. I recline the seat slightly, which lessens the discomfort and broadens the view.

It is an almost non-stop ascent to Potosí. The bus climbs and climbs, slowly, through brown mountains. We pass a petrol tanker lying on its side, undone coming too fast around a bend in the opposite direction. Occasionally, the bus moves out of its grinding, low gear and speeds on, before, once more, climbing upwards. Eventually, we crest a peak and for a time are on flat ground.

Here, patches of tilled, brown earth sit near isolated dwellings. Outside one farmhouse, newly formed, wet, mud bricks dry in the sun. In the road, workers with a hand-cart apply road markings, guided by a rope; colleagues with green and red flags regulate the sparse traffic. Further on, crosses peek over the wall of a small graveyard leaning on the side of a hill. Unsteady stone walls by the roadside look like those in the west of Ireland.

As we reach the end of the journey, the conical Cerro de Potosí (also called Cerro Rico, Rich Mountain) lies ahead. The city of Potosí, at the foot of the *cerro*, was once the largest in the New World. Three decades after silver was discovered here in 1545, its population had boomed to 150,000. At the time, all commerce between Alto Perú and Spain was conducted via Panama. Mule trains brought the silver from Potosí to the Pacific coast. It was then shipped north, and transported across the isthmus of Panama to the shores of the Caribbean. From there, treasure fleets sailed for Spain, tempting targets for the pirates of the Spanish Main. Enormous quantities of silver were mined here, and Cerro Rico is a honeycomb of tunnels. The city was famous for its wealth; in Spanish, if you're rich, you are 'worth a potosí' ('*valer un potosí*').

Today, its wealth diminished, Potosí is bleak and red-bricked and tin-roofed. The bus weaves through city streets and deposits us at a modern, domed terminal. Inside, ticket desks run around the circumference of the building on the second floor. The shouts of attendants at ticket-desk windows echo around this empty shell of a place. The echoes become louder and more insistent as the evening wears on, and the time available to fill empty seats runs short. It is 40 bolivianos for the overnight TRANSCHILENO Jumbo Buss (sic) to Villazón. It leaves at 10pm, and has, I'm assured, TV and air conditioning.

On board, the bus has no air conditioning and a TV that remains switched off. Alternative entertainment is provided by the guy beside me. He's drunk and, as we pull away, he leans heavily to his right, drooping over the aisle. The bus jolts to a halt at the station exit, and my neighbour straightens up. En route again, he topples over, inch by inch, in my direction. Soon, his head lands on my shoulder. I gently nudge him, he gives me a half-eyed, watery smile and settles into a more upright position. By this time, a teenager to the rear has switched on a CD player. It's going to be a long night.

It is still dark at 5am, when we reach Villazón, where Bolivia meets Argentina. The trip has gone well. My neighbour's toppling head didn't trouble my shoulder for the remainder of the journey; the music-playing teenager plugged in headphones. At the hold of the bus, passengers push and shove to retrieve luggage. Nearby, on the main street in town, bus company agents tout for business from early-morning arrivals. At an office there, I buy a 230-boliviano ticket to Salta. Two French girls explain that the bus will leave from La Quiaca, on the Argentinian side of the border, and that before then, passengers will be led first to *Migraciones*, and from there to the station on the other side. It's a freezing early morning. In the tiny, busy office, I put on an extra pair of socks and sit on my luggage, the only available seat. Soon, the day brightens and a guide leads the short walk to *la frontera*. Helpfully, Bolivian and Argentinian *Migraciones* are side by side. A few blocks on the other side of a bridge is the bus station at La Quiaca. Some welcome Argentinian pesos lurking in my money belt are enough for pastries at a nearby, early-opening bakery. I donate some to the hungry, peso-less French girls. Soon, we're on our way, on a good Argentinian road, in a good Argentinian bus, with TV, air conditioning, reclining seats and sober passengers. More comfortable, for sure, and far less entertaining.

67

It's Monday morning, and a guy lingering outside McDonald's in Miraflores is selling foreign-language newspapers. The papers are folded in half and layered in the crook of his arm, to show their titles.

'*Algo en Inglés?*', I ask.

He hands me the *International Herald Tribune*. I shake my head at a *Newsweek*.

'Eight *soles*', he says.

I run a forefinger across the day and date at the top of the front page. It's the Fri/Sat edition.

'Five *soles*, five *soles!*' He's keen for a sale.

I take some coins from my pocket, but change my mind and move on, across the road, to Parque 7 de Junio.

In the Parque, a small, paved, circular area is dotted with thick, round concrete stools, the workplace of local shoeshine guys. There are three of them here just now, in uniform dark blue fleeces and baseball caps. Each has a small, wooden workbox that holds brushes and polish. The workboxes also function as footrests for customers seated on the concrete stools.

It is after 10am and Miraflores is not fully awake. On Avenida Larco, on the other side of the Parque, half-empty buses lined up by the *paradero* (bus stop) wait for traffic lights to change. A sidekick approaches and points at his bus; 'Arequipa! Arequipa! Arequipa!', he rapid-fires at me. His sales patter is not quite enough to persuade me to take a lengthy and unplanned journey to the other end of the country. Further on, and in case I'd missed his bright blue official jacket, a *Cambio* guy raises a calculator towards my face. At the next corner, a man in a shirt and tie leans his upper body in my direction as I pass: 'Taxi service sir?' It's a slow business day in Lima.

It is more than a month now since I left Bolivia. I caught up with the girl I was due to meet in Salta and we passed a few pleasant days in the city. We did think we might go travelling together. In the end we went our separate ways. Via a sojourn in the Atacama Desert, I am back in Lima. My time in South America is coming to a close. The Peruvian capital is a stop-off on my leisurely way to Guayaquil in southern Ecuador, from where I will catch my return flight to London.

From Miraflores, I aim for the centre of the city. En route, the bus runs along a dedicated lane in the middle of the motorway. Traffic zips by on either side. Off the road, a steep, green, grassy bank forms a natural billboard; businesses use low foliage of different colours to advertise themselves – Capital Radio 96.7, *Paginas Amarillas* (Yellow Pages), *Radio Felicidad*.

From the final stop, it's a short walk to Plaza Mayor, the centre of old Lima. The plaza is thronged. Police stand around in groups, some with riot shields and helmets with raised visors. The throng seems thickest in a near corner, where the square meets Calle Callao. Here, a statue is hoisted above the heads of a pressing crowd. The statue faces away from the plaza, towards a handsome building off the side of the square. From the rear, I can see a 'sunburst' halo behind, and slightly above, its head; a black cloak sparsely decorated with golden stars falls the length of its body. The statue sits on a heavy-looking, gold-coloured base; arrangements of flowers rest at its feet. Police with bayonet rifles flank the base; beside them, on each side, a line of people carry the flags of the Vatican, and the US and Italy, among others.

A bell tinkles, and then, a round of applause. Those carrying the base (I can't see them over the heads of the crowd) turn away from the building, face forward, and shuffle towards the corner of the square. The crowd moves with them. To the rear, a small brass band, quiet while the statue was motionless, strikes up dirge-like music. The procession halts at the corner and all becomes quiet.

After more bell-tinkling and applause, the band resumes its funereal beat. The statue sways from side to side in the same spot for several moments before its bearers step slowly forward, turn right at the junction and move away from the plaza, down Callao.

I stop at the corner and watch after them. Behind the band, a section of uniformed female police officers wear green skirts and jackets. On each jacket, a white braid loops from a button on the right breast, under the armpit and back over the shoulder to the button. The policewomen are bored and chat among themselves. One runs to rejoin the group. She needn't have rushed. They haven't gone far. It's extremely slow progress.

Down Callao, red and white flower petals are thrown over the passing procession from a first-floor office window. I leave the corner and struggle down the heaving footpath, past the statue. Somewhere up ahead, a woman with a loudhailer keeps up a commentary. I hadn't noticed earlier, but the procession is led by three ancient women dressed in black; their grim faces could curdle milk. They're followed by nuns thumbing rosary beads against forefingers, and men and women who walk backwards, facing the statue, mouthing prayers. After more uniformed police comes the statue itself, the Virgin and Child. A shield at the feet of the Virgin bears the coat of arms of the *Policía Nacional del Perú*. Those carrying the heavy base are visible now: a group of men wearing black shoes, black trousers and white, buttonless, knee-length coats. Each wears a black cowl and a short, thick, white rope around the neck, knotted at the breast.

I escape the bustling, bumping crowd and squeeze my way back up the footpath to the plaza. There, a policeman tells me that today is *El Día de Santa Rosa de Lima* (St Rose of Lima, the first Catholic saint in the Americas). Which means that the statue in the procession is likely to be of her, rather than the Virgin. It's a public holiday in Peru, which explains the lazy start to the day in the city.

68

After lunch in Miraflores, I stroll towards the sea and reach Parque del Amor, a small, manicured patch of greenery perched on a cliff-top. A railing runs along the cliff edge; far below, a road separates the cliff from the sea shore. From the water's edge, a broad boardwalk threads through the centre of a breakwater formed of massive stone blocks. I follow a path through the Parque, descend steep steps and cross a wooden bridge to the shore.

To the left of the breakwater, waves crash heavily up the steep slope of a pebble beach. A rumble like thunder accompanies the receding water as it rushes back over shifting stones. I stroll along the boardwalk to its furthest point. Ahead is a swelling green ocean. Close at hand, a black-bodied bird with a red beak and red feet dives into the water, re-emerges and flies off (it's an Inca tern, Google tells me later). Other birds speed low, just above the waves. Onshore, the bare, brown cliff face looks to the ocean; in every other direction, a sea haze limits the view. To the north, somewhere in the fuzzy distance, is Callao, the port for Lima, into which Cochrane sailed in 1817 on his first outing for Bernardo O'Higgins, and where, in 1842, the Libertador died before he had had a chance to return to Chile. This was also the location, in the following decade, of an unlikely Irish colony.

John Gallagher, a former Royal Navy surgeon, had sunk an inheritance into land near Lima. He had plans for a sugar plantation and persuaded 180 of his countrymen to join him there; they reached Callao on July 20, 1851. Within three years, the small colony had broken up. Cholera and dysentery had taken their toll, and most of the immigrants returned to Ireland, or left for Australia or the gold-fields of California. One who stayed on was William Grace. The young Irishman had travelled to Peru with his father and two siblings as part of the mini-colonisation. Once there, he had steered clear of the sugar plantation, and instead, found work with John Bryce & Co., ship chandlers in Callao. By the time the colony had failed in 1854, Grace was a partner in the firm.

William Russell Grace was born at Riverstown, near Cobh, in County Cork, on May 10, 1832. His parents soon moved to Ballylinan, Queen's County (County Laois) to take up family holdings there. During the Famine, William's father worked as a tax inspector in Dublin, and they lived comfortably in the city, on Love Lane (now Donore Avenue).

William ran away to sea aged fourteen. Two years later, he returned to Dublin, and attended Belvedere House (now College). By 1850, he had set himself up as a passage broker, a middleman assisting people emigrating to the United States. The following year, he closed the business and left for South America.

At this time, Peru was rich in guano (bird excrement, used as a fertiliser). The heaviest deposits in the country lay on the three Chincha Islands, 190 kilometres south of Callao. The islands were little more than rocks rising from the ocean, but, over time, guano had accumulated there, almost 60 metres deep in places. Often, a fleet of over 100 ships lay off the Chinchas. Guano was loaded on to barges and transported to the waiting vessels. It took three months to fill the hold of a ship.

For those waiting off the islands, reprovisioning meant a journey to Callao, a costly impediment to business. William Grace came up with the idea of keeping a store ship at the Chinchas. He got hold of an old hulk, stocked it and towed it to the islands. It proved a great success. It was in this unlikely setting that he met his wife-to-be, Lillius Gilchrest, daughter of an American ship captain. They married in the Baptist church at Tenants Harbor, near Thomaston, Maine on September 11, 1859.

In time, William's brother Michael returned to Peru (he had left for Ireland when Gallagher's sugar plantation failed) and joined him at John Bryce and Co. In 1865, William's health failed, and he returned to Ireland. Later that year, sufficiently recovered, he made his way to post-Civil War New York, which was at that time bulging with opportunity. He set up in business on Wall Street, as a charterer and part-owner of ships. In time, he founded a sailing line that operated from the east coast of the US to Chile and Peru. In 1880, after a crop failure in Ireland, William Grace all but took charge of a campaign to supply and fit out a vessel to deliver aid to Ireland. This work brought him into contact with political leaders in the city. He would go on to serve as the first Irish Catholic mayor of New York, in opposition to the Irish of Tammany Hall (the political machine of the Democratic Party in the city); in 1885, he accepted the Statue of Liberty from the people of France.

With William in New York, Michael Grace looked after affairs in Peru. John Bryce and Co. became Bryce, Grace & Co. and ultimately Grace Brothers & Co. Although William remained involved, the Peruvian house would become Michael Grace's concern.

While Peru was harvesting guano, it cared little about the rich nitrate deposits in the barren south of the country. Here, progressive Chile took the lead and moved into Bolivian and Peruvian territory. This, in time, led to the War of the Pacific.

After the war, Peru was in dire straits. It had a defaulted foreign debt of £33m, which, with overdue interest, reached £51m. The priority, in order to make the country attractive again to outside investment, was to come to a settlement with foreign bondholders. The person most responsible for making this happen was Michael Grace.

While everyone claimed to be in favour of Peru's recovery, when it came down to it, the (mostly English) bondholders simply wanted their money back. In London, a committee was formed to determine how this could be done. In Lima, over several long sessions with the Peruvian president, Michael Grace drafted a letter to the bondholders, outlining his own suggestions. This involved giving the bondholders interests in Peru's mines and railroads, such that they could claim revenues from these industries over the term of extended leases. Grace wanted them to take a long-term view and to work to rehabilitate Peru. The bondholders came back with amendments (eg: longer leases than had originally been suggested). Michael agreed and urged the Peruvians to accept.

However, a change of government in Lima had seen the installation of the hard-line President Cáceres. He thought the bondholders should negotiate with Chile for repayment of the loans. After all, when the war ended, it had taken Peru's most valuable collateral, the nitrate provinces in the south.

The bondholders wanted Michael Grace to work on their behalf. He declined, preferring to mediate between the two parties. Instead, the bondholders chose the Earl of Donoughmore to represent them (an Irish nobleman whose family seat was at Knocklofty House, near Clonmel in County Tipperary). In effect, Donoughmore was window-dressing. Grace was the man in charge.

Michael Grace travelled to Lima for meetings with Cáceres. He gained the president's confidence and in February 1887 left for London with the minister of the treasury, José Araníbar, to arrange a deal. With the help of pressure from Baring Brothers, hefty holders of defaulted debt, the initially hostile bondholders agreed to a contract.

The terms stated that the Peruvian Corporation Ltd (representing the bondholders' interests) would cancel half of Peru's outstanding debt and pursue Chile for the balance. Chile protested, saying that the contract was not in the interests of Latin America and that it infringed on the terms of an 1883 treaty (in which they attempted to limit their liability to Peru's creditors). In Lima, the Grace–Aranibar contract was withdrawn from consideration by Congress.

Grace enlisted the help of the British Foreign Office, then the leading force in international diplomacy. By letter, he urged them to be firm with Chile, and to warn them not to interfere in dealings between Peru and its creditors. William Grace went to London to speak to the Foreign Office. They, in turn, notified Chile that they had advised Peru to accept an amended contract.

Michael hurried to Lima with Donoughmore. A revised contract (the Donoughmore Contract in the English press, the Grace Contract in the US) was signed in October 1888 and put to Congress. Chile again protested, and ignored a firm rebuke from Britain. In Congress, a minority stood against the contract. They feared Chile's reaction if it was passed. The impasse continued through December and January. Eventually, the minority walked out of Congress. There was now no longer a quorum to conduct business.

Michael Grace and Cáceres came up with a plan. Elections were called to replace the members who had walked out. Pro-contract representatives were elected, Congress reconvened in July and the contract was approved.

Again, Chile stated that it broke the terms of the 1883 treaty. Britain lost patience and protested again against Chile's interference.

This time, Chile backed down and agreed to make payments to the bondholders. Overnight, Peru's international credibility was restored. It would not have happened without the efforts of Michael Grace. He had spent five years and more than $250,000 of his own money in getting to this point.

As a postscript, in 1901, Michael Grace's daughter Elena María married Richard Hely-Hutchinson, who, the year before, had succeeded his father as the Earl of Donoughmore. Their son, John Hely-Hutchinson, the 7th Earl, was kidnapped with his wife by the IRA in June 1974, and released after a week.

The Graces' businesses flourished. In time, they operated six commercial houses and had agencies on three continents. Originally a series of partnerships, W. R. Grace & Co. was incorporated towards the end of the nineteenth century. Some of its many businesses were better known than others. The Grace National Bank was established in 1914 and existed until the 1960s when it merged with Marine Midland Bank (now part of HSBC). In 1916, the Grace Steamship Company was formed, a consolidation of two separate Grace operations. In the same year, William Grace put in place a passenger service that connected New York to the west coast of South America. As the Grace Line (*La Linea Grace*), it continued operating until 1969 when W. R. Grace & Co. exited shipping to concentrate on other business. In 1928, Pan-American Airways came together with Grace to form Pan American-Grace Airways (Panagra), the first air link between North and South America.

W. R. Grace & Co. exists today, a large conglomerate based in Maryland, in the United States, with an annual turnover in excess of $2.5bn. In 1987, it became the first wholly foreign-owned company to do business in China. The Grace family remained involved over the years. In 1992, J Peter Grace resigned as CEO. William Grace's grandson had held the position for 48 years, the longest-ever reign of a CEO of a public company.

69

The following day, before leaving for Guayaquil, I return to the centre of Lima to visit San Pedro. At the gates, an old woman in black, slouched against a pillar, reaches out with a plastic cup. Inside, at the rear of the church, an elderly man kneels on the tiled floor. His head is bowed in front of a statue of Our Lady, the *Virgen Medalla Milagrosa* (Virgin of the Miraculous Medal). Our Lady is in flowing blue and white; her bare feet tread on a gasping snake. In front of the statue, what look like lighted candles are in fact light bulbs with flickering red filaments. The old man gets off his knees and dips his fingers in a holy water font. At the bottom of the main aisle, he offers a lengthy genuflection, turns and leaves. In front of the statue, another old man is on his knees.

A line of altars runs down the right-hand side of the church, a series of tall arches over the side-aisle leading from one to the next. Paintings hang above and to the side of each arch. The altars are ornate, intricately engraved and reach high to the ceiling; the centrepiece of each is a statue of the person to whom the altar is dedicated. The eighteenth-century wooden statue of the *Virgen de la O* sits on the first altar, with, beneath her, *Niño Jesus de Huana*. This child Jesus wears a woollen hat with ear flaps, and a bright multi-coloured poncho. Pan pipes dangle from His hand.

Ahead, there's a mumbling to my left. A confession box sits at the outside edge of the pews of the main aisle. Here, the penitent kneels *outside* the box, his back to the side of the church; people lined up by the side-altars wait their turn.

Further on, a marble plaque is affixed to a side wall. It was erected in 1966, by the *Instituto de Conmemoración Histórica de Chile*:

Barón de Ballenary, Marqués de Osorno.	Baron of Ballenary, Marquis of Osorno.
Ilustre gobernador del Reino de Chile,	Illustrious governor of the kingdom of Chile,
Fortificó y Pacificó La Frontera de Arauco, y Fundó las Villas de Illapel,	Fortified and pacified The Frontier of Araucania and founded the towns of Illapel,
Sta Rosa de los Andes, Combarbalá, Vallenar, Nueva Bilbao,	Santa Rosa de los Andes, Combarbalá, Vallenar, Nueva
S. José de Maipo, Linares y Parral.	Bilbao, S. José de Maipo, Linares y Parral.
Esclarecido Virrey del Perú.	Distinguished Viceroy of Peru.
En este templo reposan sus cenizas.	His remains lie in this church.

San Pedro, burial site of Ambrose O'Higgins, the viceroy of Peru, father of the Libertador, and the man with whom my occasional search for things Irish in South America had begun, months before, in Chile.

Note on references

Books used as sources of information are listed in the Bibliography. Quotations from books and websites are sometimes attributed within the text itself; where they are not, their source can be found in the Endnotes, which are divided by chapter. The Endnotes also list additional sources of information.

Endnotes

Chapter 3

Pinochet quote from Beckett, Andy, *Pinochet in Piccadilly* (Faber and Faber Limited, 2002).

Chapter 5

Murray, Edmundo, 'Ambrose [Ambrosio] O'Higgins (c. 1721–1801)' in "Irish Migration Studies in Latin America" 4:4, October 2006 (www.irlandeses.org).

Murray, Edmundo, 'John [Juan] Mackenna (1771–1814)' in "Irish Migration Studies in Latin America" 4:4, October 2006 (www.irlandeses.org).

Murray, Edmundo, 'Benjamín Vicuña Mackenna (1831–1886)' in "Irish Migration Studies in Latin America" 4:4, October 2006 (www.irlandeses.org).

Information on Alaskan islands from www.explorenorth.com/articles/rey/spanish-irish.html

Chapter 8

Sepúlveda, Alfredo, 'Bernardo O'Higgins: The Rebel Son of a
  Viceroy' in "Irish Migration Studies in Latin America" 4:4,
  October 2006 (www.irlandeses.org).

Chapter 9

'José de San Martín', *Encyclopædia Britannica* (www.britannica.com/
  biography/Jose-de-San-Martin).

Chapter 10

de Brún, Pádraig, *Valparaíso* (www.ireland-calling.com/valparaiso).

Chapter 12

'Retail shops…' Graham, Maria, *Journal of a Residence in Chile,
  During the Year 1822* (London, 1824), quoted in Beckett, Andy,
  Pinochet in Piccadilly (Faber and Faber Limited, 2002).
'conservative and law-abiding…' Smith, W Anderson, *Temperate
  Chile: A Progressive Spain* (Black, 1899), quoted in Beckett, Andy,
  Pinochet in Piccadilly (Faber and Faber Limited, 2002).

Chapter 13

Rodríguez, Moises Enrique, 'Patricio Lynch (1825–1886)' in "Irish
  Migration Studies in Latin America" 7:3, March 2010 (www.
  irlandeses.org).
Murray, Edmundo, 'John Thomond O'Brien (1786–1861)' in "Irish
  Migration Studies in Latin America" 2:3, July–August 2004 (www.
  irlandeses.org).
Information on O'Brien railway station from www.irlandeses.org/
  ipnl_obrien2.htm

Chapter 18

Arthur Quinlan quotes from www.scotsman.com/lifestyle/the-night-che-guevara-came-to-limerick-1-1-1297544

Murray, Edmundo, 'Ernesto [Che] Guevara (1928–1967)' in "Irish Migration Studies in Latin America" 3:6, November–December 2005 (www.irlandeses.org).

www.jimfitzpatrick.com

Chapter 22

Murray, Edmundo, 'Edelmiro Julián Farrell (1887–1980)' in "Irish Migration Studies in Latin America" 3:6, November–December 2005 (www.irlandeses.org).

Murray, Edmundo, 'Rodolfo Walsh (1927–1977)' in "Irish Migration Studies in Latin America" 2:1, March–April 2004 (www.irlandeses.org).

Geraghty, Michael John, 'Rodolfo Walsh: An Argentine Irishman' in *Buenos Aires Herald*, March 29, 2002 (www.irlandeses.org/rodolfowalsh.htm).

Chapter 24

Edmundo Murray quote from www.history.ac.uk/ihr/Focus/Migration/articles/murray.html

Chapter 25

Cooney, Jerry W, 'Thomas O'Gorman (c.1760–?)' in "Irish Migration Studies in Latin America" 4:4, October 2006 (www.irlandeses.org).

Chapter 28

'sheep farmers, shepherds...' Edmundo Murray (www.history.ac.uk/ihr/Focus/Migration/articles/murray.html)

Chapter 29

All quotes from Murray, Thomas, *The Story of the Irish in Argentina* (P. J. Kennedy & Sons, 1919).

Chapter 30

Murray, Edmundo, 'James Gaynor (c. 1802–1892)' (www.irlandeses.org/dilab_gaynorj.htm).

Murray, Edmundo, 'Eduardo Pedro Maguire (1865–1929)' (www.irlandeses.org/dilab_maguireep.htm).

Murray, Edmundo, 'Leo Alfred Duggan (1903–1964)' (www.irlandeses.org/dilab_dugganla.htm).

Cané, Gonzalo, 'Margarita Morgan (1839–1923)' (www.irlandeses.org/dilab_morganm.htm).

Chapter 33

All quotes from Kelly, Helen, *Irish 'Ingleses'* (Irish Academic Press, 2009).

Murray, Edmundo, 'Eamon Bulfin (1892–1968)' in "Irish Migration Studies in Latin America" 2:1, March–April 2004 (www.irlandeses.org).

Quinn, Ronnie, 'Catholic, Male and Working-class: The Evolution of the Hurling Club into a Wide-Ranging Irish-Argentine Institution (1920–1980)' in "Irish Migration Studies in Latin America" 6:1, March 2008 (www.irlandeses.org).

Chapter 34

Murray, Edmundo, 'Camila O'Gorman (1828–1848)' in "Irish Migration Studies in Latin America" 2:2, May–June 2004 (www.irlandeses.org).

Julianello, Maria Teresa, 'The Scarlet Trinity: The Doomed Struggle of Camila O'Gorman against Family, Church and State in 19th-Century Buenos Aires' (www.irlandeses.org/julianello.htm).

Chapter 36

'Uruguay', *Encyclopædia Britannica* (www.britannica.com/place/Uruguay).

Chapter 38

All quotes from Mason, Tony, *Passion of the People? Football in South America* (Verso, 1995).

Chapter 39

www.lummifilm.com/grafspee/history.html
www.defencejournal.com/dec99/river.htm
www.nzhistory.net.nz/war/battle-of-river-plate

Chapter 40

Quotes about Peter Campbell from Robertson, J P and W P, *Letters on South America* (John Murray, 1843) and Pyne, Peter, *The Invasions of Buenos Aires 1806–1807: The Irish Dimension* (University of Liverpool, Institute of Latin American Studies, 1996): both quoted in Newark, Tim, *The Fighting Irish* (Constable & Robinson Ltd, 2012).

Chapter 42

All quotes from Jawad, Hyder, *Four Weeks in Montevideo* (Seventeen Media, 2009).

Chapter 43

www.glaniad.com, accessed 2012 (website no longer active).

Chapter 44

www.glaniad.com, accessed 2012 (website no longer active).

Sources:

R Bryn Williams, *Y Wladfa* (Cardiff, 1962).

E MacDonald, *Yr Hirdaith* (Llandysul, 1999).

Chapter 45

www.glaniad.com, accessed 2012 (website no longer active).

Sources:

R Bryn Williams, *Y Wladfa* (Cardiff, 1962).

K E Skinner, *Railway in the Desert* (Wolverhampton, 1984).

Chapter 46

www.glaniad.com, accessed 2012 (website no longer active).

Sources:

R Bryn Williams, *Y Wladfa* (Cardiff, 1962).

Chapter 48
Geraghty, Michael John, 'Argentina: Land of Broken Promises'
in *Buenos Aires Herald*, March 17, 1999, at www.irlandeses.org/
dresden.htm.

Chapter 51
Murray, Edmundo, 'John James Murphy (1822–1909)' (www.
irlandeses.org/dilab_murphyjj.htm).

Chapter 52
Wallace, José Bernardo, 'Eduardo Casey (1847–1906)' (www.
irlandeses.org/dilab_caseye.htm).
MacLoughlin Bréard, Guillermo, 'From Shepherds to Polo Players:
Irish-Argentines from the First to the Last Chukker' in "Irish
Migration Studies in Latin America" 6:1, March 2008 (www.
irlandeses.org).

Chapter 53
Wallace, José Bernardo, 'Eduardo Casey (1847–1906)' (www.
irlandeses.org/dilab_caseye.htm).
Landaburu, Roberto. *Irlandeses: Eduardo Casey, Vida y Obra* (Fondo
Editor Mutual de Venado Tuerto, 1995).

Chapter 57
'Polygamy was the…' Cardozo, Ephraim, *El Paraguay Colonial*
(1959), quoted in Lillis, Michael and Fanning, Ronan, *The Lives of
Eliza Lynch* (Gill & Macmillan Ltd, 2009).

Chapter 58

'social downfall ...' Kahle, Günter, quoted in Lillis, Michael and
Fanning, Ronan, *The Lives of Eliza Lynch* (Gill & Macmillan Ltd,
2009).

'cohabitation or "visiting rights" ...' Potthast, Professor Barbara,
quoted in Lillis, Michael and Fanning, Ronan, *The Lives of Eliza
Lynch* (Gill & Macmillan Ltd, 2009).

Chapter 60

Murray, Edmundo, 'Juan Emiliano O'Leary (1879–1969)' in "Irish
Migration Studies in Latin America" 4:1, January–February 2006
(www.irlandeses.org).

Information on John Thomas McGill at www.irlandeses.org/
biblioparuru.htm

Chapter 62

Huner, Michael Kenneth, 'Saving Republics: General Martin
Thomas McMahon, the Paraguayan War and the Fate of the
Americas (1864–1870)' in "Irish Migration Studies in Latin
America" 7:3, March 2010 (www.irlandeses.org).

Dictionary of Canadian Biography Online:
O'Callaghan, Edmund Bailey: www.biographi.ca/009004-119.01-e.
php?id_nbr=5193
Tracey, Daniel: www.biographi.ca/009004-119.01-e.php?&id_
nbr=3175

Bibliography

Beckett, Andy. *Pinochet in Piccadilly* (Faber and Faber Limited, 2002)

Williamson, Edwin. *The Penguin History of Latin America* (Penguin Group, revised edition 2009)

Wheeler, Sara. *Chile: Travels in a Thin Country* (Abacus, revised edition 2006)

Wilson, Jason. *The Andes: A Cultural History* (Signal Books, 2009)

McKenna, Patrick, 'Irish migration to Argentina' in *Patterns of Migration*, edited by Patrick O'Sullivan (Leicester University Press, 1997)

Kelly, Helen. *Irish 'Ingleses'* (Irish Academic Press, 2009)

Pyne, Peter. *The Invasions of Buenos Aires, 1806–1807: The Irish Dimension* (University of Liverpool: Institute of Latin American Studies, 1996)

Graham-Yooll, Andrew. *The Forgotten Colony* (Hutchinson & Co. [Publishers] Ltd, 1991)

Murray, Thomas. *The Story of the Irish in Argentina* (P. J. Kennedy & Sons, 1919)

Byrne, James Patrick; Coleman, Philip; King, Jason Francis. Editors. *Ireland and the Americas: Culture, Politics, and History* (ABC-CLIO, 2008)

Mason, Tony. *Passion of the People? Football in South America* (Verso, 1995)

Newark, Tim. *The Fighting Irish* (Constable & Robinson Ltd, 2012)

Graham-Yooll, Andrew. *Imperial Skirmishes* (Signal Books Limited, 2002)

Parrado, Nando. *Miracle in the Andes* (Orion, 2007 edition)

Jawad, Hyder. *Four Weeks in Montevideo* (Seventeen Media, 2009)

Chatwin, Bruce. *In Patagonia* (Vintage, 2005)

Rough Guides. *The Rough Guide to South America on a Budget* (Rough Guides, 2009)

Murray, Edmundo. *Becoming Irlandés* (L. O. L. A. [Literature of Latin America], 2006)

Lillis, Michael and Fanning, Ronan. *The Lives of Eliza Lynch* (Gill & Macmillan Ltd, 2009)

James, Marquis. *Merchant Adventurer* (Scholarly Resources Inc., 1993)

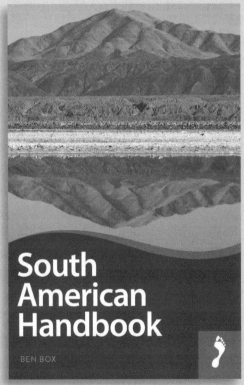